In an ambitious attempt to delve into and create links between the physical, intellectual, and spiritual realms Phillip M<sup>c</sup>Kerrow generously communicates a lifetime of experiences in his book *Faith of a Maker*. Phillip's many fields of interest include engineering, robotics and artificial intelligence, mathematics, and design. He is not content with surface understandings and combines factual accounts with meaningful and sometimes very personal stories. A passion for making things is intricately interwoven with his deep Christian faith. Phillip brings challenges and insights to any reader who is not afraid to ask questions. And I would highly recommend *Faith of a Maker* to those who are prepared to adventure into both familiar and unfamiliar territories.

**Anne Marie,**
Retired Visual Arts teacher

I have known Phillip M<sup>c</sup>Kerrow for almost thirty-five Years. Phil is a mature intelligent Christian with a wonderful evangelistic heart who is passionate about applying his faith to life. He is gifted with many unusual qualities. In particular, he is a maker with great skills in carpentry and design. He is a distinguished, respected academic within his speciality of Robotics and has published a well-received textbook in that field. Phil has spent a lifetime reflecting on the intersection of the areas of faith, work, science, and life. His new book *Faith of a Maker* draws these threads together in a unique way. Its particular merit is at least two fold. While there are many books on faith and science there are not many that discuss topics such as robotics, computer design or artificial intelligence in the way Phil's background enables him to do. At the same time, Phil colours his narrative with interesting and sometime moving stories taken from his own personal journey. From teaching undergraduate and post graduate student Phil is well versed with young intelligent inquiring minds who wish to pursue their studies but also engage in the big questions of the existence of God, the truth of the Christian faith, or the place of humanity in the greater scheme of things. Naturally this book will not answer every question but will provide ongoing stimulus to explore such issues for student and non-student alike.

**Rev. Dr. Rod Irvine,**
Retired Science Teacher and Anglican Church Pastor

One of my favourite Bible passages is found in the book of Ephesians (chapter 2, verse 10). "For we are God's handiwork, created in Christ Jesus to do good works, which God prepared in advance for us to do." God made us – we are his handiwork! Again, God made us – created us – specifically in Christ. Why? So we, in turn, might make good – this is what we are to do. It is this theme of making that Phillip M<sup>c</sup>Kerrow takes up in his new book. Not only is God a Maker, but our own making can point us to God. M<sup>c</sup>Kerrow develops this theme in engineering and design, but extends it to more fundamental spheres, including science, mathematics, and axioms, and further applies it to life and death and faith. The abstract ideas are illustrated by concrete examples, including many episodes from the author's own life. Quirky and eclectic, this book provides a new perspective on the "maker of heaven and earth" from one whose faith is entwined with his own making.

**Senior Professor Roger Lewis,**
Faculty of Engineering and Information Sciences, University of Wollongong

What is making? How does it shape our lives? Is our existence the result of an infinitely powerful maker or an infinitely impossible chance? In *Faith of a Maker*, Dr. Philip M<sup>c</sup>Kerrow draws upon his years of expertise in the areas of science, technology, engineering, and mathematics to skilfully debunk some of the common myths and beliefs surrounding making and its multifaceted relationship with the Christian faith. In each chapter he journeys into a different area of STEM, offering novel and transformative ideas that have the power to fundamentally change your perspective on both making and faith in God." Through an abundance of creative stories and personal anecdotes, M<sup>c</sup>Kerrow provides a unique insight into the influence of the Christian faith on the life of a maker. His clear and concise language makes it a straightforward and engaging read, yet it is bound to expose you to fascinating disciplines you never knew existed.

**Matej Groombridge,**
Year 10 student, Baulkham Hills High School, Australia

# FAITH OF A
# MAKER

REASONS FOR BELIEVING IN JESUS

DR. PHILLIP M<sup>C</sup>KERROW

Ark House Press
arkhousepress.com

© 2024  Dr. Phillip M<sup>c</sup>Kerrow

All rights reserved. Apart from any fair dealing for the purpose of study, research, criticism, or review, as permitted under the Copyright Act,  no part may be reproduced by any process without written permission.

Scripture quotations are taken from The Holy Bible, New International Version® NIV® Copyright ©"1973, 1978, 1984, 2011 by Biblica, Inc.® Used by permission. All rights reserved worldwide.

Cataloguing in Publication Data:
Title: Faith of a Maker: *Reasons for believing in Jesus*
ISBN: 978-0-9756331-1-3 (pbk)
Subjects: REL083000   [RELIGION / Christianity / Christian Science] REL013000   [RELIGION / Christianity / Literature & the Arts]; REL106000   [RELIGION / Religion & Science];

Design by initiateagency.com

## DEDICATION

To my wife Ann, whose faith in Jesus encourages me.

For God so loved the world that he gave his one and only Son, that whoever believes in him shall not perish but have eternal life. John 3:16 NIV

# CONTENTS

Acknowledgements ................................................................. xi

Introduction ........................................................................ xiii

Chapter 1:   Maker Movement ........................................... 1
Chapter 2:   Faith ............................................................. 22
Chapter 3:   Engineering ................................................... 51
Chapter 4:   Science .......................................................... 80
Chapter 5:   Mathematics ................................................ 128
Chapter 6:   Axioms ........................................................ 161
Chapter 7:   Time ............................................................ 186
Chapter 8:   Design ......................................................... 211
Chapter 9:   Robots and AI .............................................. 239
Chapter 10:  Death ........................................................... 271
Chapter 11:  Jesus ............................................................ 300

Other books by author ........................................................ 332
About the author ................................................................ 333

# ACKNOWLEDGEMENTS

Many of the things that I have written are not new. Over the last fifty-five years I have read many papers and books, listened to many talks, and discussed issues with many people. I have tried to acknowledge each source where I can, but I often don't remember exactly who wrote or said it. I apologize if I have not attributed to you something that you said or wrote. Also, I have referenced online sources including Wikipedia, YouTube, and Popular Mechanics in preference to journal papers because they are easier for the reader to access.

Each chapter is a mix of stories, quotations, and technical discussions. My aim is to integrate various thoughts about making into unified themes. While the ideas presented in the technical sections are my understanding of reality, some of the stories are allegories. When the word *story* is included in a section title the story is made up. It uses fictional characters and events to describe the subject by suggestive resemblances. Otherwise, the story is true, but may have names changed.

I wish to thank my wife Ann and my friend Anne Marie for reading each chapter as I wrote it. I thank Ann for her patient encouragement and her gentle corrections as she competed for my time when I disappeared into the study to write this book. I thank Anne Marie for her critical reviews and subsequent modifications to the text, her research into the topics that I was writing on, and her contribution of a story to begin the design chapter.

I wish to thank Rev Dr Rod Irvine, Senior Professor Rev Dr Roger Lewis and my grandson Matej Groombridge for reading the draft manuscript and writing extensive reviews that guided a revision of the manuscript. Rev Dr Rod Irvine has retired after a career as a science teacher and church pastor. His review was thorough and detailed, showing the breadth of his knowledge.

Senior Professor Rev Dr Roger Lewis is the Associate Dean of research in the Faculty of Engineering and Information Sciences, at the University of Wollongong. The depth of his knowledge enabled him to get a good overview of the book. Matej, a year ten student in a top high school, provided a young person's view of the contents. Each reviewer made significant contributions to this book.

I wish to thank Lynn Goldsmith (Journalist, Editor, Author) for her excellent work in editing my manuscript to fit the style guidelines used at Ark House. Also, I wish to thank Nicole Danswan and her team for creating the cover graphics.

Finally, I wish to acknowledge the promptings of the Holy Spirit in all aspects of writing this book. In answer to prayer, the Holy Spirit guided the selection of which material to include and encouraged me when the going felt tough.

# INTRODUCTION

I was watching a virtual robot run around the screen of the Macintosh computer sitting on my desk when a student walked into my office. She stopped and stared at the screen. "Wow, it's so cute," she exclaimed. "Oh, what is it? Is it a computer game?"

"No, it's a robot simulator," I replied. The student grinned in amusement as she walked out of the room and away from my influence.

I was developing the simulator for students to use in assignments. My research has focused on the application of ultrasonic sensing to mobile robot navigation. I had developed the *outline segment algorithm* to model data from ultrasonic sensors and to use this model when mapping the environment.[1] The assignment required the students to add the code for a sensor module to the simulator based on the real data in Figures 0.1 and 0.2, and to use it to navigate the simulated robot in the simulated environment.

As the simulated robot navigated around the simulated room, I could see it on the computer screen and observe its actions, but it could not see me. It existed within the bounds of the simulator code that I was writing. The only way it could tell that I existed was when I entered its world to change that world in a way that could be detected by one of its sensors.

---

[1] McKerrow, P.J. 1993. Echolocation - From Range to Outline Segments, intelligent Autonomous Systems 11, IOS Press, Amsterdam, pp 205-211.

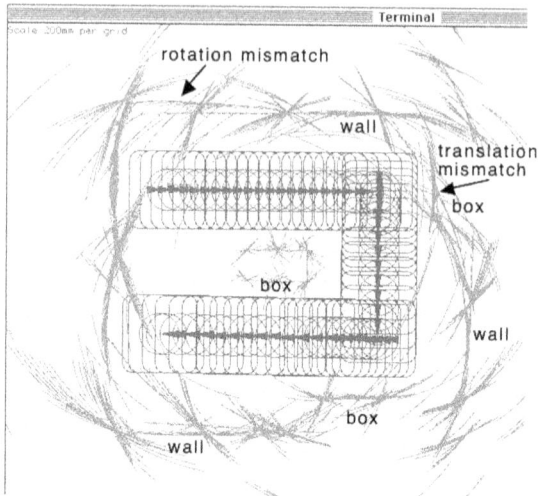

**Figure 0.1** *Data from ultrasonic ring mounted on a mobile robot. Rounded squares are robot locations. Arcs show range to objects.*

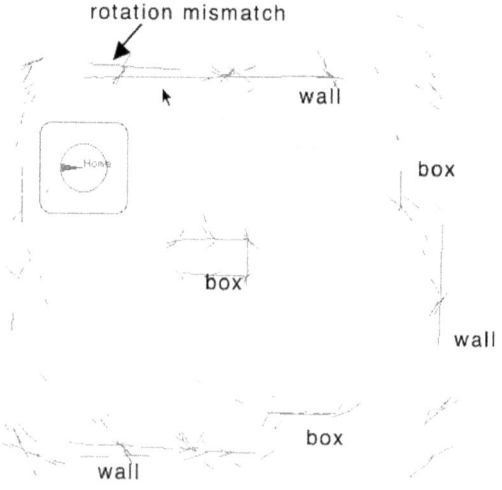

**Figure 0.2** *Map of room. Produced by Outline Segment algorithm from data in Figure 0.1 for use by an expert system to navigate the robot.*

## INTRODUCTION

Similarly, God watches me as I live in space-time, but I cannot see him unless he enters my world. Christians believe that God has entered space-time in the person of Jesus. Makers often express an interest in faith, but they walk away from the influence of God in their lives because they cannot see him. In each chapter of this book, I explore reasons for believing in Jesus by looking at examples from a specific maker realm. With these examples, I will take you on a journey through the realms involved in making things.

Also, I will take you into the realm of the Bible[2] to help you understand faith. The Bible contains the knowledge that faith in Jesus is based on. I seek to integrate faith and making using examples from my own life as a maker. Many of these examples are my thoughts about questions that students have asked me about faith and its influence on my making.

Come with me as I explore reasons for believing in Jesus. In the first chapter, I start with an overview of the Maker Movement.

*"Engines and steel!*
*Loud, pounding hammers!*
*Sing to the Lord a new song!*
*Limestone and beams!*
*Strong building workers!*
*Sing to the Lord a new Song!*
*God has done marvellous things.*
*We too will praise him with a new song."*
*Herbert F. Brokering.*[3]

---

[2] The Bible consists of two sets of books: the Jewish set of 39 books written before the birth of Jesus (called the Old Testament) and the Christian set of 27 books starting with the birth of Jesus (called the New Testament). To make Bible passages easy to find they are referenced by book name, chapter number and verse number. For example, the reference (Matthew 1:18) refers to verse 18 of the first chapter of the book written by Matthew. Matthew is the first book in the Christian set.

[3] Brokering, H. F. "Earth and All Stars" (1926 - 2009) traditionalmusic.co.uk/presbyterian-hymnal/earth-and-all-stars-loud-rushing-planets.htm

# 1

# MAKER MOVEMENT

Figure 1.1 *A wood carving exercise*

"What I cannot create I do not understand." Professor Richard Feynman of Caltech, who received the Nobel Prize in Physics in 1965 jointly with Julian Schwinger and Shin'ichirō Tomonaga.[1]

"Human creativity is definitive evidence that humans are made in the image of the Creator who made them" - The Everlasting Man, Chesterton, 1925.[2]

For since the creation of the world God's invisible qualities—his eternal power and divine nature—have been clearly seen, being understood from what has been made, so that people are without excuse. (Romans 1:20)

## WOOD CARVING

"Watch the grain or it will get you," the instructor said, as he peered over my shoulder.

I felt a desire to create, just like the God I worship, so I enrolled in a course at the Wood Carving School in Elbigenalp, Austria.[3]

Years before, when I was a child, I taught myself to carve. I would borrow one of my father's knives, cut a limb off a Camphor Laurel tree and carve a model boat. For many years I had no opportunity to carve, but a desire burned within. Eventually, I found a course near my home in Australia and began many years of fulfilling my carving desire. My nascent

---

[1] Professor Richard Feynman was a Nobel laureate who has sometimes been called "The Great Explainer". *The Feynman Lectures on Physics* may be the most popular physics book ever written. This quote was written on his blackboard at the time of his death in 1988. jcs.biologists.org/content/joces/130/18/2941.full.pdf
[2] Quoted in Richards, 2016. *The Sinister student*, Marylebone House, page P109.
[3] woodcarvingschool.com

longing to create bloomed into creative work. To develop my skills further I had travelled to Austria.

The skew chisel that I was holding bit into the wood. I shifted my grip and sliced sideways to cut across the grain rather than follow it. The instructor moved on to the next student.

As it left the wood, the tip of the chisel reflected the lights hanging from the ceiling and the chip fell away. I loved the feeling of a sharp chisel peeling away wood. Somehow it satisfied my need to create. Slowly, painstakingly, I could feel a face taking shape (Figure 1.1).[4] When asked how to carve a face, a comedian once said, "You just remove the bits that don't belong to the face."

This Austrian woodcarving school had pioneered a technique for face carving.[5] Carving involved creating a three-dimensional image of a three-dimensional object. It doesn't have to be a clone of nature to create a three-dimensional illusion. In *relief carving*, the planes that are seen from the front are carved closer together. I was carving *in the round* and would attempt to follow a three-dimensional model.

As I learned the school's technique my enjoyment of carving grew. The technique involved thinking about a face as a set of intersecting planes. "Look closely at the model and visualize her right cheek, the plane you have carved tilts too far forward," pointed out the instructor.

To relieve my frustration at not getting it right I went to the sharpening station and honed my chisel. Carving is much easier with sharp tools. Once all the planes are carved at the correct depth and three-dimensional angle the next step is to carve details. A sense of satisfaction welled up in my chest as I watched a face take shape, with each cut revealing more beauty. The

---

[4] Wood carving exercise, Elbigenalp, Austria, M<sup>c</sup>Kerrow, 26/11/2009.
[5] Geisler-Moroder, M. 2006. Carving the Head in the Classic European Tradition, Fox Chapel Publishing.

grain enhanced the shape of the facial features. My need to create morphed into a desire to carve beautiful figures.

My mind moved into a world of its own. A world where the beauty of a human face appeared as the chips fell. I might not be able to create like God can, but I can carve images of creation. Lost in this state of mind, some call it right brain thinking - time stood still while all that mattered was the carving. My need to create was satisfied, for now!

## MAKERS AND THE MAKER MOVEMENT

Making is any creative activity that produces a physical product, including activities - such as quilting, wood carving, and soldering wearable electronics. Often the activity of making is made possible by our understanding of the science and technology used in a creative process, along with the thought that goes into designing and making the product. A wide range of disciplines is involved. Throughout this book, I consider the influence of faith in Jesus on how a maker thinks about some of these disciplines. In this chapter, I look at the Maker Movement.

The Maker Movement is a culture in which people with creative gifts express their deepest feelings when they make both utilitarian and beautiful objects. Their mind is focused on making and time slips by unnoticed. The popularity of television reality shows based on making, like *Myth Busters, Making It,* and *Lego Masters,* demonstrates the worldwide interest in the Maker Movement.

Makers make things using every imaginable technology. Interest in creating physical items with digital design tools using plans shared over the internet started the Maker Movement.[6] Making is not restricted to mechanical and electronic devices. It includes arts and crafts, programming

---

[6] Rozenfeld, M. 2017. IEEE Joins the Maker Movement, The Institute, September, p 6-7.

and dress making, game design and videography. Often it draws inspiration from nature.

Makers took the approach that hackers use to develop software and adopted it to developing tools for making physical devices. The open-source software movement of the 1980s encouraged programmers to develop and distribute software. One example is the first port of the code of the Unix operating system from a DEC PDP-11 computer to run on an Interdata 7/32, which was done by my colleagues Richard Miller, Ross Nealon and Professor Juris Reinfelds at the University of Wollongong (UOW).[7]

Computer manufacturers tried to stop the development and distribution of free software but the advent of personal computers and a rapid growth in the number of programmers resulted in the development of significant amounts of freeware. The development of the Linux operating system in 1991 provided an open-source platform for program development.

Writing programs to replace commercial software became common place. The provision of tools to develop and market iPhone apps in 2008 had created opportunities for software development by anyone who had the necessary programming skills.

Software was just one of the many technologies that people used to make objects. Potter's clay was another. Similarly, a poet smiths his words to express his imagination. "A poet uses words not to explain something and not to describe something but to make something." Peterson, 2017.[8]

The word *poet* comes from a Greek word meaning *to make*.[9] A poem is a thing despite it being called an illusion of the imagination by some people. A poem may express an emotion or record an event. Like many things made by artists a poem is made to communicate to people. David, King of

---

[7] Miller, R. 2008. The First Unix Port -- A Personal History, C and the AT&T, 29/05/08 roguelife.org/~fujita/COOKIES/HISTORY/USENIX/miller.html.

[8] Peterson, E.H., 2017. As Kingfishers catch fire, Hodder & Stoughton, p369.

[9] merriam-webster.com/words-at-play/the-history-of-the-word-poet

ancient Israel, wrote songs of praise to God showing that poetry, praise, and creativity work together in worship.[10]

> The LORD is my shepherd, I lack nothing.
> He makes me lie down in green pastures,
> he leads me beside quiet waters,
> (Psalm 23:1-2)

The God presented in the Bible is both an Engineer and an Artist. He is the designer and creator of everything from galaxies in distant space to the flavors of quarks and leptons from which protons are made. His creativity includes the glory of a sunset and the beauty of the most intricate flower. But does such a God exist or is he a myth? Is there an infinitely capable maker or is everything the result of an infinitesimal chance? Are we likely to find answers to these questions at a meeting of makers called a Maker Fair?

## MAKER FAIRS

Before us stretched a collection of exciting and dynamic displays. We had entered a mini Maker Fair in Sydney's Powerhouse Museum. Fascinated parents were trying to calm excited children and help them understand the displays. The heads of 3D printers shuttled back and forth as they made simple plastic objects. Arduino micro-controllers executed code.[11] Robots moved around.

---

[10] Billingham, J. 2016. Art and prayer, Encounter with God, March, p 70.
[11] arduino.cc

## MAKER MOVEMENT

**Figure 1.2** *Philippa made a sphere at a Mini Maker Fair*

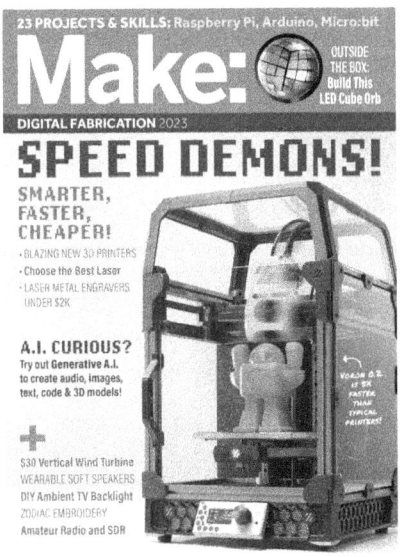

**Figure 1.3** *Make magazine*

Students spruiked their projects. Vendors sold electronic and mechanical kits. Children queued to make things. They became immersed in the displays: soldering simple circuits, feeling the texture of materials, and chasing mobile robots. Being around makers inspired them to become makers and gave them the opportunity to learn skills with tools (Figure 1.2).[12]

While certain aspects of the Maker Movement, such as arts and craft groups, school classes, practical education, science fairs, and hobby clubs have existed for ages, it was the launch of *Make magazine* in 2005 (Figure 1.3), to publish information about maker-related projects, that gave the contemporary Maker Movement its impetus.[13]

In 2006, the first Maker Fair was launched in San Francisco to showcase innovation in technology and art.[14] The movement to make and display the things you made grew quickly. In 2014, 133 Maker Fares were held in cities across the globe. That year, 215,000 people attended the flagship Maker Fairs in San Francisco and New York, with 61% first time attendees in New York. Half the attendees took their children. In 2017, over 220 independently-produced Maker Fairs took place around the world.

Maker Fairs are like a country fair that features makers and the things they have made. Makers work in the full range of metals, materials, art forms, and technologies. Each Maker is keen to share with others the objects they have made and how they made them. It is a boon for anyone who dabbles in making things, including the professionals, who develop new products. People of all ages and backgrounds gather to learn, share, play, and make. All their senses (touch, feel, sight, sound, and in some cases taste) are involved, making the experience much more enjoyable than watching virtual objects on a computer screen.

---

[12] Philippa made a sphere at a Mini Maker Fair, Powerhouse Museum, Sydney 2015.
[13] Make magazine, Vol 84, 2023.
[14] Burke, J. J. 2014. Makerspaces: a practical guide for librarians (Vol. 8). Lanham, MD: Rowman & Littlefield.

Wooden boat festivals are one of many fairs held around the world that display the creativity of people who make things. Every two years, the *MyState Wooden Boat Festival* is held in Hobart Tasmania. The festival attracts more people to the city than its population. Over 500 boats are on display from dinghies to tall ships, such as the James Craig. In February 2019, a key attraction was a group from *North-Western Boat School* in Washington who brought a container full of boats with them. During the two weeks before the festival they made a boat, which was auctioned during the festival.

The official Maker website defines a Maker Fair as:

> 'The Greatest Show (& Tell) on Earth. As a celebration of the Maker Movement, it's a family-friendly showcase of invention and creativity that brings together tech enthusiasts, crafters, educators, tinkerers, food artisans, hobbyists, engineers, science clubs, artists, students, and commercial exhibitors. Makers come to show their creations. Attendees come to glimpse the future...and to learn to become makers themselves.'[15]

At Maker Fairs, makers are often challenged to make objects and devices that will make a difference in peoples' lives in the future. In the December 4, 2003, issue of the 'The Economist' William Gibson wrote: "The future is already here, it's not very evenly distributed."[16]

Silicon Valley web strategist, Jeremiah Owang observed: "This Maker Movement puts power in the hands of the people to fund, design, prototype, produce, manufacture, distribute, market and sell their own goods."[17]

---

[15] makerfaire.com
[16] goodreads.com/quotes/681-the-future-is-already-here-it-s-just-not-evenly
[17] apbspeakers.com/speaker/jeremiah-owyang/

I believe that when we make something we reflect the character of the God who made us. The writer of Psalm 104 clearly believes that God created everything. Do we reflect his concern for the welfare of people?

> "How many are your works, LORD!
> In wisdom you made them all;
> the earth is full of your creatures.
> There is the sea, vast and spacious,
> teeming with creatures beyond number—
> living things both large and small."
> (Psalm 104:24-25)

## MAKER SPACES

Makers have always needed workshops and studios equipped with tools to make things. The Maker Movement quickly gave rise to 'maker spaces'. A maker space is a room where makers can get together to share ideas, to read designs in project books and to loan tools.[18] They are used to run courses and to make things. They are often setup to support STEAM (science, technology, engineering, art, and mathematics) programs in schools and libraries. In 2021, Newsweek published a list of the best Maker Schools in the world.[19] It includes my alma mater.

They are locations which allow students and their families to work together in project-based learning. Students can self-select their project and choose who they want to work with, which is normally not possible in a

---

[18] shop.popularmechanics.com/100-steam-activities-kids-won-t-learn-in-school.html?source=steam_book_ed_product_embed-

[19] Blakeslee, J. And Hammond, K. 2021. Best Maker Schools 2021, Make Vol 79, pp14-17.
makezine.com/best-maker-schools-2021-from-make-and-newsweek

traditional classroom. There are many different definitions of maker spaces, but most agree they enable inquiry-based learning in cooperative groups.[20]

Maker spaces allow people to share tools that they can't purchase for themselves, such as 3D printers. 3D printing enables makers to produce small runs of high-quality product. Just as the development of the LaserWriter revolutionized the printing industry, so the development of 3D printers is revolutionizing the manufacturing industry. In a special article for USA TODAY in October 2013, Martha Stewart reported that: "Makers pump some $29 billion into the economy each year."[21]

During the 2020 COVID19 pandemic countries ran short of personal protective equipment (PPE), ventilators and other medical equipment. Makers worked together and with companies to make PPE. 3D printing farms were set up to make face masks. A Wollongong (NSW) 3D printer manufacturer set up a printer farm in an empty classroom at UOW with 140 printers to make 2,000 face shields a day.

Engineering firms retooled to produce ventilators. Gin manufacturers used their stills to make alcohol for hand sanitizers. Without the Maker Movement turning its hand to medical equipment more people would have suffered from the lack of adequate supplies.

To implement new ideas, makers need access to funds and markets. Several sources of crowd funding have sprung up to meet this need. Kickstarter is an example of a group that enables makers to present proposals for new products online. These proposals include an option for financial backing, a deadline to back the project, and a version of the product.

---

[20] Spencer, R., & Huss, J. 2013. Playgrounds for the mind. Children & Libraries: The Journal of the Association for Library Service to Children, 11(3), 41-46.

[21] usatoday.com/story/money/business/2013/10/14/martha-stewart-column-meet-the-makers/2980701/

Software developers build, deliver, and maintain their software on software-repositories such as GitHub.[22] Companies have sprung up to supply the materials, electronics, and computer hardware used to make things, including Core Electronics[23] and Adafruit.[24]

## MAKING TOOLS

Makers make tools to extend human capabilities and jigs to hold workpieces in place. When you pick up a pencil to draw it becomes part of your hand. You can determine where to hold the pencil by its shape and surface texture, all using touch. In his book *Fearfully & Wonderfully, The Marvel of Bearing God's Image*, Dr. Paul Brand claims that the sensitivity of your fingertips is second only to the sensitivity of the tip of your tongue.[25] Your fingertips are wonderfully made to be highly sensitive to anything you touch, enabling you to manipulate a pencil to draw an object or to write your name.

According to researchers at the Claude Bernard Lyon 1 University in France: "Our brains treat tools as extensions of our bodies."[26] They claim: "Humans have the uncanny ability to very closely approximate where one object, like a finger, comes into contact with another object being used as a tool, like a pencil, as long as the tool is in direct contact with skin."[27] In a Youtube video,[28] a blind woman illustrates how she uses a white cane as

---

[22] github.com
[23] core-electronics.com.au
[24] adafruit.com
[25] Brand P. 2019. Fearfully and Wonderfully, Hodder, Chapter 7.
[26] Miller L.E. et al. 2019. Somatosensory Cortex Efficiently Processes Touch Located Beyond the Body, Current Biology, Volume 29, Issue 24, 16 December, Pages 4276-4283.
[27] popularmechanics.com/science/a30361970/sense-of-touch/
[28] youtube.com/watch?v=xi0JMS1rulo&t=235s

an extension of her body. When she navigates in a street, she uses the white cane to sense objects with both touch and sound (Figure 1.4).[29]

**Figure 1.4** *White cane used to extend sense of touch*

As an exercise in perception, collect a friend, a piece of paper, and a pencil. Place the paper on a table within reach. Close your eyes and keep them closed. Ask your friend to pass you the pencil by placing the tip of the pencil between your fingertips on one hand. While holding the tip of the pencil with your fingertips, reach out with your other hand and touch the other end of the pencil.

Keeping your eyes closed, adjust your hold on the pencil to the position you use for writing. Now find the edge of the paper and write your name on the paper. Open your eyes. At what steps during the exercise did you feel that the pencil was part of your body?

---

[29] White cane extending sense of touch.
youtube.com/watch?v=xi0JMS1rulo&t=235s

Just as you can think that a pencil is an extension of your body in contact with a sheet of paper, people who believe in Jesus can think of themselves as an extension of God in contact with people in this world. When you are drawing with a pencil you protect it from damage so that you can use it to write in the future. Psalm 91 tells us that when we are in God's hands, he protects us from spiritual enemies so that we can glorify his name in the future.

> For he will command his angels concerning you
> to guard you in all your ways;
> they will lift you up in their hands,
> so that you will not strike your foot against a stone.
> (Psalm 91:11-12)

## MAKING IT ON TELEVISION

As making became a popular activity it also became popular with viewers of television shows. *Making It Australia* went to air in September 2021.[30] Based on a format produced by NBC in the USA, co-hosts Susie Youssef and Harley Breen, challenge a group of contestants to demonstrate their maker skills. They were challenged to make something amazing within a given time.

Every episode revolved around a central theme that drew inspiration from the Maker Movement. At the end of each episode two judges critiqued the objects that the contestants made. The judges accentuated the positive by finding something nice to say about each design. In the first episode the contestants faced two challenges, one called a faster craft and the other a master craft.

---

[30] tvtonight.com.au/2021/09/making-it-australia.html

In the faster craft they had three hours to build a secret beast. Each contestant made a different beast, including a colorful panda, a blue octopus with moving legs, a wolf, a drop bear, and even a disco themed bat. At the first judging it became obvious that the judges were looking for color, movement, and creative ideas.

In the master craft they each made a shrine that represented something from their life. After judging, one contestant was sent home. In the second week, they built a billy cart and a cubby. The whole show appeared to be targeted at children who like to make things. The hosts maintained a fun atmosphere by cracking *dad* jokes.

*Making It Australia* is a friendly competition that focuses on the character and camaraderie of makers. Contestant Dan, summed up his feelings about making: "Making and creating is my way to feel special, my way to feel different… I'm gifted with being amazing at making and creating." Like many makers, Dan enjoys thinking about how to make an object and then seeing it come to reality as he constructs it.

## THINKING LIKE A MAKER

To successfully design objects to craft a maker must think. The process of design involves thinking about objects and shapes, patterns and relationships, and materials and processes. Making something involves problem solving. The approach of step-wise-refinement, where a problem is solved by breaking it up into smaller problems, that is taught in computer science, is used by many makers.

To make a wooden table, a craftsman thinks about the steps involved, the order in which those steps should be executed, and the processes needed to achieve each step. Masters of every creative discipline teach their students to thoughtfully and intuitively use skills that have been developed by generations of makers. When a new design is to be made the old ways may only go so far and lateral thinking is required.[31]

I have observed that many makers are concrete thinkers. Generally, they express their ideas in a simple concrete style. They start with an image in their head of what they want to make. Examples include visual artists who often have an idea that comes to fruition in paint on canvas. Writers plan a storyline to follow when writing text in their chosen media. Electronic engineers solder up a prototype on a breadboard when testing circuit ideas. All are reflecting part of the character of the creator God, who makes a new artwork in the sky every evening. We call it a sunset.

Another area that requires a maker to think is how to ship their product to people who will use it. Steve Jobs famously said: *Real artists ship*[32] to challenge computer scientists to write quality code that other people will use. One result of this challenge is the App store.

A year after the release of the iPhone, Apple released the software tools to write Apps and an on-line App store to sell them. To be accepted for sale in the App store the software had to meet certain quality restrictions. Initially, a lot of people questioned the wisdom of this policy, but App developers soon realized the advantage of launching their Apps in a secure environment. The iPhone App quickly became the preferred way to ship software.

## MAKING AND MY FAITH

People have asked me many questions about the interaction of making with faith, including: "How can an intelligent, rational maker believe in a

---

[31] Chernyak, Y.B. and Rose, R.M. 1996. The Chicken from Minsk, Weidenfeld and Nicolson, London.
[32] fantartic.com/buy/posters/real-artists-ship

creator?" For over fifty-five years, I have thought about this interaction as I made various objects, including an electronic interface card for an Apple 2 personal computer (Figure 1.5) .[33] and a wooden boat.

**Figure 1.5** *Computer interface project for makers. Designed by the author and published in Electronics Today International.*

I became a believer in Jesus partly through observing design in nature when studying science at a public high school. I wanted to know more

---

[33] Computer interface project for makers, McKerrow, P.J. 1983. General purpose analogue and digital interface card for Apple II, Electronics Today International (ETI), March, pp 36-43.

about the God who made me, so I set out to find reasons for believing in Jesus, specifically, answers to two questions: "How can I know that God exists?" and "If God made me then does he have a purpose for my life?"

To answer these questions, I looked for evidence for an infinitely intelligent God. I learned that belief in Jesus is based on the evidence for his resurrection. When Jesus rose from the dead, he made the greatest escape story ever known.

I was challenged to do justice to that evidence by thinking about the influence that faith in Jesus would have on my life. I found that it requires wisdom to believe in Jesus, just as it requires wisdom to combine knowledge and experience with common sense and insight to produce an excellent object when making.

Wisdom is the collected knowledge of a trade or discipline coupled with the experience to apply that knowledge. It includes the skills passed on from a master to an apprentice. For example, I was taught by a master boat builder to fix problems when they occur. The longer I left a problem the harder it became to fix.

My experience contrasts to those makers whose 'making' does not include faith in God. They are not able to enhance their maker wisdom with spiritual wisdom. Spiritual wisdom is the collected knowledge about God recorded in the Bible coupled with the desire to obey his commands.

Grant Imahara was one such maker. He was a presenter in the popular television series *Myth Busters*. Grant died in 2020, at the age of 49, after suffering a ruptured intracranial aneurysm. Mike Senese, the Executive Editor of Make magazine wrote:

> "I also look back and appreciate that we were all graced with Grant's skills, as a builder, a presenter, and as a fantastic person overall. He made science cool. He made engineering fun. I changed my life because of him. Many

people changed their lives because of him. The world is a better place because of what he gave us."[34]

It was obvious that Grant loved making, but he did not have faith, he was non-religious, yet many people became makers after watching him on television. Even though I have not been in a television series, my faith in Jesus, my maker, has encouraged other makers to believe in him.

## OUR MAKER

Some makers choose to believe in an infinitely creative God, others choose not to. The God presented in the Bible gives people the skills to be a maker. For example, when God wanted Moses to build a tent of worship, he gave a craftsman expertise in all kinds of crafts.

> See, the LORD has chosen Bezalel son of Uri, the son of Hur, of the tribe of Judah, and he has filled him with the Spirit of God, with wisdom, with understanding, with knowledge and with all kinds of skills— to make artistic designs for work in gold, silver and bronze, to cut and set stones, to work in wood and to engage in all kinds of artistic crafts. (Exodus 35:30-32)

By inspecting an item that I have made you can get some idea of my character (Figure 1.6). Is the item precise or rough? Is the object functional or artistic? Have I given attention to detail? The Bible claims that we can observe the character of God by looking at the earth and sky.

---

[34] makezine.com/2020/07/14/how-grant-imahara-made-me-a-better-maker/

**Figure 1.6** *Peeler Skiff wooden motorboat made by the author, Photographer Rochelle Groombridge*

According to Psalm 100 verse 3 God is our Maker. He created us to serve and enjoy him forever. He made us to be like himself and to have a relationship with him. As our Maker he set up commands for us to live by. These commands are in the form of a covenant that defines life, love, and death. Life is our relationship with our Maker. Love is the outcome of keeping the covenant and death is the result of breaking the covenant.

> "Know that the LORD is God.
> It is he who made us, and we are his;
> we are his people, the sheep of his pasture."
> (Psalm 100:3)

In a Gospel Coalition Blog, Wheaton College Professor Trevin Wax cynically claimed that Psalm 100:3 "may be the most offensive verse in the Bible."[35] He claims that it is morally offensive to the modern mind because it states that God is our maker and we do not belong to ourselves. In an interview with Christian influencer Alisa Childers,[36] Michael Kruger,[37] Professor of New Testament at Reformed Theological Seminary, Charlotte, NC says that one of the main reasons that modern students reject Christianity is this teaching that "the content of the Bible is morally offensive." Does such a God exist or is he a myth?

A maker can support a bridge with a wire rope or with a steel girder. Each chapter in this book builds a wire into the rope to support the claim that God is our Maker. The last chapter studies the girder: the resurrection of Jesus. We finish this chapter with the question: Is there a master maker? - an infinitely capable maker who made us makers to be like himself. To explore this question further, as we look for reasons for believing in Jesus, we will plunge into the realm of faith to see what we can see.

---

[35] Wax, T. 2020. Why This May Be the Most Offensive Verse in the Bible, Gospel Coalition Blog, October 14.
thegospelcoalition.org/blogs/trevin-wax/the-most-offensive-verse-in-the-bible/

[36] Childers, A. 2020. Another Gospel?: A Lifelong Christian Seeks Truth in Response to Progressive Christianity, Tyndale Momentum.

[37] Kruger, M. 2021. Surviving Religion 101, Crossway.
youtube.com/watch?v=5UQsJWCerho

# 2

# FAITH

**Figure 2.1** *Training course for sighted trainers of blind people*

I am a fundamental atheist and genuinely have never had faith or interest in spiritual matters. Because I admire him as a mathematician, I have read Rob Hydman's book which describes his journey of *deconversion*.[1] It is a very interesting and readable book. I like his quote: "Faith is the gap between evidence and truth. The Bible agrees with this: Faith shows the reality of what we hope for; it is the evidence of things we cannot see." (Hebrews 11:1). - Professor Hugh Durrant-Whyte, NSW Chief Scientist & Engineer.[2]

"All I have seen teaches me to trust the creator for all I have not seen." - Ralph Waldo Emerson. 1803-82.[3]

"Faith is to believe what you do not see, and the reward of this faith is to see what you believe." - Augustine.[4]

"Unless there is an element of risk in our exploits for God, there is no need for faith." - Hudson Taylor, 1832-1905.[5]

## ADVENTURE IN FAITH

Ann (my wife) and I went on an organized tour of China for two weeks. Several days before we left one of our sons said, "Don't take Bibles to China, you will end up in gaol. Chinese gaols are not nice."

---

[1] robjhyndman.com/unbelievable/
[2] sydney.edu.au/engineering/about/our-people/academic-staff/hugh-durrantwhyte.html
[3] American Philosopher and poet.
[4] azquotes.com/quote/12927
[5] wikipedia.org/wiki/Hudson_Taylor

Three days before we left for China, we received an email from Jane in Wuhan.[6] She became a believer in Jesus while she was studying at the University Of Wollongong in NSW. She wrote:

"I am so sorry that I left the Bible that you gave me in Australia. If you can come to my city, would you please carry a Bible for me? Sometimes I really want to read it word by word. The Bible on my phone is not always available from the internet …

Our itinerary in China included a flight from Shanghai to Wuhan, followed by a bus trip to Yichang. We arranged to meet Jane at Wuhan airport. The day before we left Australia was a public holiday and the bookshops were shut. I prayed, "Lord where do I get a Bible from?"

A suitable Bible was locked in a cupboard in the church building. I had a key to the cupboard but not to the building. I drove to the building, to find it was deserted, then I went to the pastor's house, no one was home. As I walked back across the road to the church building, I prayed, "Lord if you want me to take a Bible to China, I have to get into that building."

I thought I would try the doors before I rang the building supervisor. I went to the door at the rear of the children's hall. The doorknob would not turn, it was locked. But, to my surprise, as I pulled my hand away and turned to go the latch clicked and the door flew open. So, I went inside and got a Bible. On the way out, I checked the door; it was still locked. Later, the building supervisor told me that they had been having trouble with that door, but they thought they had fixed it.

---

[6] True story, names changed

# FAITH

At home we opened a Bible to Proverbs 18;16: "Giving a gift can open doors; it gives access to important people!" (NLT). We were convinced that the door opening was more than a coincidence and prayed that this Bible would open doors in China and give many people access to Jesus.

When we got to Shanghai, I asked our tour guide for information on our flight to Wuhan. She said, "You are not going to Wuhan - the itinerary has been changed, you are flying directly to Yichang. I prayed, "Lord we have a Bible in our bag, what do we do with it?"

If we tried to post it, we would arouse suspicion because we had never been in a Chinese post office and couldn't speak the language. That night we had dinner with a Christian friend in Shanghai. He is a member of an underground church with about 100 members. They meet in a community room in a large block of units.

We asked him if he would post the Bible to Jane. He agreed to mail it to her. We gave him the Bible on Friday evening. He mailed it on Saturday and no questions were asked. Jane received it on Sunday. I asked Jane for her thoughts on why it is so good to have a Bible. She wrote:

> "It is really a big question why we need a Bible to read. Yes, it is natural just like water to fish, air to life, and sun to trees. Bible offers us spiritual nutrition that helps us growing up.
>
> I am not a good reader, neither well, nor often. But I like to read it when I am tired, sad, confused, and lost. The words on Bible just like spring water when I feel thirsty. I am just a beginner on the way, expecting better inspiration after longer period study." – Jane.

## FAITH

To look at the influence of faith in the life of a maker, we will examine what faith is. Then we will use this definition to help order out thoughts as we look at reasons for believing in Jesus. Our understanding of faith is the basis for answering the question: Why believe in Jesus?

Faith is defined in the bible as "confidence in what we hope for and assurance about what we do not see." (Hebrews 11:1) There are two assumptions in that definition. First, there are things that we cannot see with our eyes. Second, there are other forms of evidence than vision. In this chapter we meet the master maker: a God we cannot see who offers to give us the eternal life we hope for.

Christians are often accused of having blind faith because they believe in a God they cannot see. They respond that just because they cannot see something doesn't mean it doesn't exist. I have worked with electricity for many years. I can't see it but boy it gave me a kick when I touched a bare wire!

At UOW we developed a training course to teach sighted people how a blind person uses an ultrasonic mobility aid, giving us insight into the problem of sensing what we cannot see (Figure 2.1).[7] For more information see the section on 'Echolocation' later in this chapter.

Critics say that believing in God is a leap in the dark. In the sense that I cannot see God this may be true. But a blind person can know me even though they can't see me. They use their other senses: touch, sound, and smell. It is true that I cannot detect God with any of my physical senses unless God chooses to reveal himself to me. Christians claim that when

---

[7] DVD training course for sighted trainers of blind people using K-Sonar (Figure 2.3) developed by the author and his students, 30/5/2008

# FAITH

they believed in Jesus, God sent his Holy Spirit to communicate with them. Knowing God is like having an additional sense.

I have never jumped from a bridge attached to a bungee cord. My children tell me the exhilaration is very real. Faith is like a bungee jump. You strap a harness on. One end of the bungee cord is tied to the harness, the other to the bridge you plan to jump off.

In faith that the cord won't break, and you won't crash, you launch yourself into space and fall down, down, down into the canyon below until the cord stretches to bring you to a halt before you hit the ground. Faith is taking the hand of Jesus, knowing that he will not let you go as you launch out into the rest of your life.

Your faith that the bungee cord will stop your flight is based on the evidence that others have jumped before you. You experience exhilaration as you fall, having let go of all means of support other than the cord. It is not a blind leap, you can see where you are going, even though you have little control over where you are going. When you have faith in Jesus, you trust him to control where you are going because he has proved trustworthy in the past. Christians live by faith.

> "Without faith it is impossible to please God, because anyone who comes to him must believe that he exists and that he rewards those who earnestly seek him." (Hebrews 11:6)

Faith in Jesus, based on non-visual evidence, is belief in a personal creator who loves you. Jesus was born as a human to reveal God to you. The experience of knowing God by faith is recorded in the Bible for us to read. The personal experience of many Christians is their reason for believing in Jesus.

## IN OUR LANGUAGE

Paul White was known throughout Australia as the *Jungle Doctor*.[8] In 1941, he started a weekly radio broadcast where he told stories of faith featuring African animals. The names of the animals are their Swahili names, for example, Twiga the giraffe. He rewrote some of the stories as the *Jungle Doctor* series of illustrated children's books.[9]

**Figure 2.2** *The monkeys who didn't believe in crocodiles*

---

[8] jungledoctorcomics.com
[9] Figure 2.2 The monkeys who didn't believe in crocodiles Paul White jungledoctorcomics.com/jungle-doctors-fables

# FAITH

One story featured Tip and Top the twin monkeys who didn't believe in crocodiles (Figure 2.2). But their unbelief didn't make any difference when they met Crunch the Crocodile in the middle of the night on the banks of the Great River. They needed someone strong and wise to save them from Crunch. A split second before Crunch's jaws slammed shut, Twiga's strong neck had swept down, carrying two small, terrified monkeys to safety.

Paul White was invited to speak at a civic reception in a New South Wales city.[10]

> After his speech the mayor said publicly, "I don't believe the Bible, it is full of contradictions."

White took a $50 note out of his pocket, placed it in a Bible and handed it to the mayor with the words:

> "If you can show me a contradiction you can have the $50."

The mayor admitted that he couldn't because he had never read the Bible.

The teachings of the Christian faith are found in the Bible. It is a book containing 66 individual books written over a period of roughly 1600 years between 1500 BC and 100 AD. It is divided into two sections, one deals with God's relationship with people before the birth of Jesus, in particular the Israelites. The other deals with God's relationship with people after the birth of Jesus.

Believers in Jesus put their faith in the Bible's teaching. They believe by faith that God has welcomed them into eternal life. They claim that the Bible is the Word of God in human language. The Bible was originally

---

[10] This story was shared with me by Paul's protege Clifford Warne.

written in Hebrew, Aramaic, and Greek.[11] Today it has been translated into all the major languages in the world. The Holy Spirit ensures that it remains God's Word through the translation process.

From beginning to end the Bible is about Jesus. It claims to be the big story of faith. The focal point is the death and resurrection of Jesus from the dead. If Jesus didn't rise from the dead, then the Bible is not true and consequently believing in Jesus is a waste of your life and faith in him is useless. If Jesus did rise from the dead, then the Bible is true and consequently, believing in Jesus is the path to eternal life, and faith is the confidence that you are on that path.

Theologians use big words to describe the character of God that is revealed in the Bible, words that start with the prefix omni, meaning all or infinite. Omniscience means God has infinite knowledge and nothing is hidden from him. Omnipresence means God is everywhere at once in space-time. Omnipotence means God has infinite power and will bring people to justice. Notice, we are talking about a God with infinite capabilities.

## EVIDENCE

Faith in Jesus is based on the Bible's claim that we were created by an infinitely powerful and intelligent God. Many atheists believe that humans are the result of one chance in an infinite number of possibilities. Each one of us is required to choose between faith in an infinitely intelligent God or faith in something that is not God, such as an infinitesimal chance. Both beliefs can seem to be impossible. Christians and atheists agree that to be an intelligent thinker you should do justice to the evidence. One aim of this book is to look at some of that evidence.

---

[11] At the time of Jesus the old testament was written in Hebrew. Aramaic was the common language in Israel and Greek was the language of learning.

# FAITH

There are several types of evidence for the existence of God, including design, history, revelation, and personal experience. The Bible claims that we can see God's character by observing the design and beauty of his creation. Christians believe they know about God because Jesus was born as a human to reveal God to us. His words are recorded in the gospels. They are history books that record the birth, life, death, and resurrection of Jesus.

When people believe in Jesus, the Holy Spirit moves into their life to reveal the truth of these words. What you think of this evidence is often determined by your understanding of revelation by faith. Revelation is the source of information about God.

It seems that a lot of atheists define faith as "belief without evidence." The atheist who is celebrated in the world today is Oxford evolutionary biologist Richard Dawkins. He states that: "religious faith ... does not depend on rational justification" and he claims that religions demand "unquestioned faith."[12] While some atheists disagree with Dawkins, it is his views that have been popularized in the media.

Naturally, believers in Jesus don't agree with Dawkins. Their reasons for believing in Jesus are based on evidence, specifically the historical evidence for Jesus rising from the dead. Also, believers point to the profit that comes from believing as evidence of the Holy Spirit working in their lives, such as joy, peace, and wisdom. Bible commentator Nigel Wright wrote about those who don't believe:

> "Those who are hostile to the bible (and there are many) are destined never to profit from its wisdom."[13]

---

[12] Dawkins, R. 2016. The God Delusion Bantam Press, 2006
[13] Wright, N. 2021, Encounter with God, January - March, p 60.

**Figure 2.3** *K-Sonar. Sonic navigation device for the blind and used in ultrasonic sensing research.*

## ECHOLOCATION

An example of people putting their faith in something they cannot see is the use of echolocation by blind people. A group of blind children were attending a live-in training course in a two-story house.[14] They were on the bottom floor, and they knew that there was a ceiling above them. James was exploring the ceiling with a K-Sonar ultrasonic mobility aid (Figure 2.3).[15]

He asked, "Teacher, why is there a big hole in the ceiling?"

She replied, "When you go to bed at night you will walk up the steps to the floor above us?"

---

[14] Story told to me by the late Nora Kay, wife of Professor Leslie Kay, University of Canterbury, New Zealand. the inventor of the K-Sonar:

[15] Figure 2.3 McKerrow, P.J. and Kristiansen, B.E. 2006. Classifying surface roughness with CTFM ultrasonic sensing, IEEE Sensors Journal, Vol. 6. No. 5. October, pp 1267-1279

"Yes," James replied.

"Well, the hole is for the steps to go through. You walk through it when you go up to bed."

To understand the echoes, he was hearing James needed to know about the room he was in. This context helped him perceive what he was sensing.

A blind person observes their world through heightened touch and sound. Echolocation is the location and recognition of objects by bouncing sound waves off them, as used by bats and dolphin. Some people can echolocate naturally using their mouth to produce clicks of sound.[16] Others use electronic aids, such as the K-Sonar developed by Professor Leslie Kay, to produce chirps of ultrasonic energy, and still others bang the end of their white cane against objects.[17]

The sensor in the K-Sonar blind aid consists of a transmitter and a receiver. The transmitter sends a beam of ultrasonic energy toward an object where it is reflected back towards the receiver. The number, spacing and amplitude of the echoes detected by the receiver is determined by the shape of the object (Figure 2.4).[18]

The electronic circuits in the sensor convert the range information into a set of audio tones that act as a signature for object recognition. A glass window has a sharp narrow set of tones. A row of books has a wider rougher set of tones. A curtain has a softer set of tone.

A blind user learns to convert this audio information into a mental view of the environment containing the range to and direction of objects. The echo from the object is as complex as the geometry of the object, enabling

---

[16] Gordon, A. 2014. Echoes of an Angel, Tyndale House Publishers.
[17] Kay, L. 2000. Auditory perception of objects by blind persons using a bioacoustic high resolution air sonar, Journal Acoustical Society of America. Vol 107, No 6, June, pp 3266-3275.
[18] Echolocation with ultrasonic sensor (https://www.youtube.com/watch?v=zpifkY2C5og)

the user to recognize some objects. It is thought that people use the part of the brain normally used for vision to build a 3D acoustic model of their world.

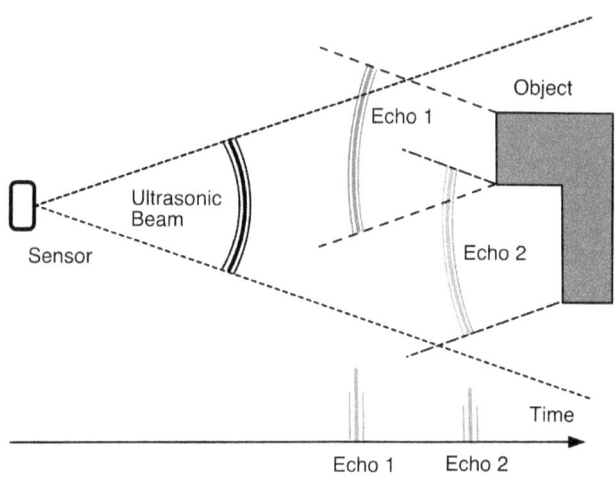

**Figure 2.4** *Echolocation with ultrasonic sensor*

One problem, when training blind people to use this aid, is that their trainers, who can see, cannot see the ultrasonic beam and are not sure what object is producing the echoes. Much work has been done by sighted people to try and understand how the blind navigate with echolocation. One goal is to produce a training video for people who can see, so that they can help people who can't see to understand how to train blind people (Figure 2.1).[19]

The best teachers of the blind are blind people who have learned to recognize objects and navigate using the aid.[20] In an attempt to explain

---

[19] McKerrow, P.J. and Vita, F. 2008. K-Sonar, Seeing the world with sound, Video Training Course, Department of Computer Science, University of Wollongong.

[20] sites.aph.org/files/manuals/ksonar.pdf

how he navigated with echolocation, one blind man made a set of audio recordings. Most blind people just use the aid and cannot explain how they do it.[21]

To move freely in a room, you must perceive the environment and then trust your perception before taking your next step. That is, you should put your faith in your interpretation of the signals from a sensor based on the evidence of your previous experience. Similarly, to find your way to God by faith you must believe that he exists and that you can hear him (Hebrews 11:6).

## LISTENING TO GOD

The Bible says that the moment a person trusts in Jesus the Holy Spirit enters their spirit and sets up communication between them and God. In effect, it is like receiving an extra sense of perception. It takes time to learn to echolocate, likewise it takes time to learn to listen to God.

It is nearly impossible for a sighted person to explain vision to a blind person, similarly it is nearly impossible for a believer in Jesus to explain faith to a non-believer. Vision is real for most people. Faith is just as real for believers in Jesus.

God often speaks to believers by putting words in their minds. The Holy Spirit confirms these words with spiritual prompts in their spirit. Sometimes God speaks through an audible voice, an image, or a dream. The believer confirms it is God's voice they are hearing by comparing the message to the directions and stories written in the Bible.

Christians believe that the Holy Spirit inspired the writing of the bible, so anything God says will be consistent with the bible when it is interpreted correctly. If the message is not consistent with the bible, it is not from God.

---

[21] Gissoni, F. 1966. My cane is twenty feet long, The New Outlook for the blind, February.

## READING THE BIBLE IN CONTEXT

Faith in Jesus is based on trusting in the teaching about him that is recorded in the Bible. The claim that the Bible is God's Word in human language implies that humans can understand it. For example, Psalm 119 is a celebration of the benefits of reading the Bible as God's Word. To understand the Bible, or any other piece of literature, we must know its context. Context is the most powerful tool we have for interpreting the Bible and, hence, for understanding its message.

The Bible is not always easy to understand. We may find a command that God gives offensive to our modern mind because we are unaware of the cultural context in which it was given, or we may not like the command. In their book, titled 'The Bible Handbook of Difficult Verses', Josh and Sean McDowell discuss many of these difficulties.[22]

The first context we will consider is how meaning is given to words, including the way words are used to describe time. In the book of Genesis, God is described as having created life on earth in six days. In the beginning he had created the heavens and the earth. But the earth was empty. Then he spent six days creating plants, animals, and humans to fill the earth with life. Such a feat would require an infinitely powerful God.

Many scholars believe that Moses wrote the first five books of the Jewish Bible using previous writings, tribal stories, and revelation from God to correct the first two sources. Many parts of the Bible were written to correct false ideas in the surrounding culture. To understand this claim of creation in six days we need to understand the culture in which he was writing. Hebrew is a Semitic language (named after Noah's son Shem), possibly derived from the Canaanite language. One problem is that much knowl-

---

[22] McDowell Josh and McDowell Sean, 2013. The Bible Handbook of Difficult Verses: A Complete Guide to Answering the Tough Questions, Harvest House Publishers

edge about the surrounding Egyptian culture has been lost. The Bible is one ancient document that we have intact. This is one evidence for its divine origin.

To get our minds in tune with the Hebrew culture of Moses, we can ask a variety of questions. When asked to describe an object, did they talk about its form or its function? For example, when asked to describe a spear - did they describe its shape, length, etc. or say it has a sharp point to kill the enemy? When speaking of an abstract concept - did they use a concrete example? For example, instead of saying, "She is in love with him,", they may have said, "Her face is covered in smiles when she is with him."

> "Hebrew makes extensive use of terms for physical attitudes to describe psychological states, or organs of the body are associated with mental states. … The imagery of Hebrew is largely drawn from the things and activities of everyday life. It has, therefore, a universal quality and lends itself without difficulty to translation. … Hebrew speaks about the 'head' of a mountain, the 'face' of the earth, the 'lip' (shore) of the sea, …" *The Illustrated Bible Dictionary*[23]

How did they think about the passing of time? We talk of going forward into the future while the ancient Greeks talked about going forward into the past because we can see the past, but we can't see the future. We think of an hour as a fixed length of time and a day as a fixed number of hours. People in ancient societies are believed to have defined a day as the time from sunrise to sunset, so the length of a day varied with the seasons. In some cultures, time is circular with sunrise, noon, sunset and the watches of the night forming a repeating cycle.

---

[23] Language of the old Testament, The Illustrated Bible Dictionary, 1980. Part 2, page 875, IVP.

We measure time with mechanical devices that give us a linear view of time. The Hebrews had a linear view of time based on events, not based on an abstract continuity but based on the concept of God given appointed times for particular events.[24] So, in the Bible time moves from creation to the first sin, from expulsion from the garden to Abraham, from Abraham to King David, from David to the birth of Jesus, from his birth to his resurrection and finally from his resurrection to the consummation of all events in his second coming.

Two dates are proposed for the exodus of Israel from Egypt led by Moses: 1270BC and 1440BC. At that time, the word day was in common use. It described a concrete event: the period from sunrise to sunset.[25] The timing of the agricultural seasons, which is determined by the passage of the sun, was described with the word 'month.' Using the word 'hour' to describe the time of day was in common use by the time of Jesus.[26]

The word 'minute' does not occur in the Bible. It is an abstract term. It wasn't until 1670 that William Clement made a clock precise enough to establish the second as a unit of time.[27] Today we divide time even further and use seconds to describe the length of ordinary events and nanoseconds to describe the speed of our computers.

The word day was a natural way to describe a period of time in the language of Moses' day. To describe creation as taking billions of years would have been so abstract that they would not have been able to comprehend it. Can we? Also, the writers of the Bible often didn't present events in chronological order. They were more interested in the interaction between

---

[24] Time, The Illustrated Bible Dictionary, 1980. Part 3, page 1566, IVP.
[25] In the first three chapters of Genesis the word day is used 12 times with 1366 occurrences in the rest of the bible.
[26] Jesus said a day was 12 hours. Hour is used only 4 times in the old testament and 20 times in the new.
[27] theuijunkie.com/second-length/

God and people. The Bible was written in the language of the day using their concepts of time.

## READING THE BIBLE IN PERSPECTIVE

A second context is the perspective from which the story of creation was transcribed. It is written in the third person from the perspective of an observer. An observer standing on the surface of the earth will see events differently to an observer in space or to an observer in eternity.

A third context is the type of literature: history, poetry, soliloquy, fiction, formal, dialog, allegory, etc. Moses wrote in the language of the Hebrews so the people could understand him. He did not write in a science-based language.

The Bible is not a scientific textbook. It was written using concrete terms to describe abstract ideas. Some people read it literally, which results in a conflict with science, which we will look at in later chapters. Others consider the description of creation in Genesis 1 to be poetry. Poetry can be true while using language that evokes emotions.

The creation story is repeated in Genesis 2 from a different point of view with events in a different order. In Genesis 1 human beings were made on the sixth day. In Genesis 2 God appears to create humans at roughly the same time as the land sprouts vegetation on the third day. This appears to be a contradiction but could simply be the result of viewing the events from a different perspective. In Genesis 1 the events are related by the theme of the days of creation. In Genesis 2 they are related by the theme of the earth becoming fertile and bearing fruit.

A fourth context is theological. Biblical scholar Emeritus Professor David Clines, from the University of Sheffield, discusses creation from a theological perspective in his paper: 'Varieties of Creation in the Bible.'.[28] The Hebrews were a monotheistic people, worshiping one God, while the nations around them were polytheistic, worshiping nature and man-made idols. The theological thrust of "God created" in Genesis 1 is that we should worship the one God who created everything, not the things he created, or idols made to represent the seasons.

## PURPOSE OF THE BIBLE

This raises the question: "What was Moses' purpose in writing Genesis?" The writers of the Bible believed that they were writing the Word of God in human language. An angel did not dictate the words to them, as in some other religions. They were inspired by the Holy Spirit to think about life in the context of the big story of God seeking a people for himself and then they wrote down their thoughts, feelings, and recollections.

Their purpose was to tell us about the God who created humans and about our relationship with that God, so that we can put our faith in him. Faith that results from wonder at the beauty of the earth we live on. Wonder that expresses itself in praise.

Genesis is not a scientific textbook. It is a record of creation from the perspective of God creating a people to enjoy a relationship with himself. We learn several things about this creation. First, God is the creator. Second, he is so powerful that he spoke and life in its various forms sprung into being.

Third, this process of creation occurred in several stages, each stage taking a period of time that was described as a day. Fourth, he created the earth to provide a home for people. Fifth, he desired a relationship with people. Sixth, when he completed his work of creation he rested and enjoyed

---

[28] academia.edu/2381241/Varieties_of_Creation_in_the_Bible

his creation. Seventh, he ensures that the physical universe continues to function.

## SEX

God ensures that the process he began at creation will continue with his command to each species to be fruitful and multiply. One characteristic of creation is that God created male and female humans so that the two will couple to make the next generation of humans. He reveals in the Bible that he created male and female to be equal and different.

Christian marriage is a commitment by a man and a woman to belong to each other, exclusively. The couple are to abstain from sexual intercourse before marriage and be faithful to each other in marriage. At a deeper level, it models the relationship between Jesus and the church.

The couple commit to one another for life by going through a wedding ceremony. In an act of faith, they express their trust in one another. A wedding consists of three parts. One, the couple sign a legal document that states that they are married according to the laws of their country. Two, they ask God to bless their marriage as they leave their parents. Three, they couple in sexual intercourse to become united into one.

In future, they will work together as a team to build their home. They will seek to establish it as a secure, warm, and gentle environment for their children, where the man loves his wife, and the woman respects her husband. Also, their home will be a place where they provide hospitality to friends and strangers.

A loving relationship between a man and woman is one of the most beautiful things God created. The breakdown of that relationship is one of the saddest things that can happen. Recently Ann and I celebrated 50 years of joyous intimate marriage. Some would say that this is a miracle, but we know it is a consequence of our faith in Jesus.

## MIRACLES

Another characteristic of creation is that our maker can enter into it to make events that we find impossible. Before God created the earth, he created the laws of physics. These laws control what we can do in space-time. When an event occurs that is contrary to one of these laws, we call it a miracle.

For example, a group of prophets found a suitable place to build a meeting house beside the Jordan river (2 Kings 6: 1-7). They began cutting down trees, under the supervision of Elisha the chief prophet. But as one of them was cutting a tree, his ax head fell into the river.

> "Oh no, my lord!" he cried to Elisha. "It was borrowed!"

> "Where did it fall?" the man of God asked.

When he showed him the place, Elisha cut a stick and threw it into the water at that spot. Then the ax head floated to the surface.

> "Lift it out," Elisha said. And the prophet reached out and grabbed it.

We all know that ax heads don't float. Iron is denser than water so the head would weigh more than the volume of water it displaced, and it would sink, which it did. The force due to gravity was greater than the force due to buoyancy, causing it to sink.

Throwing a stick in the water would not make the ax head float. For it to float the force due to buoyancy would have to be supplemented by another force so that the combined force is greater than the force due to gravity.

This event is called a miracle because it is physically impossible, but the Bible writer presents it as a true story. We see two things about miracles: (1) the seemingly impossible occurs in response to an act of faith in God, and (2) the required faith is demonstrated by doing something that could not achieve the desired outcome.

Elisha knew that throwing a stick into the water would not, by itself, raise the ax. God had asked him to do something that cannot achieve the desired outcome to show that the ax head was raised by God, because only God can adjust the laws of physics. Once again, the writer of the Bible is asking us to believe in an infinitely powerful God.

## SEEING

Another example of an incredible miracle, where a man exercised faith in Jesus, is illustrated by the following event:

> "Some people brought a blind man and begged Jesus to touch him. He took the blind man by the hand and led him outside the village. When he had spit on the man's eyes and put his hands on him, Jesus asked, "Do you see anything?"
>
> He looked up and said, "I see people; they look like trees walking around."
>
> Once more Jesus put his hands on the man's eyes. Then his eyes were opened, his sight was restored, and he saw everything clearly." (Mark 8:22-25)

Again, the person wanting the miracle is asked to do something by faith that can't achieve the desired result. Spitting on someone's eyes might wash away the sleep but it will not cure blindness. Jesus demonstrated that he is God by healing the man.

However, seeing is more than fixing up someone's eyes so they can sense light. The man could not understand the visual patterns falling on his working eyes. So, Jesus did something even more incredible; he gave the man a lifetime of visual experience. Now he could perceive as well as sense.

The crowd, who were following Jesus, saw the miracle. However, they didn't get the message that they needed their eyes opened to see who Jesus is. This miracle illustrates that faith is often a two-step process: knowing about Jesus followed by knowing him personally.

The God who created the laws of nature usually lets them run their course, but he can change them to produce a miracle. He normally works through everyday events that obey the laws of the universe, after all he created those laws to govern life on earth.

He created physical laws to govern physical activity, such as gravity, and chemical laws to govern chemical reactions, such as fermentation. Also, he created moral laws to govern social activity, such as you shall not commit adultery, and relationship laws to govern your relationship with other people, such as love your neighbor as yourself. Importantly, he created spiritual laws to govern your relationship with God, such as, "You must not have any other god but me."

## CROSSING THE SEA OF REEDS.

The realm of faith has even greater challenges for us. Possibly, the story in the Bible that people find the most difficult to believe is the crossing of the Sea of Reeds when the Israelites escaped from slavery. It is the great saving event of the *Hebrew Bible*. To escape from Egypt the people of Israel had to cross the Eastern border of Egypt into the wilderness of Shur. The border was along a string of lakes and marshes that ran from the Gulf of Suez to the Mediterranean Sea (roughly where the Suez Canal is today).

The Egyptians had garrisons along the border, at the crossing points into the wilderness. Three main roads crossed the border. The northern road went along the Mediterranean Sea coast to Canaan, the middle road went through the wilderness to Canaan and the southern road went through the Sinai desert towards Arabia.

The northern road was the shortest, but God led the Israelites away from it because they were not ready to fight a war.[29] They were slaves fleeing from a cruel master and were yet to become a nation. The following experiences would start the process of forging them into a nation. So, God led them along the desert road that ran through the marshes to the southeast. However, it would have had an Egyptian garrison on the border also.

Having neared the border between Egypt and the wilderness the Israelites turned north and followed the border until they came to a body of water too large to ford and camped there. The author pinpoints the exact location of this camp, but we do not know the location of the towns he used as reference points— the passage of time often erases useful historical knowledge.

The Egyptians thought that the Israelites didn't know where they were going. Which was true, they didn't but God did. So, the Egyptian army blocked their retreat planning to drive them into the water to their death. Both the Egyptians and the Israelites thought that the Egyptians had succeeded in trapping the Israelites.

Next, we see both the power and the strategy of God. He revealed his power by clearing a path through the Sea of Reeds. It is known that a wind

---

[29] Exodus 14

can move water about but usually only to a shallow depth. God moved the water in a supernatural act and used the wind to dry out the ground so that they could walk over it.

By taking this supernatural path God led them out of Egypt without having to fight one of the Egyptian garrisons. When the water returned it cut off any possible retreat by the Israelites, effectively shutting them out of Egypt. So, the only way forward was into the wilderness, probably along the road to Arabia.

Escaping from Egypt was one step in making a group of slaves into a nation under the rule of God. Here we see God using both normal physical events (don't travel the road to a garrison) in conjunction with supernatural intervention (using an east wind to clear a path through the water).

## LOGISTICS

Another supernatural act was the organization of the people. The Bible says there were 600,000 men. With the addition of women and children the total number of people would be roughly 2.4 million.[30]

But there is a logistical problem. For the sake of calculation, let us divide the people into 12 equal tribes of 200,000 people (50,000 men + 50,000 women + 100,000 children). Then let each tribe march four abreast making a column 50,000 people long and four people wide. If each person took up an area 1.5 m long by 1.5 m wide the column would be 75 kms long and 6 m wide.

If the road was narrow (6m wide), and the 12 tribes marched in sequence, then the total column would be 900 kms long. If the road was

---

[30] 70 of Jacob's direct descendants went into Egypt 400 years before. If we start with 50 males and double the number of boys born every generation with a generation span of 30 years we get 810,200 born in the 14th generation, over 420 years ($2^{14}$ = 819,200). Thus, it is feasible that there were 600,000 men.

very wide (>72m = 12 * 6) and the 12 tribes marched in parallel, the total column would be 75 kms long.

If the people marched at 5.5 kms per hour - the marching speed of trained troops - it would take 13.6 hours for the wide column to pass a single location. By comparison, in the American Civil War 26,000 rebel troops, marching four abreast, stretched over 10 kms.

This is the logistical problem, no other march was close to this distance, except for Syrian refugees across Europe in 2018. According to UNHCR, there were more than 584,000 Syrian refugees and asylum-seekers living in Germany in 2019.[31] Videos of them walking across Europe were shown in the television news. The logistical problem becomes worse when we include the herds of goats and flocks of sheep that they drove before them.

The distance from Raamses to Succoth is about 36Kms, taking 6.5 hours, which is a long day's march.[32] They probably took two days. Marching from Succoth to the border would have been a further 20k or 4hrs. So, it would have taken them at least three days to flee to the border. Faced with these logistical problems some people question the figure of 600,000 men and the truth of the crossing of the Sea of Reeds.[33] Again, we are faced with putting our faith in an infinitely powerful God, a God who helps his people.

---

[31] pbs.org/wgbh/frontline/article/numbers-syrian-refugees-around-world/

[32] 5hrs is considered to be a day's march - need daylight to setup camp at night and pack up in the morning.

[33] This number is verified in Exodus 38:25-26 where the men over 20 are counted in a census (Exodus 30:11-16) by each giving half a shekel. The weight of silver given was 100 talents and 1,775 shekels which is equivalent to 603,550 men, where one talent = 3,000 shekels. A second census, at a later date, recorded in Numbers 26:51 counted 601,730 men.

## MYTHS AND MISCONCEPTIONS

A myth is a traditional story, accepted as history, that is used to explain the worldview of a group of people. A myth may be used to pass information from one generation to the next - for example sailing routes around New Zealand are recorded in Maori myths. Maori sailors put their faith in these myths because their ancestors told them they were true.

A misconception is something that is incorrect. When someone doesn't accept the Bible at face value, they often invent a myth or create a misconception. The myth may be based around a fantasy, or a straw man, or a different interpretation of the Bible, or a non-biblical text. The proponents of misconceptions often twist Bible passages to support their misconceptions.

One deliberate misconception, which is found in the popular fiction novel *The Da Vinci Code* by Dan Brown, is the claim that the Bible was changed during translation, making it historically unreliable.[34] When the Christian Bible is tested by comparing current copies to fragments from the earlier periods (of which we have 17,000 compared to only a handful of Caesar's *Gallic Wars*) it is shown to be accurately translated. What we have is what was written.

Some myths are pure fantasy. For example, the myth that Adam had a wife before Eve named Lilith. In Judaic mythology Lilith is the primordial she-demon and first wife of Adam. The myth claims that the night creature mentioned in Isaiah 34:14 is the Hebrew Lilith.

One way to create a misconception is to infer the nature of God from the nature of people. We should do the inverse, start with nature of God and from it, infer the nature of people. For example, a common misconception is that people are evil - therefore God is either evil or powerless against evil. The Bible says God designed human beings not robots. Beings

---

[34] Pearcey, N. 2010. Saving Leonardo, B&H Publishing, pages 10-11

have the freedom to choose, robots don't. When given the opportunity to choose between good and evil, people often choose evil.

From time to time the media discovers a *new* gospel - really an old book. Two such books are the *Gospel of Barnabas*[35] and the *Gospel of Judas*.[36] The atheist Richard Dawkins likes the Gospel of Judas because it contradicts the *New Testament*. "*It suggests that* Judas was the only one of the 12 disciples who really understood Jesus' mission."[37] At the Council of Nicaea in 325 AD the whole church agreed on which books should be included in the Bible, leaving out these *new* gospels because they were not considered to be divinely inspired.

The four gospels (*Matthew, Mark, Luke,* and *John*) are considered to be divinely inspired because they record the memories of eyewitnesses who accompanied Jesus during his public ministry. They are a true history. Professor C. S. Lewis, author of the Narnia series, stated, "Christianity is both a myth and a fact. It's unique. It's the true myth."[38]

## THE CREATOR WHO MADE US

Faith shows us the reality of things we cannot see. In the realm of faith, we learned that trust in Jesus is based on revelation. Faith is believing in a God of miracles. Faith is the assurance that our hope to receive eternal life will come to pass. Christian faith is choosing to believe in an infinitely powerful God. Faith is the foundation of our reasons for believing in Jesus.

---

[35] mahustlerszone.wordpress.com/2014/05/04/turkish-authorities-find-new-gospel-stating-that-jesus-was-not-crucified-but-ascended-to-heaven-alive/

[36] nationalgeographic.com/science/article/lost-gospel-judas-revealed-jesus-archaeology

[37] express.co.uk/news/weird/1186373/bible-news-gospel-judas-jesus-christ-egypt-richard-dawkins-outgroing-god-spt

[38] patheos.com/topics/religion-and-myth/cs-lewis-on-christianity-as-the-true-myth-michael-ward-03-09-2016

We put our faith in God because we have seen his creation. His making points us to his existence. Does our making point us to God? We put our faith in the work of engineers because we have seen abstract ideas in their minds coalesce into concrete objects. Objects that we use in everyday life.

# 3

# ENGINEERING

**Figure 3.1** *Mobile robot used in proof of correctness research*

"The end result of science and engineering is a set of objective outcomes. But the beginning of any scientific or engineering project engages our deepest values: what projects do we undertake? What insights and creativity do we bring? How do we build and nurture a team? In all those areas, my Christian call to "do justice, love mercy, and walk humbly with my God" deeply influences my life, and makes me a better researcher and professor" - Professor Chuck Thorpe, Provost Clarkson University[1]

"During my years with Elon I became familiar with a distinctly and deeply tribal mentality known as Engineers. Once when my dad came to visit, I was taking him to see Elon … and he saw these lengthy dudes in jeans and tee shirts. They were racing these remote-controlled contraptions around the parking lot and banging them into cars, and my dad said to me, "Are these the children of the engineers?" And I said, "No. Dad these are the engineers " - Justine Musk, first wife of Elon Musk[2]

## CORRECTNESS

I visited the University of Essex in England to do robotics research with my late friend Ulrich Nehmzow. One of his students presented a paper on a way to learn a complex robot behavior from measurements of the robot's

---

[1] clarkson.edu/people/chuck-thorpe
[2] Elon Musk's first wife Justine describes their relationship youtube.com/watch?v=9lkQPpSOtz8

# ENGINEERING

motion (Figure 3.1). As I listened, I thought: *is he claiming that he can prove that a robot exhibits a certain behavior?*

Proof of correctness of algorithms is a major field of research in Computer Science. For example, the world's financial systems are dependent on computers calculating the correct amounts of interest. There could be great benefits if we could prove that a robot performed a behavior correctly.

The thesis of this research is: If we can obtain a model of the robot's behavior from measurements of its motion and match this model to the desired behavior then we may be able to prove that the robot behaved correctly. I was not convinced and questioned the student's claim.

After much discussion we started a research project. Our approach was to select a simple task and program a mobile robot to execute that task. While executing the task the robot collected motion data. We used this data to develop a model using a system identification tool (Narmax[3]) and compared the model to the task.

For a simple task, we chose a behavior that moves the robot to follow a straight wall (Figure 3.2). This behavior commands the robot to follow a path along a straight wall at a desired distance from the wall with a fixed linear velocity. If it is not at the desired distance, then its angular velocity is controlled to turn it to move toward the desired distance and then to turn in the opposite direction to come parallel to the wall at the desired distance.

The robot calculates the angular velocity using successive measurements of range to the wall on its left. We found a simple equation that calculated the robot's turning speed as a function of the range data from the laser range finder.

---

[3] sysidentpy.org/landing-page/ch0-narmax-intro/

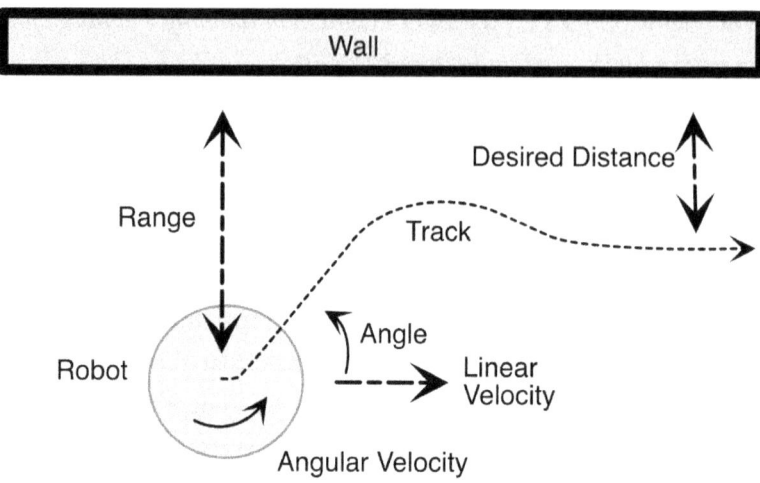

**Figure 3.2** *Following a straight wall behavior*

This idea that we can prove that a robot exhibits a certain behavior is contrary to the views of many roboticists. We were able to get good results with simple behaviors, but we needed more complex and realistic examples. A slightly more complex behavior, that is built on the behavior to follow a wall, is a behavior to drive around the inside of a room by following the wall on the left (Figure 3.3). We were in the process of studying this behavior when Ulrich developed cancer.

This room navigation behavior followed a path around the inside of a room using the measurements of range to the left and range to the front. The left range measurements were used to follow the wall. The front range measurements were used to detect a wall in front at ninety degrees to the current wall. When it approached this wall, the robot turned to the right and followed the path along the new wall.

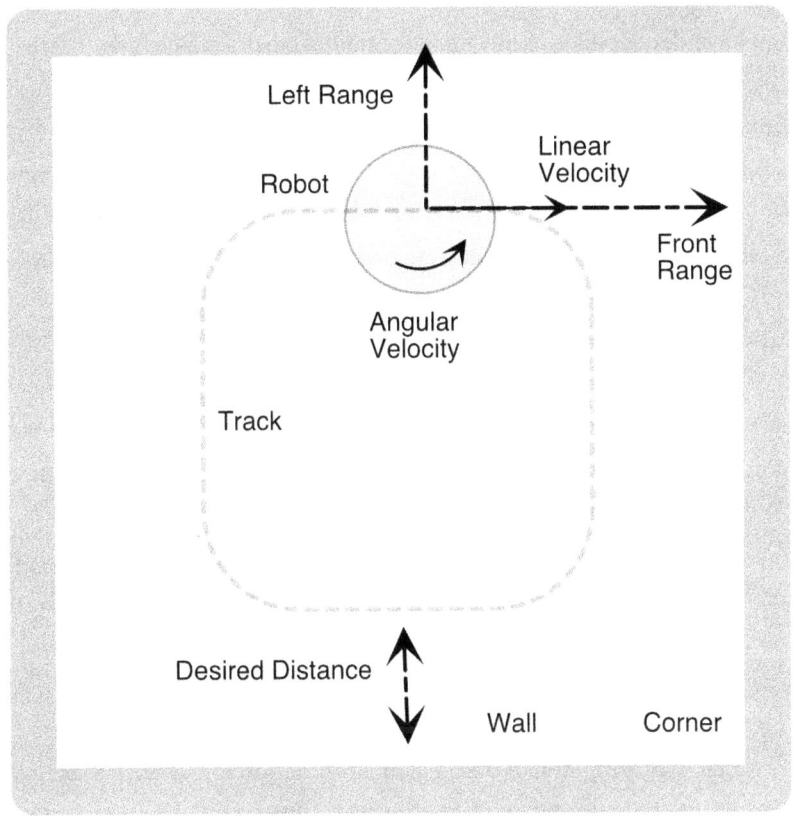

Figure 3.3 *Room navigation behavior*

A paper that presented some results from this research had been accepted at a conference in Paris.[4] Before he died Ulrich asked me to present his paper. His death was a sad loss for his family, his students, and robotics research. Ulrich trusted in Jesus so I believe he is now in eternity.

---

[4] Nehmzow, U. M<sup>c</sup>Kerrow P.J. and Billings S.A. 2010. "Do Empirical Models of Robot-Environment Interaction have a Meaning?", Animals to Animats 11, Proceedings 11th International Conference on Simulation of Adaptive Behavior, SAB 2010, Paris - Clos Lucé, France, August 25-28, 2010.

During the course of the research, I had become convinced that Ulrich may have developed a useful tool for modelling robot behavior. I went to the conference and presented the paper. In the question time Rod Brooks, a leading roboticist, said, "You have not proved it."

I had not expected that comment and it threw me into a spin. Rod was right, I hadn't proved it. I had fallen into the trap that I had accused Ulrich of at the beginning of the project. I was claiming something to be true without sufficient evidence. I was embarrassed and handled the question badly. I felt that I had let Ulrich down.

When I reexamined the results of the left-wall-following experiment I realized that we had missed an important result. The model that the system identification software had developed was not that of a left-wall follower but that of a right-wall follower.

The reason was that the rectangular room where we were doing the experiments was enclosed and symmetrical. We can follow the walls of a small, enclosed room by controlling either left range or right range. The system had discovered a model that did not match the robot control software and didn't discover the model that did.

When reporting this work, I had unintentionally failed to act with integrity and was found out. As Proverbs 10:9 says: "Whoever walks in integrity walks securely, but whoever takes crooked paths will be found out." Engineers make both things and the infrastructure required to enable us to use those things. We put our faith in these engineers to act with integrity. They build their integrity by their rigorous application of the results of research using the processes they learned from their role models.

ENGINEERING

## ROLE MODELS

"It's not rocket science." Every time I hear that phrase I wince. Engineers design rockets not scientists. In many fields engineers take a back seat to scientists by designing and building their experimental equipment for them. Regularly we hear politicians call for more funding for science because they think it will result in new products. The scientists may discover new physics, chemistry, or biology but it is the engineers who make the new product. Engineers turn abstract ideas into concrete reality.

An engineer is a person who uses scientific knowledge to solve practical problems. Engineers are versed in the design, construction, testing, application, and maintenance of devices. Each branch of engineering specializes in a particular type of device determined by the underlying science. For example, computer engineers implement electronic computers to execute software developed to solve problems using computer science.

I have benefited greatly from older men investing in me. In the 1960s Neil Brain ran a television repair business. He gathered an informal group of Christian technologists with the aim of providing audio and video production facilities for significant Christian events such as the relay of the 1968 Billy Graham Crusade from the Sydney Show Ground to the Wollongong Town Hall.

Neil received a request to build a recording studio for the Msalato Bible School in Dodoma, Tanzania. The use of reliable solid state audio equipment was in its infancy and a suitable audio mixer was not available for purchase.[5] So he decided to attempt to build one using circuit designs found in the magazine *Electronics Australia*.[6] My task was to design and make the printed circuit boards for the microphone preamplifiers.

---

[5] australianroadcrew.com.au/images/downloads/30_years_of_live_production.pdf
[6] archive.org/details/electronics_australia

Most of the boards etched perfectly, but a couple had poorly defined copper tracks with fuzzy edges, making them useless. A friend, Ken Kitchen, and I presented the bad ones to Neil with the comment: "It all went wrong, and the boards are useless." He looked aghast. It was all we could do to hold a straight face. Then with much glee we showed him the good ones. He was so relieved that he laughed with us at the trick we had played on him.

When I was a trainee engineer, I was blessed with good role models. The company I worked for, *John Lysaghts Australia Ltd*, had an engineering department whose role was to build, install and maintain steel processing lines.[7] They understood that good engineering training involved three components: understanding theory, hands on skills with tools, and research and development of new equipment.

We were taught the theory at university, how to use tools through apprentice training and the design of electronic controllers by working with engineers on the job. Professor Brian Smith was head of electrical engineering at UOW when I was an undergraduate. He drummed one sentence into our brains: "To solve a problem go back to first principles."

Roger Evans was Chief Electrical Engineer at Lysaghts. He was an excellent design engineer, who championed in-house development where possible. He emphasized the use of rules of thumb, when designing electronics and control systems, over theory.[8]

I found that the rules of thumb worked because an engineer had previously developed them from the theory. Consequently, when we came across a control system where the rules of thumb didn't work, Roger turned to me to work out the theory from first principles and from it to design and set up the control loops.

---

[7] now Blue Scope Coated Products
[8] Rule of thumb - A rule or principle that provides guidance to appropriate behavior usually derived from experience and used as a short cut to achieve a goal.

# ENGINEERING

In a parallel area of life, I was taught how to communicate using technology by another role model, the late Clifford Warne.[9] The central corridor in Channel Seven television studios in Sydney is *Seven's wall of fame*. It is lined with photographs of the greats of television. Clifford's photo is included for his work as a pioneer of children's television in Australia.

He ran a communications course one evening a week especially for Christian Asian students. Ann and I were privileged to be asked to join that course. We enjoyed it greatly. I didn't know at the time that I would spend much of my life teaching Asian students both computer science at UOW and the Bible at Keiraville International church (KIC). I have often looked up my course notes.

Clifford was a great entertainer. Not only did he have us laughing but he taught us how to read aloud, how to write a script and how to communicate the love of Jesus. He was a master story writer who loved to tell stories, often humorous and always with a point. Much of the material he taught us, I repeated in the multimedia subject that I taught in the Computer Science Master's program. He inspired me to use my communication gifts to help others meet Jesus.

Another important role model was R.G. Le Tourneau. I cherish his autobiography: *Mover of men and mountains* (Moody1967). In it, he challenged me to think biblically about the issues of being both a practicing Christian and a practicing engineer. It was a life affirming story. Le Tourneau was an engineer who designed and manufactured machines to build roads. His inventive genius was ahead of his time. What stood out for me was that here was a maker who believed in God.

I was a student engineer and a young believer in Jesus. Here was a man who was doing what I wanted to do - serve Jesus as an engineer. When he failed, he brought the situation to God in prayer, confessed his sins and

---

[9] sydneyanglicans.net/mediareleases/758a

then got up and had another go. He combined engineering and Christian commitment to sponsor many mission and education projects.

From reading his book it was obvious that Le Tourneau believed that God sustains the universe that he created. He believed in an infinitely capable maker, a maker who keeps the universe running so it all holds together and doesn't fly apart. The alternative is to believe that by a one in infinity chance everything is in balance. The following quote describes the role of Jesus in holding the universe together:

> "For in him all things were created: things in heaven and on earth, visible and invisible, whether thrones or powers or rulers or authorities; all things have been created through him and for him. He is before all things, and in him all things hold together." (Colossians 1:16-17)

Role models play an important part in our development as people. The Bible encourages us to choose them carefully: "Join together in following my example, brothers and sisters, and just as you have us as a model, keep your eyes on those who live as we do." (Philippians 3:17). The lives of our role models show us who they are and who we could be. Do your role models give you reason for believing in Jesus?

## ROCKET ENGINEERING

No, it's not rocket science, it's rocket engineering! Rockets are designed by engineers: aero engineers, mechanical engineers, combustion engineers, electrical engineers, and software engineers. Rocket engineers use scientific knowledge to solve practical problems in rocket design. Rocket trajectories are calculated by mathematicians. Control engineers design control systems to fly rockets along those trajectories.

# ENGINEERING

My experience is in the design of robots and steel mill controls. While robots are often used by scientists they are designed and built by engineers - for example, the Martian rovers. In 1985, a small group of engineers from various projects in the Robotics Institute at CMU met with leading roboticists Mark Raibert and Mat Mason to discuss robotics research. Each one of us was given a paper to present. The paper was either the latest or the best in the area. The rest of the group would critique both the paper and our presentation of it.

Raibert often emphasized the distinction between robotics engineering and the science of robotics. Robotics engineering is concerned with the design, construction, and application of robots. While robots are built to enable scientific research, the goal of robotics science is not the development of machines, but to understand the physical and information processes underlying perception and action. Once basic principles are established, they can be used in the design of new robots.

While theory is used in design, the design is tested by building prototypes. During 2022 and 2023 Space X has been developing a starship with the aim of going to Mars. They have had three spectacular explosions when attempting to land. Trial and error can be expensive, but it is needed to confirm that a design works as expected, particularly when the theory is still being researched.

Mechanical engineers build models. Electrical engineers build prototypes. Myth busters like to blow things up - it's called stress testing. A product should be thoroughly tested before it goes to market. In 2023, the implosion of a submarine diving to the wreck of the Titanic generated much comment among engineers about the maker's lack of adequate testing.

## BRILLIANT MAKERS FROM PREVIOUS SOCIETIES

We all admire brilliant makers and use them as role models. The challenge for believers is to find a brilliant maker, who uses his mind and hands in the service of Jesus, to model their life on. The following examples are of brilliant makers that you could model your making on but not your life.

At various times through history the invention of a new device has changed people's lives. The design and construction of these devices had reached a peak. The infrastructure had been established to support their manufacture and usage. The design of these devices had usually come about from the insight of one or more very intelligent makers.

For example, we are on the cusp of an electric car revolution. During the last decade Tesla has set up Giga Factories to make electric cars and has installed recharging stations along major highways to enable their use.[10] Elon Musk recruited a team of very capable engineers to make these electric cars.

A much earlier example of technology at its peak is the Parthenon on the Acropolis in Athens (Figure 3.4).[11] It was built between 447 and 438 BC as a temple dedicated to the goddess Athena Parthenos - parthénos meaning virgin. It was richly decorated with sculptures that were designed by the famous artist Pheidias.

The art of sculpture in stone had reached a peak, as had the design of a building to give the illusion of aesthetic perfection. On a visit to Athens, I sat on the Acropolis and marveled at what remains of the building. It was built to seem perfect to the eye.

---

[10] Tesla the car maker is named after Nikola Tesla who pioneered the use of alternating current electrical supply to homes.
popularmechanics.com/science/a33561982/nikola-tesla-interesting-facts/

[11] blog.britishmuseum.org/an-introduction-to-the-parthenon-and-its-sculptures
And britannica.com/topic/Parthenon

# ENGINEERING

**Figure 3.4** *Parthenon*

The Parthenon's design included many golden rectangles, which are visually pleasing. The length of the long side or a golden rectangle is approximately 1.628 times the length of the short side. In addition, many rectangular features were measured in proportions that allowed them to be divided equally into a series of Pythagorean triangles. A Pythagorean triangle is a right-angle triangle with integer side lengths such as 3-4-5.

However, the Parthenon's dynamic appearance of perfection is an illusion. Variations in architectural features were included to make the building look symmetric and the lines appear straight when viewed from a distance. One variation from actual symmetry to achieve visual symmetry is an upward curvature of the base along the ends of the building. A second is that the diameter of columns decreased toward the top with a delicate convexity that is almost imperceptible. The four corner columns are thicker to counteract the visual impact of the thinning effect on the corner columns when silhouetted against the sky from a distance.

Another example in ancient history of technology reaching a peak is the mosaics made by artisans in the Roman Empire. About the year 200AD, a Roman villa, was built in the city of Sepphoris.[12] It contains an elaborate mosaic floor in what is believed to have been a banquet hall.

Seating would have been arranged in a U-shape around the mosaic for guests to recline as they ate, drank, and socialized. The mosaic depicts a wine-drinking contest between the gods Dionysus and Hercules. It includes a famous image of a young woman, possibly representing Venus, who has been called the *Mona Lisa of the Galilee* (Figure 3.5).

Small mosaic tesserae were used, allowing greater detail and a more lifelike result. The excellent workmanship is reminiscent of a painting. The artist has achieved a tonal modeling of the curves of her face with highlights reflecting from her nose, chin and forehead and has created the blush of her cheeks. The artist has created the illusion of a three-dimensional form through modeling in light and shade with a subtle gradation into the shadows on the side of her face, and through focusing her eyes as if she is looking at you.

The detail in the mosaic, including the subtle shading, show that the technology had reached a peak. The creation of a mosaic of this quality requires ready access to a source of tesserae that included subtle variations in color, tone, and size.

---

[12] wikipedia.org/wiki/Sepphoris

## ENGINEERING

Figure 3.5 *Mona Lisa of Galilee Mosaic*

## A MODERN MAKER WHO CHANGED SOCIETY

In 2007, I was sitting in the Moscone Center in San Francisco with over 5,000 software developers at Apple's *Worldwide Developers Conference* (WWDC 2007) when Steve Jobs came onto the stage to preview the iPhone to eager developers.[13] I suspect that most of us who listened to Jobs extol

---

[13] Apple's Worldwide Developer Conference, where new hardware and software is released to the developer community.

the features of the original iPhone did not realize the huge impact it would have. Jobs was larger than life, a show man, and a master communicator.

Two years later, at WWDC 2009, we were treated to two musical items by the *Stanford University iPhone Orchestra* playing two iPhone apps made by *Smule*: an ocarina[14] and a leaf trombone. These are two of the very early creative apps.

Jobs is a modern example of a strong willed, visionary maker who had ideas of what the future could be like and set out to design consumer-oriented products to make the future happen. Jobs was an artist in consumer design. His colleague Steve Wozniak said:

> "All through his time in Apple products, even from our very first ones, that's how Jobs looked at the world, that you don't really want a piece of technology, a certain type of chip. What you want is a solution to a problem in life, some cause, some issue that you want in your life that'll help you. And it's how do you make that almost one step - say it and it happens." Steve Wozniak, Engineer.[15]

In 1985, Apple CEO John Scully persuaded the board of directors to remove Jobs from head of the Macintosh division. Jobs left Apple and started NeXT to make his vision of a personal computer and bought Pixar to make digital movies.[16] Apple failed badly under Scully's management. Jobs sold NeXT to Apple and became its CEO in 1997.

---

[14] An ocarina is a egg-shaped terracotta wind instrument with a mouthpiece and four finger holes. The ocarina app is played by blowing into the iPhone microphone and closing virtual holes on the touch display.
[15] quotemaster.org/q4a0b378b4d2e28213344a1eb1ff414ff
[16] Catmull, E. 2014. Creativity, INC. Random House, New York.

## ENGINEERING

Together with designer Jony Ive he revived Apple to develop the creative products we use today.[17] Walter Isaacson, the biographer of Steve Jobs, commented on an aspect of his character that enabled Jobs to be a great maker:

> Jobs insisted that Apple focus on just two or three priorities at a time. "There is no one better at turning off the noise that is going on around him," Cook said. "That allows him to focus on a few things and say no to many things. Few people are really good at that." Walter Isaacson.[18]

Steve Jobs was a practitioner of *Zen Buddhism*. He died of respiratory arrest related to a pancreatic neuroendocrine tumor in 2011.[19] His faith in alternative medicine probably cost him his life. He had the only kind of pancreatic cancer that is treatable and curable. Steve's final words were: "Oh wow. Oh wow. Oh wow." He then lost consciousness and died several hours later. Walter Issacson recorded the following interview prior to his death:

> I remember sitting in his backyard in his garden, one day, and he started talking about God. He [Jobs] said, "Sometimes I believe in God, sometimes I don't. I think it's 50/50, maybe. But ever since I've had cancer, I've been thinking about it more, and I find myself believing a bit more, maybe it's because I want to believe in an afterlife, that when you die, it doesn't just all disappear. The wisdom you've accumulated, somehow it lives on." Walter Isaacson, Steve Jobs.

---

[17] goodreads.com/quotes/tag/apple
[18] Isaacson W. 2011. Steve Jobs: The Exclusive Biography, Walter Isaacson, Little, Brown.
[19] wikipedia.org/wiki/Steve_Jobs#Death

These examples are just some of the intelligent makers who made devices and artworks that both represented and changed the society they lived in. They made things for the pleasure, enjoyment, and benefit of others. All were brilliant and all tried to make things that met a societal need. All these makers put their faith in something, especially in their own ability to make. Very few were believers in Jesus. The challenge for believers who are brilliant makers is to use their minds and hands in the service of Jesus:

> "Whatever you do, work at it with all your heart, as working for the Lord, not for human masters, since you know that you will receive an inheritance from the Lord as a reward. It is the Lord Christ you are serving." (Colossians 3:23-24)

## MY TOWER IS BIGGER THAN YOURS

Other, less humble makers build monuments to themselves. Scattered across Britain and Europe are cathedrals with high spires. Some were built to point to God, others to conform to the gothic architectural style of the time. All contain lightning rods to protect them from lightning strikes. Today, some have telecommunications towers hidden inside them. Often the higher the spire the more important the bishop thought he was.

The cathedral in Londonderry (Figure 3.6) is a classic example of what can happen.[20] In 1776, the bishop raised the total height of the building to 67 m (221 feet) by increasing the height of the tower by 6.4 m (21 feet) and adding a very tall spire. The additions to the tower were too heavy and, as a result, the spire lasted only two decades before it threatened to collapse and had to be dismantled and rebuilt.

---

[20] wikipedia.org/wiki/St_Columb%27s_Cathedral

## ENGINEERING

**Figure 3.6** *Tower and spire loom above St Columb's Cathedral Londonderry*

During the last century the competition has been to see who can build the tallest skyscraper. At 829.8 meters (2,722 ft) the Burj Khalifa in Dubai has been the world's tallest skyscraper since it was completed in 2010. It has 163 floors, with 30,000 residences, and nine hotels, in 19 residential towers.

A major task was the design and construction of the foundation of the building.[21] The Burj Khalifa's foundation is a pile supported raft, made from 125 piles that are 1.5 meters in diameter and 50 meters in length, comprising 45,000 cubic meters of concrete, reinforced with steel. The groundwater in which the Burj Dubai substructure is constructed is par-

---

[21] aboutcivil.org/burj-khalifa-design-construction-structural-details.html

ticularly severe, with chloride and sulfate concentrations higher than their concentrations in sea water.

The *Jeddah Tower* in Saudi Arabia is scheduled to replace it at 1,000 meters (3,280 feet) when it is completed. Makers are tempted to make a name for themselves and become like God. In the ancient world, before the time of Abraham, the go to project was the tower of Babel:

> "Then they said, "Come, let us build ourselves a city, with a tower that reaches to the heavens, so that we may make a name for ourselves; otherwise we will be scattered over the face of the whole earth." (Genesis 11:4)

In the biblical narrative God had commanded the people to spread around the globe. But, instead, they chose to stay put and build a tower in defiance. God stopped the construction by breaking their ability to communicate with one another. Interestingly, the reason God confused their speech is that when people unite, they think they can make anything. God put a limit on the extent of human rebellion that he would tolerate:

> "But the LORD came down to see the city and the tower the people were building. The LORD said, "If as one people speaking the same language they have begun to do this, then nothing they plan to do will be impossible for them. Come, let us go down and confuse their language so they will not understand each other." (Genesis 11:5-7)

## MORAL RESPONSIBILITY

We have seen, in previous sections, that engineers and other makers can change the world. Often the good devices that they make are turned to evil purposes by selfish people. A recent survey concluded that 70% of teenage boys are watching pornography on their data phones. They see abusive behavior in the porn videos and copy it resulting in the sexual abuse of young women. It is the responsibility of makers and parents to help their children resist this evil. The inventor of the iPad set us an example of responsible use of technology by children.

> "So, your kids must love the iPad?" I asked Mr. [Steve] Jobs, trying to change the subject. The company's first tablet was just hitting the shelves. "They haven't used it," he told me. "We limit how much technology our kids use at home." - Nick Bilton.[22]

When an intelligent maker sets out to make something one of the areas that he must research is the social impact of the object he wants to make. The Institution of Electrical and Electronic Engineers (IEEE) has a code of ethics which starts with a commitment:[23]

> "We, the members of the IEEE, in recognition of the importance of our technologies in affecting the quality of life throughout the world, and in accepting a personal obligation to our profession, its members and the communities we serve, do hereby commit ourselves to the highest ethical and professional conduct ..." (June 2020).

The intelligent maker who wants to serve God will think about his values. He will look in the Bible for examples of the best biblical practice to guide his thinking. He will seek answers to the question: "Do my values

---

[22] Nytimes article, Sept. 10, 2014
[23] ieee.org/about/corporate/governance/p7-8.html

encourage me to or prevent me from making this object?" The Christian maker will look to God for guidance.

> "Good and upright is the LORD;
> therefore he instructs sinners in his ways.
> He guides the humble in what is right
> and teaches them his way."
> (Psalm 25:8-9)

## SECOND FIDDLE

On many projects engineers are not considered to be as important as the salesman, or the scientist, or the medical doctor. Regularly, people in these professions are paid a higher salary than the engineers. "Engineers could not quite figure out why it was that the suits made the big money when the engineers actually made the stuff they were selling." - Justine Musk.[24]

Often this happens because the engineer would prefer to make than to manage. I was at a Christian conference when the speaker, Don Carson, quoted an old saying, "It takes more grace than I can tell to play the second fiddle well."[25]

Leonard Bernstein was the conductor of the New York Philharmonic orchestra.[26] When asked what he thought was the most difficult instrument to play he immediately replied, "The second fiddle." Everyone in the audience is watching the person who plays the first violin. But if the second fiddler doesn't play well, she makes the lead instrument sound very bad.

---

[24] Elon Musk's first wife describes their relationship, youtube.com/watch?v=9lkQPpSOtz8
[25] Carson, D. A. 2018. Basics for Believers: The Core of Christian Faith and Life, Baker Books.
[26] Brooks, J. 2014. Playing for an Audience of One, Paperback, 2nd edition, Redemption Press.

## ENGINEERING

By comparison, if the second fiddler plays well she can make the first fiddler sound very good. Similarly, engineers have the capacity to make a project succeed or fail by their attitude to being second in charge.

Occasionally an engineer is recognized by the users of the technology. Professor John Grant-Thompson's work was recognized by his nomination as a finalist in the 2019 Queensland Senior Australian of the Year Award for developing the Neocot (Figure 3.7): a transport system for sick babies, that has saved thousands of lives.[27] When he saw the previous overweight transport cot he expressed the thoughts of many engineers.

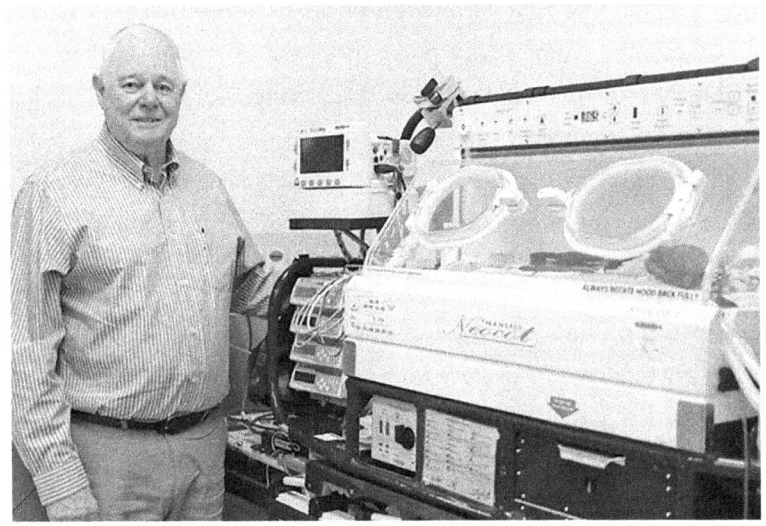

**Figure 3.7** *Professor John Grant-Thomson AM RFD with a Neocot.*

"I thought, why are engineers born if we can't do something about it? I started a student project at the University of Southern Queensland to improve what I saw." The

---

[27] Quote from TV interview in Australian Story about the making of neonatal retrieval transport cots. metronorth.health.qld.gov.au/news/engineering-the-safe-transport-of-4000-babies

Neocot is the result you see today. Yet he downplayed his contribution in a television interview where he said: "I'm just an engineer who builds tools, it's the doctors who are smart."[28]

## WOMEN IN ENGINEERING

Another group who makes good engineers, but are often not encouraged too, are women. I have supervised several female Masters and PhD students to the completion of their degrees. They have done research as good as their male colleagues. Women who build their homes as well as their careers probably do more making than men. They bring their own special creativity to any making project.

Fathers who encourage their daughters to make things enable them to achieve and not be left behind. When asked about women in STEM, Melinda Gates said:

> "It turns out that one of the single best predictors of whether a woman goes into a STEM field is whether or not her father believed in her when she was growing up. Well, my father did, in spades."[29]

Go to it fathers, encourage your daughters to make things. I have a daughter-in-law who is employed as an engineer to control the allocation of water in NSW.

Another woman, Natalie Palmquist is a Civil Engineer who works for the international aid organization Samaritan's Purse. She believes that the

---

[28] blackburnpc.org.au/images/YAHeart/YH_December_13_2020_Prof_Thompson.pdf
[29] popularmechanics.com/technology/gadgets/a22824572/melinda-gates-apple-iii/

# ENGINEERING

walls we build between faith and work should be taken down because they lead to superficial relationships. She enjoys math, building things, making puzzles, and thinking logically.

In episode 102 of the American Society of Civil Engineers (ASCE) Plot Points podcast (26 January), Palmquist talks about how her faith and her civil engineering intersect. She believes that the Bible encourages her to honor God by working hard with excellence and integrity. When you work to honor God, it throws off the pressure to chase a pay cheque. She is enthusiastic about being a civil engineer because she can love her neighbor as herself by making practical products that meet people's needs.

## RESEARCH AND DEVELOPMENT

Engineers use the results of research to design practical products. The government often expects the engineers to go to industry to get funding for research and development. Raj Reddy, the head of the Robotics Institute at CMU in 1985, called a meeting of the research staff. He told us that when you are talking to industry about funding be sure to emphasize that the cost of taking your bench prototype to market is roughly 10 times the cost of the research and development required to make the bench prototype.

When I moved from being a control engineer at *John Lysaghts* to become a project engineer in *Computer Science* at UOW, I was asked to take over a languishing research project funded by the *Australian Research Council* (ARC).[30] Three months into the project I had to do a presentation to the ARC review committee.

This was a completely new experience. I didn't do very well, partly because it wasn't clear how we were going to do the research. The problem to be solved was obviously a good one because they continued the funding.

---

[30] Australian Research Council - government funder of university research

After the interview, the engineer in charge of the review committee took me aside and explained how to formulate a research proposal.

He said that they look for four things when evaluating a research proposal. First, what is the problem? In my case, it was to work out how to measure the performance of computer software using a logic-state analyzer (an instrument that displays digital signals). My supervisor, an atomic physicist, had expressed it as follows: "Connect a logic-state analyzer to a computer and see if you can get something interesting."

Second, why is the problem significant? At that time computers were slow and improving software performance was a major issue in software development. Third, how are you going to solve it? The logic-state analyzer was a new instrument and we thought it could be used to trace the flow of execution of a program and hence measure both where it went and how long it took.

The fourth thing was, what is the outcome that will be of benefit to others? To develop this measurement system required the development of a formulation of performance measurement which became my PhD thesis and was published as a book (Figure 3.8).[31]

A decade later, another research professor said to me that when he starts a student on a research project, he gives them the best thesis in the field and asks them to reproduce the research. In the process, they learn about the research topic and if they can't reproduce the results then they have a project to work on. If they can, they have learned how to do research - research whose results may underpin the making of beautiful objects in the future.

---

[31] McKerrow, P.J. 1988. Performance Measurement of Computer Systems, Addison Wesley.

**Figure 3.8** *Performance measurement research. Author's PhD Thesis (Addison Wesley, 1988)*

## BEAUTIFUL DESIGN

I sat at a window watching the *Parade of Sail* at the *Wooden Boat Festival* in Hobart. It was led by tall ships with their sails billowing in the breeze, a beautiful sight. Each boat had been built by craftsmen and craftswomen. Each was built for a purpose. First, a designer thought about that purpose. Second, he or she envisioned its lines; how it would sit in the water when still and when underway.

Third, the designer thought about the technology that would be used to build it. Different technologies impose different design rules. For example, the design of a plywood hull is different to a wooden planked hull. We can bend a wooden plank in two dimensions, but we can only bend a sheet of ply in one-dimension.

Fourth, the designer would draw up a set of plans. Fifth, a shipwright would cut boards or sheets of ply to match the plans. Sixth, the shipwright would bend the boards around a frame to form graceful curves. When anyone looks at the boat, they see the design and praise the skill of the maker. No one questions that it was designed by a skillful designer and built by a master craftsman (Figure 3.9).

**Figure 3.9** *Peeler Skiff. Made by author from marine ply.*

In your imagination, look beyond the boat and see the human makers who designed, built, and sailed it. Every maker is also an exquisite design.

# ENGINEERING

Each one masterfully made. Each one made for a purpose. Each one a beautiful human who was made in the image of the master maker. When other people see the beauty of Jesus reflected in your character do you become a reason for them to believe in Jesus?

## REFLECTING OUR MAKER

When you look at a human do you see the invisible qualities of the maker, his eternal power and divine nature? There are people who say that humans were not made by an infinitely intelligent maker. They say people are the result of an infinitesimal chance. Each one of us can choose whether to believe that we were created by an infinitely intelligent God or that we are the result of one chance in an infinite number of possibilities.

Making elegant technology changes the world. Engineers design that technology using principles established by science. "God saw all that he had made, and it was very good." (Genesis 1:31). Do we reflect the image of the master maker who made us?

# 4

# SCIENCE

**Figure 4.1** *Titan four-wheel drive robot in a vegetable garden. Built by the author for navigation research.*

# SCIENCE

"As a Christian who is also a scientist, I find my physics informs my faith. Physics phenomena may appear to defy logic. Sometimes light acts like a particle and sometimes it acts like a wave – how can it be both? I can't dictate the nature of light, but rather need to adapt my thinking to the experimental evidence." - Senior Professor Roger Lewis, Associate Dean Research, Faculty of Engineering and Information Sciences, University of Wollongong.[1]

"Biologists must constantly keep in mind that what they see was not designed but rather evolved." - Sir Francis Crick, co-discoverer of the structure of DNA, Salk Institute for Biological Studies, 1988.[2]

"The God of the Bible … can be worshiped in the cathedral or in the laboratory." - Francis Collins, Leader of the Human Genome project, National Institutes of Health, 2007.[3]

"Music is a biological curiosity–it doesn't reproduce us, it doesn't feed us, and it doesn't shelter us, so why do humans like it and why do they like to move to it?" - D.J. Cameron, 2022.[4]

---

[1] Wave Particle Duality, youtube.com/watch?v=k581_XpaTnU
[2] Crick, F, 1988. What Mad Pursuit: A Personal View of Scientific Discovery. New York: Basic Books. p138. — co-discoverer in 1953 of the structure of DNA
[3] Leader of the human Genome project, Collins, F. C. 2007. The Language of God: A Scientist Presents Evidence for Belief. wikipedia.org/wiki/Francis_Collins
[4] Cameron, D. J. et al. 2022. Undetectable very-low frequency sound increases dancing at a live concert, Current Biology, vol 32, issue 21, quoted in (https://brighterworld.mcmaster.ca/articles/want-to-fire-up-the-dance-floor-play-low-frequency-bass/)

## GRANDAD'S STORY [5]

"Grandad how did the earth begin?" the boy asked.

The wise old man thought for a bit and said, "The world began with a voice, a strong and beautiful voice."

"Please, tell me what the voice said," asked the boy.

"Let there be light."

"Is that all?" asked his sister.

"No, each time the voice spoke something new popped into being," replied Grandad.

"You mean that before the voice there was nothing?" asked the girl.

"There was nothing. Nothing to see. Nothing to hear, nothing to touch, taste or smell. The world was a void until the voice began. A beautiful voice that filled the void. A creative voice, deep and resonant, bringing change to the void. Time and space arrived with a rush. A rush that makes warp speed seem slow."

"What is warp speed?" interrupted the boy.

"It is the fastest speed you can move inside space-time. But space-time itself can go a whole lot faster," said Grandad.

"I don't get it," said the girl.

---

[5] When the word story is included in the section title the story is made up. It uses fictional characters and events to describe the subject by suggestive resemblances.

## SCIENCE

"Imagine a boat on a river. You can move around inside the boat but only up to a walking pace. We can move in space-time but only up to warp speed. The boat is carried along much faster by the river. Space-time is carried along much faster by the voice," replied Grandad.

Grandad continued the story. "The deep, resonant voice described space-time. The voice defined the structure of the universe. An empty universe, like a piece of graph paper waiting for someone to draw on it, waiting for someone to blow on it and feel the ripples.

"The voice changed. The deep resonate notes ceased. Sharp, high-pitched notes emanated from the voice. Bing, a star popped into space-time. More bings, like the base notes played on a xylophone rang out through space-time. A galaxy swished into view. The voice rose in pitch to form planets, joyously circling the stars in a cosmic dance.

"One planet stood out. Azure pools of water formed, sparkling in the warm light of a newly created star. The voice became soft. Droplets of water formed and resonated with the voice as it continued. They began to shimmer. As the voice grew in strength, they began to shake and quiver swaying with the voice."

"Grandad, did the world really begin that way?" inquired the boy.

"Yes, my son," answered Grandad.

"Grandad that is an intriguing story, but I don't believe it," the boy said.

"Why don't you believe it?" asked his grandfather with a slight edge in his voice.

"My science teacher told us that everything happened by chance. There was a big explosion, and everything came from that. It's called the big bang," replied the girl.

"You mean one moment there was nothing, then nothing blew up and made something?" asked Grandad.

"Sorta like that Grandad," replied the boy.

The old man continued, "You know the good book teaches that God made everything from nothing. When I was your age, everyone said it couldn't be true. Something can't come from nothing they said, but now science agrees with the good book."

"But science says it happened by chance not by the voice of God," replied the girl.

"Is that idea scientifically proven or is it atheism?" asked Grandad.

"My teacher says it is science, so he must believe it," replied the boy in a frustrated voice.

"Careful my son, to be truly scientific, you should question what people say and look at the evidence," said Grandad.

# SCIENCE

"A wise observer of science and faith concluded: 'If you base your beliefs on science you will have to change them regularly because science is changing all the time as new discoveries are made,'" said Grandad.

"But science is right, it is based on the observation of experimental evidence," replied the girl in frustration. She felt she was getting nowhere trying to change Grandad's beliefs.

"You are partly correct; science is based on observation. But it is limited to what we can observe in three dimensions of space and half a dimension of time. If anything exists outside of space-time then science cannot observe it, so science can neither prove nor disprove the existence of a creator God who lives in eternity," said Grandad.

"I don't get it," said the girl.

"Imagine that this room represents eternity and that space-time looks like an egg," suggested Grandad.

"I'm imagining it but the egg is small compared to the room," replied the girl.

Her grandfather explained, "Inside the egg is space-time. Outside is eternity. The egg is much smaller than the room just like space-time is much smaller than eternity."

"You mean, we are inside the egg and can't observe the rest of the room?" asked the boy.

"Kinda like that, my son," mused Grandad.

"Do you ever doubt Grandad?" the girl asked seeking to find a hole in his argument.

"Sometimes I see a nature show on TV that assumes it all happened by chance. That makes me doubt," replied Grandad.

"Then why do you still believe?" asked the boy.

"I do some research to find out how much we actually know about the topic of the TV show. Often the view being popularized by the TV presenter is based on assumptions that are not correct," replied Grandad.

"What if they are correct?" asked the boy.

"Then I wait to see the results of further research in that field, before making a decision about that view," said Grandad.

"What if it supports your doubt?" asked the boy.

"So far, my research has taught me to doubt my doubts and believe my beliefs," replied Grandad.

Suddenly, it clicked in the boy's mind - his grandfather had good reasons for believing. The frustration of not convincing Grandad went away, to be replaced by the joy of believing in a loving creator God. A God who created everything from nothing with his voice. It was a great relief to believe that God created him for a purpose.

# SCIENCE

"Grandad, I think you are right," the boy said and he gave his grandfather a hug. "What do you think sis?" he asked his sister.

"I want to see more evidence," she replied.

## WHO BELIEVES?

This story creates real problems for many people. If we can believe science in our making, then shouldn't we also believe science in our religion? Makers look to science to understand the objects they are making. In a real sense makers put their faith in science. Science is the realm where the observable world is modelled and measured. To find evidence to support theories scientists asks the question: Why is it so?

Harry's white teeth flashed in his brown face. He grinned as he asked, "Are you the only scientist who believes in God?" It wasn't a trick question but rather the expression of a desire to affirm his belief in God. Harry knew very few engineers and scientists who believed in Jesus. He was having difficulty believing that an infinitely powerful and loving God made the universe. So, he was looking for reasons for believing in Jesus.

Harry had moved from India to Saudi Arabia as a child. There, he became a follower of Jesus and was baptized in secret on the roof of an apartment block. In both the Hindu culture in India and the Muslim culture in Saudi Arabia he met people who believed in unattractive gods. By contrast, he found Jesus to be attractive. In a lecture in Melbourne, Professor John Pilbrow commented:

> "People of faith have nothing to fear from scientific discoveries. From time-to-time science will challenge us to

rethink aspects of our faith. That makes the journey for a follower of Jesus Christ exciting and worth living."[6]

When I was looking for quotes to use in this book, I found a lot more from scientists than from engineers, so I asked my friends for their thoughts about how their faith impacts their engineering or vice versa. Some came back with brilliant insights that have enriched this book.

Also, I found people who believe that science and faith are incompatible. Some believe that space-time is all there is and, therefore, since God cannot be observed in space-time He does not exist. Others believe that if God exists then science must be wrong.[7] Some merge science and faith by suggesting that God caused the big events by special creation and evolution occurs between those events.[8]

At every stage of my career, I have met engineers, scientists, and other makers who believe in Jesus. While doing post-doctoral research in the Robotics Institute at Carnegie Mellon University (CMU) in Pittsburgh Pennsylvania, I joined a group of engineers who met to study the Bible. To keep up with robotics research, I regularly visited universities around the world to collaborate in research and attend conferences. I was stimulated by discussions with PhD students about the making of robots (Figure 4.1) and about my research in ultrasonic sensing (echolocation). During my travels I met distinguished engineers who put their faith in Jesus.

I was inspired to think about the influence of faith on science by Professor Donald McKay, a 20th century British Christian thinker, whom I visited in the Department of Communications and Neuroscience at the

---

[6] Professor John Pilbrow, 2009. Lecture in Melbourne, Science and Faith, the Intersection
[7] Ashton, J.F. 2001. In Six Days: Why Fifty Scientists Choose to Believe in Creation, Master Books
[8] Ross, H. 1989. The Fingerprint of God, Promise Publishing Company.

# SCIENCE

University of Keele.[9] Also, I was challenged to think about the influence of my faith on the robotics technology that I was making by Dr. Stephen Garber who led the Bible study group in the Robotics Institute at CMU.[10] These two men gave me confidence that there are many reasons for believing in Jesus.

The belief that science has displaced faith is common in the 21st century. Academics who believe in Jesus are in the minority in most universities. They do exist in all disciplines, often working quietly in the background. Students may not recognize them as followers of Jesus, but they recognize the care they give. One example is Bruce Krogh who is Professor Emeritus in Electrical and Computer Engineering at CMU. One of the female robotics students said to me: "All the students like Professor Krogh because he cares for them and helps them."[11]

There are groups of Christians in western countries who work together to explore the interface between science, technology, and Christian faith. One such group is the *Society of Christian Scholars* who seek to have a Christian influence in higher education.[12] In Australia, *ISCAST*, a network of people from students to distinguished academics, seeks to engage Australian scientists in constructive conversation with Christians.[13] In the United Kingdom, *Christians in Science* (CIS) is a network of people who are interested in science and faith issues.[14] CIS works closely with the *Faraday Institute of Science and Religion*.[15]

---

[9] MacKay, D.M. 1965.Christianity in a Mechanistic Universe, IVP, London.
[10] Garber, S. 2007. The Fabric of Faithfulness, IVP
[11] Bruce Krogh ece.cmu.edu/directory/bios/krogh-bruce.html
[12] scshub.net
[13] iscast.org/vision
[14] cis.org.uk/about-cis
[15] facebook.com/TheFaradayInstitute/?__xts__[fusion_builder_column]=

In the United States, the *Veritas Forum* runs debates and lectures.[16] They aim to promote courageous discourse where the historic Christian faith is put in dialogue with other beliefs and where participants from all backgrounds are invited to pursue truth together. Many people are not as sure that Jesus is God as the members of these groups are. Science seems more believable. For example:

> "I suspect that one of the many reasons why Japanese are reluctant to take on Christianity is that Christianity appears to oppose modern science. ... If Christianity opposes all that science teaches then it seems logical to discard the Christian faith." -_ Roger Dethlefs, Ophthalmologist.

## DUALITY

Many Christians believe that there is a good coherence between science and the Christian faith.[17] Some achieve this coherence by believing that God used evolution to create the world. Others believe that God created the process of evolution, set the parameters, and let evolution run to create the universe. Still others hold science and faith as separate truths in their minds. Senior Professor Roger Lewis, Associate Dean Research, Faculty of Engineering, and Information Sciences, wrote about how he believes in both science and the Bible:

> "I carry over my experience as an experimental physicist, of accepting how the world is, to how I read the Bible. If the biblical evidence is that Jesus was fully human, but also

---

[16] veritas.org
[17] Professor Cees Dekker, 2019 Lecture at Keiraville International Church, ISCAST, one of Holland's most cited scientists.

## SCIENCE

fully God, I accept that this is how the world is. I don't presume that my limited understanding should be forced on the evidence, and either the humanity or the divinity of Jesus be abandoned."

The Bible clearly states that, "In the beginning God created"… but the earth He created was formless, empty, and dark. Genesis 1 is about God giving the earth form, filling the emptiness with life, and driving away the darkness. It is written in poetic language.

Genesis 2 repeats the story from a relational perspective. Neither story is intended to be a scientific account. A scientific account written 50 years ago would not be considered correct today and vice versa. Rather, the story of creation is written in a form that is true for all ages and all cultures.

Duality is the idea that opposite ideas can both be true at the same time.[18] Opposing ideas and forces exist in the universe, such as Newton's third law: "To every action there is an equal and opposite reaction." Duality occurs in quantum physics where some properties of light are explained best with wave theory and other properties with particle theory. Duality occurs in many fields. It is a valid way of thinking about apparent contradictions.

In a discussion about creation and evolution, I commented to a friend that there is a third way: to hold the two as both being true and to wait for a resolution at some time in the future. He said, "That is an Anglican approach to the problem." Anglicanism is considered by some to be the great middle way between Catholic and reformed teaching.

A fundamentalist requires absolute certainty - only one position can be true. To the post-modern mind truth is how you see it. In contrast, Anglicans have a long-standing practice of holding two apparently contradictory views in tension and waiting for future revelation or discovery to

---

[18] geniustypes.com/critical_thinking_101_duality/#.YL2wjS0RrTY

resolve the differences. They are comfortable with duality. For example, a poet describes the earth's rotation as a sunrise. A physicist thinks in apparent contradictions:

> "My training as a physicist actually prepares me for accepting biblical texts that a theologian or philosopher, not so used to dealing with apparent contradictions, may struggle with. Far from undermining faith, a scientific background may, in practice, enhance it." - Senior Professor Roger Lewis, Associate Dean Research, Faculty of Engineering and Information Sciences, University of Wollongong.

God created the universe, and He inspired people to write the Bible, so a Christian accepts a duality where both the Bible and creation are true. Conflict may occur between our interpretation of nature, called science, and our interpretation of the Bible, called theology, fueled by our impatience. The world is more than our observations in space-time. For example, from where do we get the name of an object? Why is a horse called a horse and not an equine?

## STORY ABOUT THE FIRST SCIENTIST[19]

Humans love to classify objects based on their observation of the shape of the object in 3D space and the motion of the object in time. Possibly, the earliest written record of a scientist is in Genesis. God gave Adam the task of naming all the animals. "He gave names to all the livestock, all the birds

---

[19] When the word story is included in the section title the story is made up. It uses fictional characters and events to describe the subject by suggestive resemblances

## SCIENCE

of the sky, and all the wild animals" (Genesis 2:20). Does this make Adam the first taxonomist?[20]

Let us imagine the first scientist observing shadows as he attempted to measure a day. He poked one (shadow) stick into the ground so that it cast a shadow. He placed a second (direction) stick toward the end of the shadow. The two sticks recorded the direction of the shadow (Figure 4.2).

> "Man, what are you doing with those sticks?" asked woman.
>
> "I am trying to work out whether the colder days are shorter than the warmer days," he replied.
>
> "What for, how is that going to help you tend the fruit trees? While you are there can you pick some apples for lunch, please," she asked.

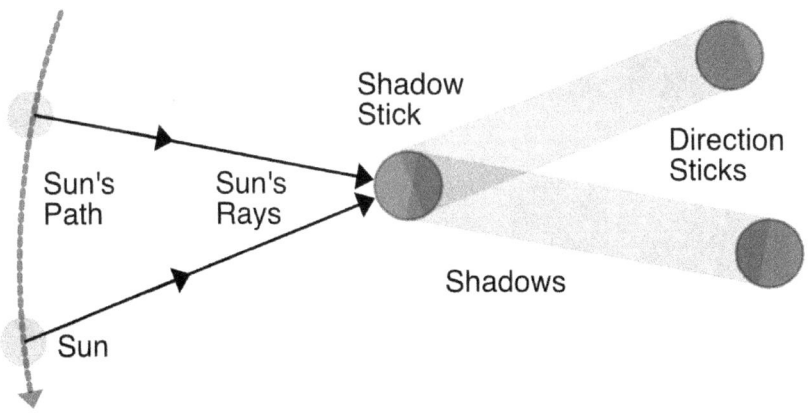

**Figure 4.2** *Plan view of a simple sundial*

---

[20] Adam means man and Eve means the mother of all

When he got back to his sticks, man noticed that the shadow had shifted. He placed a second shadow stick in the shifted shadow. He had a measurement of how far the sun moved across the sky. The next day he placed a shadow stick at sunrise and another at sunset. He had made a simple sundial to measure a day.

After many days he noticed that both shadows had moved. This puzzled him. "Why did God make the sun do this?" he asked himself. His view of how the world came to be was built on the limited knowledge he had. Some consider that since we now have much more scientific knowledge, we have no need for God.

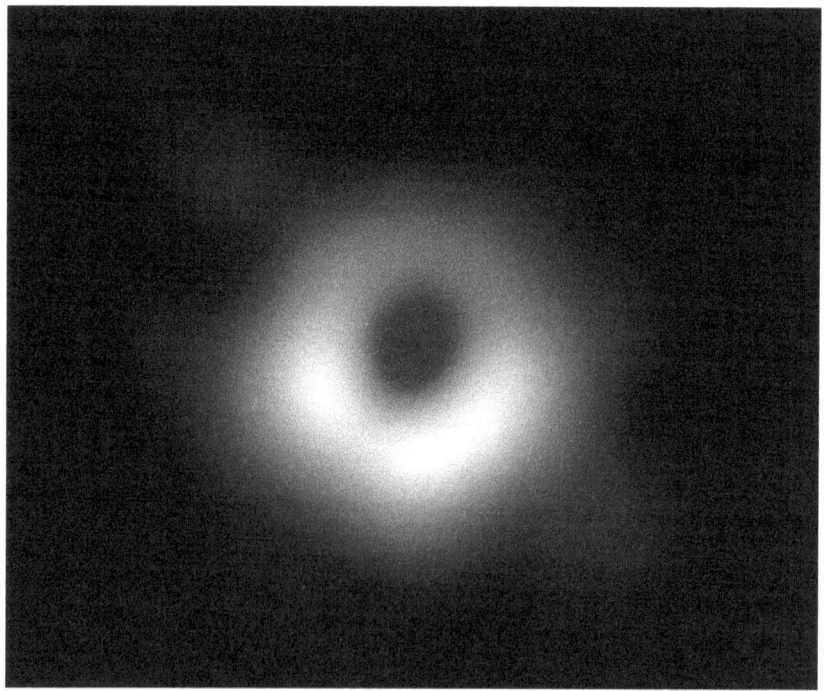

**Figure 4.3** *The first image of a supermassive black hole. Depicted in the first false-color image of radio waves by the Event Horizon Telescope, Wikimedia Commons, April 2019.*

## MODERN SCIENCE

Science is the rigorous study of the physical and natural world using theoretical models and data from observing experiments. Scientists use mathematics to model nature. For example, gravity is modeled with the equation: force-of-gravity = mass-of-object times the-acceleration-due-to-gravity ($f = m * g$, where $g$ is the acceleration due to gravity = 9.8 meters/second$^2$) known as Newton's second law.

Using these models, illustrators draw images both to record and to visualize natural phenomena. Many natural phenomena, for example molecules, cannot be directly observed, so graphic artists make computer generated visualizations of these objects from their models.

Science is made possible by engineers who make instruments to measure natural phenomena. We can't see electricity, so makers developed instruments to measure voltage and current based on Ohms law: voltage = current times resistance ($v = i * r$). In the second half of the 19th century, the first electrical engineers were the only people who knew Ohm's law. They earned their living by designing electric power networks for cities using this knowledge.

Science is dependent on makers. Scientists regularly put their faith in the measurements taken with instruments made by makers and they express their theories with illustrations made by artists. Without mathematicians, illustrators, and other makers science would be much poorer. Many of the images we see of objects in space are computer generated from models using code developed by computer scientists.

For example, the first image of a black hole (Figure 4.3) was a false-color image of radio waves taken by the Event Horizon Telescope (EHT) on 10 April 2019.[21] The EHT is made by synchronizing a global network of radio

---

[21] wikipedia.org/wiki/Black_hole

frequency telescopes. It takes images of the silhouette of the black hole against its glowing surroundings. The images are sorted and synchronized using computer algorithms.

The feature that defines a black hole is the event horizon - a boundary in space-time through which matter, and light can pass only inward towards the center of the black hole where its mass is. Hence the use of silhouettes to image it. The black region at the center of the image is the black hole. It is black because all the electromagnetic radiation that enters it is not reflected back toward earth. There is much discussion in scientific circles about the nature of black holes, some researchers even claiming that they are dark matter.

## SCIENCE AND GOD

While we all benefit from the discoveries made by scientists and put our faith in the technology made by engineers from those discoveries, science is not able to prove or disprove the existence of God. It is limited to studying phenomena that can be observed in space-time. Christians believe that God created both space and time in eternity. He is outside of space-time. So, God cannot be observed by science, unless He chooses to reveal Himself to the scientist in space-time.

Christians also believe that the creation reflects the character of the creator. Just as King David, who wrote Psalm 19 was challenged to marvel at what he observed, so are scientists.

> "The heavens declare the glory of God;
> the skies proclaim the work of his hands."
> (Psalm 19:1)

# SCIENCE

It is important to read the Bible in context. The story of creation was written in the context of human scientific knowledge around 1500 B.C. A day would have been a significant marker of time. A year was many days and included four seasons. A person's life was a multiple of years.

To the writer of Genesis, six days would have been a long time and six billion years would have been beyond his comprehension. So, the idea that God created everything in six days would have seemed reasonable to him and fitted within his scientific understanding. He describes the creation of the cosmos with beautiful poetry[22] while we describe it with mathematical models. Are his ideas wrong because they are different to ours, or are they true within his context?

While our science has moved on from Newtonian mechanics to quantum mechanics and relativity, we still assume Newtonian mechanics to be true even though it is an approximation. We choose which models to use depending on the context of the situation we are describing.

Similarly, it is argued, that a person can hold in their mind both six billion years to create and six days of creation, depending on whether they are thinking of science within the limits of space-time or faith within the limits of revelation. Will scientists in one hundred years' time look at the science we consider to be true today and scoff at it? Christians do not believe in God because of science, they believe in science because of God.

## ORIGINS OF MODERN SCIENCE

Science developed in 17th century Europe because the people who lived then believed in the Christian God who is thoughtful, coherent, and compassionate. Therefore, they believed that God created a universe that is

---

[22] For a discussion of the literary style of Genesis 1 see Dickson J, 2009 The Genre of Genesis 1, publicchristianity.org/the-genre-of-genesis-1-an-historical-approach

ordered and consistent - a universe that can be understood and described by intelligent people. On the impact of theology on science, Alfred North Whitehead, a famous Professor of Philosophy and Mathematics at the start of the 20th century, wrote:

> "But for science something more is wanted than a general sense of the order in things… faith in the possibility of science, generated antecedently to the development of modern scientific theory, is an unconscious derivative from medieval theology." - Professor A. N. Whitehead, Harvard.[23]

Today, many scientists consider the fact that science works as a way of understanding space-time is sufficient justification to practice science. Thus, some claim that God is no longer relevant. In the introduction to a biochemistry textbook three Professors of Biochemistry at the University of Wisconsin-Madison wrote:

> "The progress of science rests on a foundational assumption that is often unstated but crucial to the enterprise: that the laws governing forces und phenomena existing in the universe are not subject to change. The Nobel laureate Jacques Monod referred to this underlying assumption as the "postulate of objectivity." The natural world can therefore be understood by applying a process of inquiry — the scientific method. Science could not succeed in a universe that played tricks on us. Other than the postulate of objectivity, science makes no inviolate assumptions

---

[23] Whitehead, A.N. 1925. Science and the modern world, Macmillan, New York. - Professor of Philosophy, Harvard.

about the natural world." - David Nelson, Michael Cox and Aaron Hoskins, 2021. Lehninger Principles of Biochemistry, Eighth Edition, Macmillan International.

Many of the early scientists never thought of science as being isolated from their Christian beliefs, including Newton, Pascal, Faraday, and Maxwell.[24] Other civilizations did not believe in a coherent God, and some considered the material world to be inferior to the spiritual world and therefore not worthy of study. For example, the Chinese, who had developed a blast furnace, had an early knowledge of science but lost interest because:

> "…there was no confidence that the code of nature's laws could ever be unveiled or read … there was no assurance that a divine being, even more rational than ourselves, had ever formulated such a code capable of being read." - J. Needham, Cambridge.[25]

Also, the Christians thought in terms of a duality where both sacred and material are equally important. We cannot discover the love of God by studying science and we cannot discover the speed of light by studying theology. To think like God, we need both theology and science. Science is both possible because of the coherence of the universe and essential because of the contingency and freedom built into it.[26]

Several things came together in 17th century Christian Europe that were required for the development of science. Early examples of each thing had occurred in other cultures but not together. They included mathematics to

---

[24] Schaeffer, F. A. 1976. How Should we then Live.
[25] Needhan, J. 1969. The Grand Titration, Science and Society in East and West. London, Allen and Unwin
[26] Turner, H. 1998, The Roots of Science: An Investigative Journey Through the World's Religions, Deep Sight Publishing

form abstract models, technology to make measuring instruments, money to pay for the research, and a belief system that said science was possible.

Many of the 16th to 19th century scientists were church ministers who had a stipend to live on, God given curiosity to explore nature, and training in both theology and liberal arts. Catholic clergy who made contributions to science include Nicolaus Copernicus, Georges Lemaître and Roger Bacon.[27]

**Figure 4.4** *Sticker promoting Make: magazine*

---

[27] wikipedia.org/wiki/List_of_Catholic_clergy_scientists

# SCIENCE

In 1663 the relationship between faith and science was spelled out in the charter of the *Royal Society of London for Improving Natural Knowledge*.[28] It included the statement:

> "…whose studies are to be applied to further promoting by the authority of experiments the sciences of natural things and of useful arts, to the glory of God the Creator, and the advantage of the human race." - Royal Society of London, 1663.[29]

Makers played an important role in the development of science. Prior to the Renaissance the development of science was hindered by a lack of precision instruments to make observations. Precise instruments are needed to measure the data required to provide evidence to prove or disprove theories. To make precise instruments we require processes to accurately machine metal and grind glass lenses. In 1830 Joseph Whitworth developed a method for producing accurate flat surfaces and in 1841 he devised a standardized screw thread.[30] These advances contributed to the development of accurate instrumentation.

Another beneficiary was the development of mechanical calculators, including Babbage's Analytical Engine - a proposed mechanical general-purpose computer.[31] It was first described in 1837 and was the forerunner to ENIAC (Electronic Numerical Integrator and Computer) the first programmable, electronic, general-purpose digital computer in 1945.

Engineers are continually developing new instruments that refine and change our observations. For example, since its launch in 2021, the James

---

[28] Purver, M. 1967. The Royal Society: Concept and Creation, The MIT Press.
[29] royalsociety.org/-/media/Royal_Society_Content/about-us/history/2012-Supplemental-Charter.pdf
[30] wikipedia.org/wiki/Joseph_Whitworth#Accuracy_and_standardisation
[31] wikipedia.org/wiki/Charles_Babbage

Webb Space Telescope has been making images of galaxies right to the edge of the universe where time and space bend and warp.

## FAITH IN SCIENCE

Science is changing rapidly due to new discoveries that give us greater understanding of the universe and relegate previous theories. If your faith is based on science (Figure 4.4) then in a few years, you will have to change it. People are having difficulty keeping their beliefs up with the rapid changes in science. Some scientific discoveries have no impact on what Christians believe, while others either create or resolve apparent conflicts.

In the 20th century several discoveries changed science. Four of them are: the big bang theory, the model of matter, punctuated equilibrium, and DNA (see Chapter 8. Design). In the 21st century gravity waves were measured for the first time and a photograph was synthesized of a black hole. Just to name a few advances.

The first example, the big bang theory, has many scientists struggling with the evidence that the universe came from nothing. Creation from nothing is a teaching of the Bible that atheists had previously scoffed at. Creation out of nothing is the doctrine that matter is not eternal but had to be created by some divine creative act. This concept is found in Hebrews 11:3.

> "By faith we understand that the universe was formed at God's command, so that what is seen was not made out of what was visible." (Hebrews 11:3)

A second example of change is our model of matter. When my mother went to school, she was taught that atoms are the smallest particle of matter. When I went to school, I was taught that electrons are the smallest particle of matter. Today, an atom is still considered to be the smallest unit of ordinary matter that forms a chemical element. Every solid, liquid, gas, and plasma is composed of neutral or ionized atoms.

However, today an electron is just one particle in the *Standard Model* of an atom (Figure 4.5).[32] An excellent visual explanation of the fundamental forces and particles in the Standard Model is presented in a YouTube video by MagellanTV.[33]

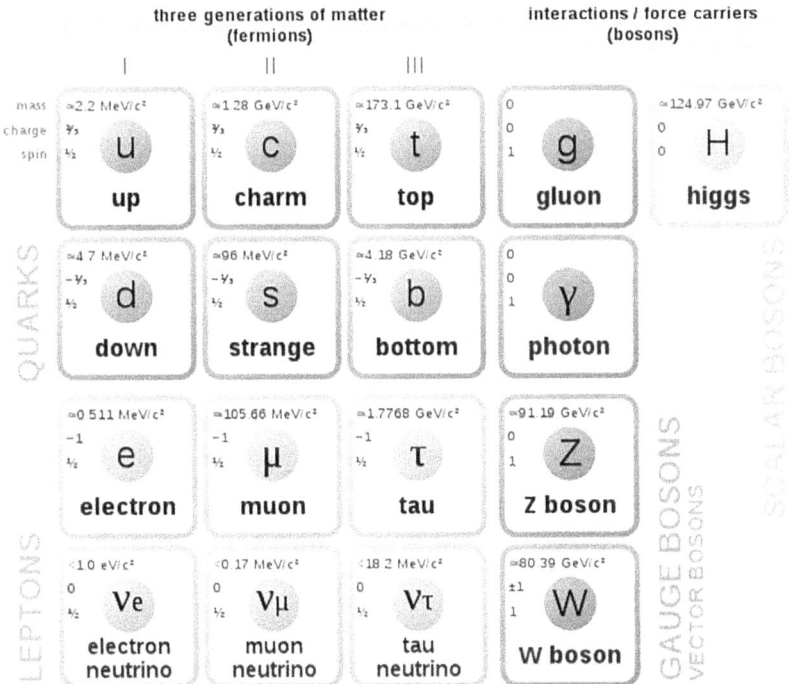

Figure 4.5 *Elementary particles included in the Standard Model in 2019*, Wikimedia Commons

---

[32] wikipedia.org/wiki/Standard_Model
[33] youtube.com/watch?v=TDYex6VSd7o&t=133s

Also, a free electron is considered to be an elemental particle because we have not found a way to split it into possible component particles. Yet, within a molecule an electron has a three degree of freedom wave function giving rise to the appearance of three quasiparticles named holon, spinon and orbiton.

By contrast, protons and neutrons were found to be composite particles that contain quarks. *Quarks* are now considered to be elementary particles. Particle physicists currently think that the elementary particles include the fundamental *fermions,* which generally speaking are matter and antimatter particles as well as the fundamental *bosons,* which are force particles that mediate interactions among fermions.

A *charm* meson, one of the six flavors of quark, is a particle that contains both a quark and an antiquark. In 2021, researchers from Oxford reported on their measurement of the masses of charm mesons in both their particle and antiparticle state using data from the Large Hadron Collider.[34] They claim that charm meson particles can alternate between states of matter and antimatter.

Charm mesons are another example of duality in nature. They can exist in a state of both matter and antimatter at the same time - in quantum superposition. Caroline Delbert and Courtney Linder report that if the research is validated, it "could shake up our assumptions about the very nature of reality."[35]

Canada television presenter Derek Muller reflected on the move away from fixed theories to a more flexible approach to science to deal with the rapid changes in theories, particularly in cosmology:

---

[34] home.cern/science/accelerators/large-hadron-collider
[35] Delbert, C. and Linder, C. 2021. A Particle Just Did Something That Changed the Nature of Reality, Popular Mechanics, July 29. popularmechanics.com/science/a36701159/charm-mesons-particle

## SCIENCE

> "I feel like non-scientists like being right, they like when things turn out the way they were expecting. But scientists, on the other hand, they want things to work out not the way they expected because that's the way we get clues into what new physics is still there to be discovered." - Muller, 2020.[36]

A third example, where there has been change to scientific theory, is the inclusion of punctuated equilibrium in the theory of evolution. Punctuated equilibrium is seen as an alternative to gradual development.[37] Many evolution researchers claim that it is a change in the mechanism of evolution, not in the theory.

In his book *On the Origin of Species*, Charles Darwin discusses at great length why, in his view, there should be a lack of fossils of intermediate forms between the geological ages. He goes so far as to say the lack of intermediate fossils is the greatest problem facing his theory.

> "Why then is not every geological formation and every stratum full of such intermediate links? Geology assuredly does not reveal any such finely graduated organic chain; and this, perhaps, is the most obvious and grave objection which can be urged against my theory. The explanation lies, as I believe, in the extreme imperfection of the geological record." - Charles Darwin, 1859.[38]

---

[36] Muller, D. 2020. Canadian science communicator, filmmaker, television personality and inventor, who is best known for his YouTube channel Veritasium. youtube.com/watch?v=Kp_kqamkYpw&feature=youtu.be

[37] sciencedirect.com/topics/earth-and-planetary-sciences/punctuated-equilibrium

[38] Darwin, C. 1859. On the Origin of Species, A Facsimile of the First Edition, Harvard University Press, Cambridge, 1966.

## FAITH OF A MAKER

Darwin believed that the process of evolution was slow, and it should be possible to derive a complete lineage of ancestors for every living creature. The late Stephen J Gould, a paleontologist at Harvard, championed the process known as punctuated equilibria as an alternative to gradual development.[39]

He pointed out that a century of digging had only made the absence of fossils of missing links more glaring. He challenged scientists to accept the fossil record on its own terms. In an article titled *Enigmas of Evolution* in Newsweek about Gould's teaching and research his view on the fossil record was put as:

> "Rather than transforming gradually, most of the species in the world appear to have evolved relatively quickly (on the scale of geologic time) and to have persisted virtually unchanged for millions of years." - Adler and Carey, 1982.[40]

Gould put his faith in his understanding of the fossil record. We have faith in science because scientists use a standard process to validate their results. We put our faith in scientists when we trust them to follow that process and we make them accountable by having their papers reviewed by their peers. However, the process can fail when scientists use the wrong assumptions when interpreting the data.

We put our faith in the results of repeatable experiments that we design to test theories based on previous results. This grounds science within spacetime to make measurements with accurate instruments built by makers.

But measurements can be falsified. For example, to return the results required to meet regulatory standards Volkswagen programmed diesel

---

[39] Eldredge, N. 1986. Progress in evolution?, New Scientist, 5 June, pp54-57.
[40] Adler, J. and Carey, J. March 1982. Enigmas of Evolution, Newsweek, pp44-47. Article about the teaching and research of the late Stephen Jay Gould

engines to activate their emissions controls only during laboratory emissions testing.[41] When driven on the road the cars were emitting up to 40 times more pollutants than the standards. The challenge to makers is to act with integrity when reporting the results of research so that others can put their faith in their results.

The theory of evolution is controversial and the cause of much debate between Christians and the popularizers of science. In the next eight sections we will look at the theory, some of its problems and its dating methods, followed by a section on the problems with creation science.

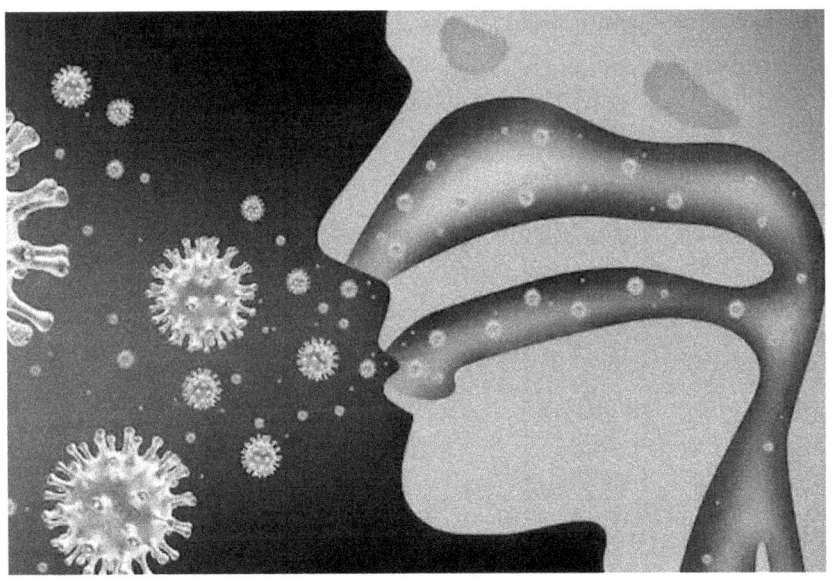

**Figure 4.6** *Visualization of COVID-19*

---

[41] wikipedia.org/wiki/Volkswagen_emissions_scandal

## EVOLUTION WITHIN SPECIES

Evolution within a species occurs due to breeding, mutations, and the survival of the fittest. People with both scientific and Christian beliefs agree that nature includes processes that result in variation between members of a species.

For example, nowadays we can order designer dogs. New breeds of dogs are bred by selective cross breeding of two exiting breeds, such as Labradoodles (Labrador Poodle cross) or Kilter (Kelpie Terrier cross). In the past dogs were bred with the characteristics desired in working dogs, such as herding and hunting. Today many dogs are bred with the characteristics of companion dogs.

In 2020 the COVID-19 virus changed the way we live (Figure 4.6). Masks became mandatory. Swabs were stuck up our nostrils every time we had symptoms due to a new outbreak. Businesses closed as suburbs were locked down. Parents had to home school their children. Many people had to cancel holidays when borders were closed.

The pandemic is thought to have been started by the mutation of an existing virus, known as Sars-CoV-2[42]. The mutation is located in the spike protein that pries open our cells to allow viruses to enter. It has since mutated further to produce even more infectious variant strains.

A mutation is any event that changes the genetic structure of the virus (DNA or RNA sequences of a genome). The genetic structure is the inherited nucleic acid sequence of the genotype of an organism that defines how the organism is made. Since the Covid-19 virus was first identified it is thought that thousands of mutations have arisen. Most of these mutations don't change the behavior of the virus. They are the *good* ones.

---

[42] bbc.com/news/science-environment-55404988

## SCIENCE

Occasionally a virus mutates in a way that helps it survive and reproduce. Viruses carrying these mutations can then increase in frequency due to natural selection in the right conditions. The problem with these 'bad' mutations is that they are aggressive. The delta variant of the COVID-19 virus is an example of evolution within a species that we prefer had not happened.

Variation within the members of a species can be the result of natural selection. As a result of global warming the sea waters around the Great Barrier Reef are heating up. While some corals are thriving in the warmer water, some are dying due to coral bleaching, and some are migrating to reefs in cooler waters to the south.

Corals are animals that have microscopic marine algae living inside their tissue. These algal plants, called zooxanthellae, give corals their color and food. Coral bleaching occurs when corals are under stress, causing them to expel the zooxanthellae. Without them, the coral's tissue becomes transparent, revealing the bright white skeleton.

When a coral bleaches, it's not dead. But if the stress is prolonged then bleached corals begin to starve without their food. If the temperature of the water returns to normal quickly enough, then corals can recover, and their resident zooxanthellae will move back in. If the water temperature stays hot for a long period, the bleached coral will eventually die. A question that arises from this: is the change in the type of corals on a given reef the result of natural selection or a biodiversity response to environment changes?

These examples of evolution within a species due to breeding, mutations, and the survival of the fittest are easy to observe. Evolution is usually portrayed as very slow, taking millions of years, but each of these examples happened quickly.[43] The formation of dangerous mutant strains of Covid-

---

[43] Le Page, M. 2011. Evolution in the fast lane, New Scientist, 2 April, pp32-36

19 appears to only take a few weeks. The evidence is that organisms evolve very rapidly in response to changes in their environment.

> "I think a superficial reading of the fossil record has given us a misleading picture of the evolutionary process. The changes seen over long intervals of geographical time are not representative of what happens on a generation-to-generation timescale." - Professor P. Gingerich, University of Michigan 1983.[44]

## EVOLUTION OF A NEW SPECIES

Having seen examples of evolution within a species we ask the question, "Does it scale up to the evolution of a new species?" In other words, do the mechanisms of breeding, mutations, and the survival of the fittest, that work for evolution in the small, work for evolution in the large? Or is some other, currently unknown, mechanism required?

While not an expert in biology, David Gelernter is a highly respected professor of Computer Science at Yale who comments from the perspective of a Computer Scientist who has recently changed his view of evolution.

> "There's no reason to doubt that Darwin successfully explained the small adjustments by which an organism adapts to local circumstances: changes to fur density or wing style or beak shape. Yet there are many reasons to doubt whether he can answer the hard questions and explain the big picture—not the fine-tuning of existing species but the emergence of new ones. The origin of species is

---

[44] Gingerich, P. 1983. Science, vol 222, p159. Referenced in Le Page, M. 2011.

# SCIENCE

exactly what Darwin cannot explain."[45] - Professor David Gelernter, Yale 2019.[46]

To get an insight into what is involved in making a new species we will look at one issue in the development of autonomous robots. The development of robots is often inspired by studies of animals, but the resulting robot may look nothing like the animal. Most roboticist argue that the exploration of other planets should be done by robots not humans. The series of mobile robots that NASA has sent to Mars are the result of this thinking.

A six-wheel rover named Perseverance landed on Mars in 2021 carrying a coaxial helicopter named Ingenuity.[47] The design of the helicopter was indeed ingenious. I presented a paper on the modeling of a coaxial helicopter at a robotics conference and appreciate the cleverness of NASA's design.[48]

Previous Mars robots have persevered for longer than expected before they failed. In response to these failures some robotics researchers have suggested that the robots should make replicas of themselves to carry on the task of Mars exploration. But for a robot to make even a copy of itself it would require a robot-building workshop equipped with plans, tools, and materials. The robot itself would have to have the skills to make things as well as its exploration skills.

Thus, the ability of a robot to self-replicate requires two things: a plan and a fully equipped workshop stocked with the right materials. Any work-

---

[45] claremontreviewofbooks.com/giving-up-darwin
[46] cpsc.yale.edu/people/david-gelernter
[47] nasa.gov/press-release/nasa-ingenuity-mars-helicopter-prepares-for-first-flight
[48] Li, C. and McKerrow, P.J. 2007. Modelling the Lama Coaxial Helicopter, accepted16/10/07, ACRA'07, Brisbane, December 2007. Due to a communication problem it doesn't appear in the proceedings

shop will not do; it must have all the tools and materials needed to make the specific robot according to the plan.

Similarly, if we are going to make a baby, we need two things: a DNA sequence and a womb.[49] If we are going to make a new species, a genome containing the mutations to describe the new species is not enough.

Normally, a male fertilises a female through sexual intercourse. In this process a sperm cell from the male penetrates the female's ovum to form a zygote with a new DNA sequence. The zygote embeds itself in the mother's womb where it grows. Fertilization will only occur when the womb is compatible with the zygote's DNA.

The functioning of the mother's womb is controlled by the zygote's DNA to produce a child with that DNA. The DNA controls the development of the fetus until it is born as a baby. As the fetus grows the parents rejoice. After birth the baby's body continues to develop as instructed by the DNA, and the parents are filled with wonder.

In order to survive, a new species has to be self-replicating. To create a self-replicating species requires both a DNA sequence to define the species and a matching womb to make the species. For fertilization to occur the male and female must be of the same species. A mule is a donkey crossed with a horse.[50] But female mules rarely get pregnant. Mules are not self-replicating. Our attempts to create a new species in the laboratory have failed, for example crossing a lion and a tiger.[51]

Thus, for evolution of a new species to occur by mutation it must mutate both the DNA and the womb at the same time. Does this make the odds of evolution creating a new species by means of mutation extremely small? It has not been shown that the process scales up.

---

[49] genoma.com/blog/en/genetics-has-a-fundamental-role-in-fetal-life-development/
[50] wikipedia.org/wiki/Mule
[51] wikipedia.org/wiki/Liger

Atheists and many Christians believe that creation by God (Psalm 33:6) and development by evolution are incompatible. What do you believe? We are back to the question: Is human life the creation of an infinitely intelligent God or the result of one chance in infinity? Researchers in evolution are working on the solutions for several problems with the theory.

**Figure 4.7** *Shaligram stones - fossils of ammonite shells*

## EVOLUTION PROBLEMS

One of the big problems that biologists are studying is: How does evolution happen?[52] While the punctuated equilibrium theory may be more popular than Darwin's gradual development theory, neither theory offers a working mechanism. The processes observed within species do not appear to scale up. Yet many people believe that evolution between species is a fact not a theory.

We have not found the missing links Darwin required to support his theory, and mutation has not been shown to be a working mechanism

---

[52] evolution.berkeley.edu/evo101/VIIBigissues.shtml

for evolution from one species to a new species. No chain of fossil links between two species has ever been found. And there are some very large gaps in the fossil record, e.g., for example the gap between single-cell and multi-cell organisms.

Other areas of science have developed procedures for verifying theories. These procedures involve observation of repeated experiments. Repeated experiments work with passive objects but may not work with dynamic objects. For example: compare dropping an apple to kissing a woman. A problem with the study of the origin of species is that we cannot go back in time and observe the creation of the earth and its inhabitants.

Also, to date we have not developed an experiment for creating a new species that we can re-run. We are limited to observing fossils and theorizing what happened. The Carnegie Museum in Pittsburgh contains one of the five skeletons that have been found of Tyrannosaurus Rex. It is an awesome but very dead structure of bones. There is a limit to what we can learn from this fossil.

Observing the remains of events that happened long ago may not be enough to prove a theory or convince a sceptic. Min Raj grew up in Nepal where he observed shaligram stones (Figure 4.7) in rocks in streams at the top of the Himalayas.[53] Shaligram stones are the coiled chambered fossil shells of extinct mollusks. When he broke them open, they looked like a snake inside - a spiral.

When I asked Min Raj, "Why are these fossils of sea creatures at the top of mountains?"

He replied, "I was told by a geologist that they were there due to continental shift. I found that hard to believe. I think a massive flood rearranged the topography of the world."

---

[53] wikipedia.org/wiki/Shaligram

## UNCONFORMITIES

A second problem is that the columns of rock stratum that geologists use to date rocks and the fossils contained in them are full of gaps. A stratum is a layer of rock or soil that was formed at the earth's surface and then buried (Figure 4.8). Geologists believe that every layer has internally consistent characteristics that distinguish it from other layers. They use the stratum of a rock to estimate the environment that existed when the layer was formed.

Sedimentary rocks are usually laid down in flat layers, although these can be tilted and folded by later events. These layers extend sideways and can often be seen in river cuttings. Layers are identified by their type, color, and physical composition. Geologists study rock layers and layering (stratification) to determine the relative date of when the layers were formed.

Layers in different places with the same characteristics are assumed to have been laid at the same time. The geologic record is the correlation of strata from different places, but the complete record has not been observed in any single place.[54] It is used as a date ruler. At any locality on the earth's surface the rock column provides a cross section of the natural history in the area during the time covered by the age of the rocks. The problem with all columns is that: "There are unconformities all through the rock record." - Francis Macdonald, 2020. University of California, Santa Barbara, Geologist.[55]

Unconformities are gaps in time within the rock record. In every column there are more layers missing than there are remaining. No stratum conforms to the standard column. In 1869, John Wesley Powell noticed the *Great Unconformity* in the layers of the Grand Canyon. In some places it indicates more than one billion years of missing rock.

---

[54] wikipedia.org/wiki/Geologic_record
[55] news.ucsb.edu/2020/019892/great-unconformity

**Figure 4.8** *King's Canyon, Central Australia*

These unconformities make calculating relative time and environmental conditions from the rock record difficult. Is the Great Unconformity a large period of geographical time that we know nothing about? This leaves us with the question: How accurate is the scientific model of the rock column?

## CARBON-14 DATING

A third problem is that all the dating methods are based on assumptions. The process of radioactive dating is used to estimate when an animal or plant died. It assumes that the rate at which radioactive isotopes impinge on an object hasn't changed over time. It assumes that the fossil stopped absorbing the isotope when it died. It assumes that the rate of decay of the

# SCIENCE

isotope in the fossil is in accordance with the isotope's half-life. Also, it assumes that there is an alternate, more accurate measurement of time that can be used to calibrate the measurement.

Carbon-14, a naturally occurring isotope that is unstable and radioactive, is measured in radiocarbon dating. The measurements assume that the concentration of carbon-14 in the atmosphere has remained constant. Its value in 1950 is used as a reference point (BP stands for age Before Present, 1950 is BP0). The half-life used in carbon-14 dating is 5568 years.

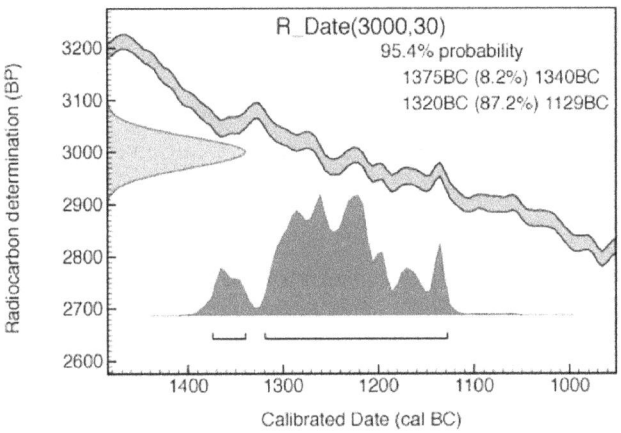

Calibration curves of a sample
Oxford Radiocarbon Accelerator Unit

**Figure 4.9** *Carbon-14 calibration curves of a sample*

Measurements must be calibrated to account for the changes in the atmospheric concentration of carbon-14.[56] These changes are the result of several factors, including fluctuations in the earth's geomagnetic moment, fossil fuel burning, and nuclear testing.

---

[56] radiocarbon.com/tree-ring-calibration.htm

To calibrate any measurement tool, we need a more accurate measuring tool. A more accurate measurement of the age of a radiocarbon measurement of a sample is found by comparing it to the radiocarbon measurement of tree rings. Libraries of tree ring measurements provide records extending back over the last 11,000 years and calendar calibration curves reach as far back as about 48,000 BC.

Figure 4.9 shows how the radiocarbon measurement of date (3000+-30BP) is calibrated.[57] The left-hand axis shows the radiocarbon concentration expressed in years BP. The bottom axis shows calendar years (derived from the tree ring data). The pair of curves sloping down to the right show the radiocarbon measurements on the tree rings (plus and minus one standard deviation).

The bell curve on the left indicates the radiocarbon concentration in the sample. The histogram on the bottom shows possible ages for the sample. The results of calibration are often given as an age range. In this case, we might say that we could be 95% sure that the sample comes from between calibrated dates 1375 BC and 1129 BC.

Inaccuracies in radiocarbon measurements are the result of two issues. One: the measurement of both the samples and the tree rings have limited precision. And two: the concentration of radiocarbon in the atmosphere has varied since 1950. As a result of these errors, the calibration gives an age range, and at times, more than one possible date.

Accurate measurement of date using radiocarbon is limited to 50,000 years. So, it cannot be used to date the earth. Other methods are required for dates further in the past. Also, measuring methods that are more accurate than the dating method are required to calibrate these methods, such as Potassium-argon dating.

---

[57] c14.arch.ox.ac.uk/calibration.html

# SCIENCE

## POTASSIUM–ARGON DATING

Potassium-argon dating is based on measuring the radioactive decay of an isotope of potassium (K-40) to form argon (Ar-40).[58] Argon escapes from molten material but is trapped by solid material and starts to accumulate after the material solidifies.

The ratio of argon-40 to potassium-40 in a mineral or rock sample is used as a measure of the age of the sample. This measure assumes that there was no argon-40 left in the sample when it solidified. If some argon-40 was left in the sample, then the measurement will be high.

The more argon-40 accumulated the longer the time since the material solidified and hence the older the sample. The amount accumulated is a function of the purity of the sample and its composition. Also, the age that is estimated is impacted by environmental factors during the formation of the sample, including melting, pressure decrease, and exposure to open-air. Again, the value is determined within error limits, due to these variations.

Research into the origin of species is constrained by the limitation that we can't go back in time and have a look. We must infer what happened by observing the residue of past events. Accurate dating of fossils is an important part of modeling past events.

In these sections, we have examined some of the problems with the theory of evolution. As you think about these issues, which one or more of the following conclusions appears to be supported by the evidence? Darwin's theory is not true, or it does not conform with nature, or it is a working hypothesis, or it is a beautiful model, or it is the best explanation we have, or it is a proven fact!

---

[58] wikipedia.org/wiki/K–Ar_dating

## EVOLUTION OF GAPS

When faced with a gap in our knowledge some Christians have fallen into the mistake of explaining the gap by saying *God did it* and some atheists fall into the same trap by saying *Evolution did it*. In the 19th-century, Henry Drummond chastised Christians for filling up gaps in science with God. He urged Christians to embrace all of nature as the work of an immanent God, including evolution.

In his 1955 book *Science and Christian Belief* Charles Alfred Coulson, a mathematics professor at Oxford and a Methodist church leader, wrote:

> "There is no 'God of the gaps' to take over at those strategic places where science fails; and the reason is that gaps of this sort have the unpreventable habit of shrinking…"

The God of the Bible is outside of creation, that is, He is not immanent (spread throughout creation). While God sustains life, the belief that He inhabits everything is not Christian. When Jesus came to earth, He entered creation as a human being to show us what God is like, not to fill gaps in our scientific knowledge. St Paul described Jesus as being supreme over all of nature.[59] In another place he said we can see God's invisible qualities through nature.[60]

In the 21st century, it is not unusual to hear the presenters of popular science programs say:

> *"We don't know how but we know it evolved."*

It seems we have an evolution of the gaps. When we don't know how an animal or plant got a particular trait or characteristic, we start with

---

[59] Colossians 1:13
[60] Romans 1:20

## SCIENCE

the assumption that it evolved so evolution must have found a way. Our knowledge is changing continuously, and gaps have the unpreventable habit of shrinking.

Some people worship evolution, saying that something evolved for evolution's sake. A recent article in Popular Mechanics had the following statement:

> "A virus like SARS-CoV-2 constantly changes by mutating, with the evolutionary goal of continuing to infect new host organisms."[61]

I wonder, does a virus have a mind that enables it to have an evolutionary goal?

**Figure 4.10** *Ghost Bat. Native to Australia. Duncan MacKenzie, published in Australian Geographic, copied from reddit.com*

---

[61] popularmechanics.com/science/health/a37200703/delta-variant-research/

## EVOLUTION OF ECHOLOCATING BATS

The development of some animals are enigmas. In his book on bat echolocation (Figure 4.10) David Pye stated that there are no fossils of pre-bats.[62] The oldest fossil is of a fully echolocating bat. A recent paper suggests that echolocating bats evolved into non-echolocating bats.[63]

In 1989, I visited Professor Neuweller in his research laboratory in Munich. He gave me a preprint of his famous paper on *Foraging ecology and audition in echolocating bats*, which had just been published.[64] He told me that the editors of the journal had approached him to write a paper on the evolution of bats. He told them that he knew nothing about their evolution. They asked him to write the paper anyway.

His response was to write a paper on a topic he had researched: how bats adapt their echolocation signal to the specific acoustical constraints of their foraging area when they hunt in different types of environments, specifically below, inside and above the tree canopy. Above the canopy they use low frequencies. Within foliage they detect fluttering targets. When bats glean, they detect very faint noises, such as a stationary prey changing its posture. The paper is quoted by others as an important paper on the evolution of bats even though it is about bat ecology, not their evolution.

## CREATION SCIENCE

The controversy between some evolutionists and some Christians has given rise to various groups with conflicting ideas. A teacher, who is a Christian,

---

[62] Pye D. 1968. Hearing in Bats, Department of Zoology, King's College, London.
[63] Jones, G. and Teeling, E.C. 2006. The evolution of echolocation in bats, Trends in Ecology and Evolution, Vol. 21, No 3. pp 149-156
[64] Neuweiler, G. 1989. Foraging ecology and audition in echolocating bats. Trends in Ecology and Evolution, 4: pp 160-166.

was teaching evolution to a science class in a public school. The class asked him how he could teach evolution and still believe that God created everything? They spent the rest of the class discussing creation (Colossians 1:16-17) and evolution.

> Later, he told another teacher what had happened. The other teacher said, "You shouldn't teach creation science - it's not science."
>
> He replied, "I agree, creation science is not science. I taught creation as the Word of God, evolution as a scientific theory and evolution by chance as atheism."

I am not a creation scientist. I am a Christian who believes in creation. I will not go into the beliefs of creation science here but rather examine why many scientists and engineers who are Christians have difficulty with creation science?

For those who wish to examine creation science further CIS have a web page with links to the web sites of various Christian and some non-Christian groups who hold differing views on the relationship between creation and evolution, including Young-Earth Creation Science (YECS), anti YECS, Christian Old-Earth, Intelligent Design, and Anti-Intelligent design.[65]

Science is restricted to answering questions about things we can observe in space-time. It can neither prove the existence of God - as falsely claimed by creation scientists - nor disprove the existence of God - as falsely claimed by atheistic evolutionists - because God is outside of space-time. Christians believe God created both space and time. The scientist who is a Christian is given the task of working out how He did it so we can praise Him.

---

[65] cis.org.uk/resources/articles-talks-and-links/creation/creationism-links/

If creation science can prove the existence of a loving creator God by scientific methods, then doesn't that put creation science above God? If it does, then creation science will have backfired. If they can prove God exists by science, then would science be God?

Creation science attempts to create an alternate science from the Bible. In doing so, they fail to recognize that the Bible is not a science text. The purpose of the writers of the Bible was to tell their readers what God has done and why He did it, not how He did it.

Also, they must make assumptions to fill in the scientific gaps in the Bible, such as the concept of created age. Imagine that I have the ability to create a tiger, and I let it run around in a jungle for a few days. Would it look a lot older than a few days? Would you be able to tell that it was created a week ago and not born two years ago?

Take the stars - they look to be millions of light years away. If the universe was created only a few thousand years ago then God would have had to create the light beam from each star to earth when He created the star. Why would He create the universe to appear much older than it is, unless it is a side effect of the physics He used? But how are we to know if these assumptions are true?

The authors of the Bible wrote in several literary genres. Each one choosing the genre that best communicated his message. The Bible is to be interpreted in the context of the writer's culture. It is to be interpreted literarily as a piece of literature, not literally as a word-for-word text about creation.

## SCIENCE FICTION

Various beliefs about science have become a fertile ground for the writers of science fiction. Makers have an innate desire to create and make worlds,

worlds that stretch their imagination and expand their ability to make. Imagination is the formation of a mental image of something that is not perceived as real and is not present to the senses. Science fiction is literary fantasy that involves the imagined impact of science on society, a fantasy that is restricted by reality. Fantasy is imagination unrestricted by current reality.

Creation stories are common in the genres of science fiction and fantasy. Someone or something is recognized as the all-powerful being who created the world and everything in it. Our desire to create is evidence that we were created in the image of God. Our creativity shows us the creative side of God's character. God spoke humans into existence:

> "Then God said, "Let us make mankind in our image, in our likeness,
> so that they may rule over the fish in the sea and the birds in the sky,
> over the livestock and all the wild animals,
> and over all the creatures that move along the ground."
> So God created mankind in his own image,
> in the image of God he created them;
> male and female he created them."
> (Genesis 1:26-27)

Two books that include creation stories, that I have enjoyed reading, are: *The Magician's Nephew* from the Narnia series written by C.S. Lewis,[66] and *The Hitchhiker's Guide to the Galaxy* written by Douglas Adams.[67]

In *The Magician's Nephew* the great lion *Aslan* creates the land of *Narnia* by singing. Like the story at the start of this chapter, his voice brought plants and animals into existence on a world that was previously in darkness. The skill of the writer is such that the reader is filled with wonder as he is transported into the creation of *Narnia*.

---

[66] Lewis C.S. 1955. "The Magicians Nephew", Chapter 8
[67] Adams D. 1979. "The Hitchhiker's Guide to the Galaxy" Chapter 24.

Lewis wrote the *Narnia* series to teach significant Bible truths. One Christian concept that permeates his writings is goodness. In contrast none of J.K. Rowling's characters in the *Harry Potter* series could be called good. They are not written from a Christian worldview.

In *The Hitchhiker's Guide to the Galaxy* the main character, Arthur Dent, is taken to a hyperspace factory where planets are built. When completed the planet is moved through hyperspace and placed in orbit around a sun.

Slartibartfast had taken Arthur there to see the construction of Earth Mark Two. This science fiction spoof is made humorous by the description of Arthur's mind as he travels through the factory in an air car at breakneck speed.

Not only is the ability to imagine and fantasize new worlds evidence of an imaginative God, so too is our ability to enjoy the music, art, poetry, fiction, and fantasy that we create. Makers regularly launch new worlds in fantasy games on Kickstarter. The desire of makers to create new worlds reflects the image of God our maker. Dr Theocharis Kyriacou sees our appreciation of all art forms as evidence of a creator God.

> "There is increasing questioning/challenging of the existence of God from scientists/engineers. Non-believers call for a 'scientific proof' but the way I like to see it is that our very ability to ask for or search for that proof is proof in itself that God exists.
>
> I also find God in music and art, both strong featuring elements in science and engineering in more ways than most scientists and engineers realize. The fact that we can produce and appreciate/enjoy these elements is, has to be, Divine." - Theocharis Kyriacou, Ph.D. Keele University.[68]

---

[68] Senior Lecturer in Computer Science, Keele, keele.ac.uk/scm/staff/drtheochariskyriacou

## SCIENCE

# WHY IS IT SO?

Physicist, Professor Julius Sumner-Miller was the presenter of the children's science show with the name *Why is it so?*[69] It became an instant hit and was known for its 'cool experiments, interesting science, and Sumner-Miller's fantastic hair'. Finding an answer to the question, "Why is it so?" is the goal of all scientific research.

The scientific method involves defining the problem to be solved, making a hypothesis, encoding the hypothesis with mathematical equations, conducting experiments, using the results to test the hypothesis, and then revising the hypothesis. When we talk to research students about knowing God, we can challenge them to use the same rigorous approach to think about questions of faith. We can teach them to pose their problem about God as a hypothesis and then do research and think about the results. Why is there something rather than nothing?

Many people claim that science is their reason for not believing in Jesus, what about you? Science can neither prove nor disprove the existence of God because He exists outside of space-time. So, was the universe created by this infinitely intelligent and loving God who lives in eternity, or did it come about by the infinitesimal chance occurrence of a ripple in the universe? People exist, you exist. Why is it so?

---

[69] wikipedia.org/wiki/Julius_Sumner_Miller

# 5

# MATHEMATICS

**Figure 5.1** *Draganflyer. Drone used in research.*

# MATHEMATICS

"The most direct relationship between my faith and my career as a professor of engineering has been in my reflections on the relationship of theory to practice. Having studied mathematics and physics as an undergraduate, I entered engineering through its theoretical side.

However, I came to realize that although engineering is informed by theory, it requires the skills and insights obtained from experience, grappling with the complexities of real problems that never distill neatly and completely into the theoretical frameworks.

"I've seen rich parallels in my spiritual life. Theology and doctrine may inform my Christian life, but these intellectual frameworks are not sufficient for living a life of faith. To live the Christian life, one must draw on and learn from experience." - Professor Bruce Krough, CMU, 2021.

"Following Jesus and obeying His loving commands helps me see the purposes in my work as engineer and as teacher of engineering." - Associate Professor Buyung Kosasih, Faculty of Engineering and Information Sciences, UOW, 2021.

## PI

Ken stuck his head through the door of my office.[1] "How can you believe in God?" he asked. "The Bible can't even get Pi right." Then he turned his head and wandered away without waiting for an answer.

---

[1] True story, name changed

Pi Day (Figure 5.2) is a fun celebration of the mathematical constant π (Pi ≈ 3.14159).[2] Pi Day is observed on March 14 since 3, 1, and 4 are the first three significant digits of π. It was founded in 1988 by Larry Shaw, an employee of the Exploratorium: a museum of science, technology, and arts in San Francisco. The Exploratorium has been described as "a mad scientist's penny arcade, a scientific funhouse, and an experimental laboratory all rolled into one."[3]

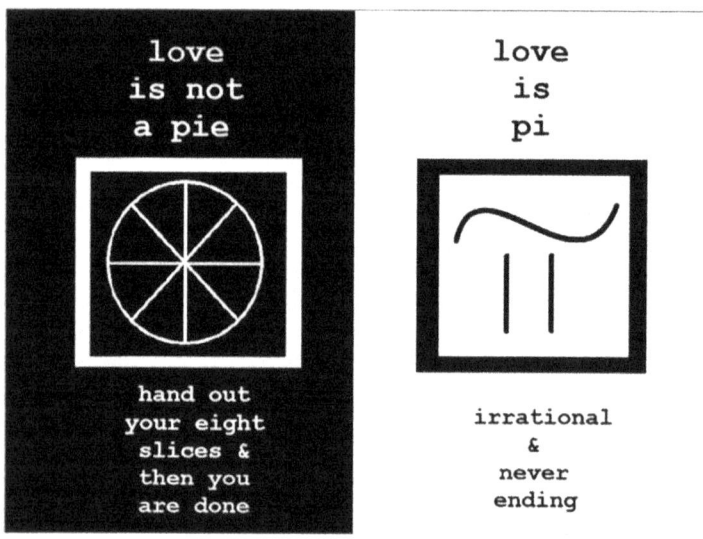

**Figure 5.2** *Pie Day Sticker, A Science Enthusiast, 2018*

Pi Day is often observed by eating and throwing pies, about as much fun as a mathematician can have. Since 2012, Massachusetts Institute of Technology (MIT) has posted its application decision letters to prospective students online on Pi Day at exactly 6:28 pm, which they have called, "Tau Time."

---

[2] wikipedia.org/wiki/Pi_Day
[3] wikipedia.org/wiki/Exploratorium

## MATHEMATICS

The number π is a mathematical constant. It is defined as the ratio of a circle's circumference to its diameter.

Pi = circumference / diameter.

Pi has been represented by the Greek letter π since the mid-18th century. Pi is an irrational number, so it cannot be expressed as a common fraction. 22 / 7 is often used to approximate it. Its decimal representation never ends and never settles into a permanently repeating pattern. Pi ≈ 3.14159 is an approximation.

The ancient Egyptians did not have a value for Pi. Instead, they used methods involving ratios. The Rhind Papyrus is a scroll recording their mathematical knowledge.[4] Written about 1650 BC it includes methods for solving 60 mathematical problems.[5] These methods were used by engineers to do the calculations to make buildings and pyramids.

An Egyptian example of where they used Pi is the calculation of the volume of a cylindrical granary. When calculating its volume, the fractional term 256 / 81 was used. It approximates the value of π as being 3.1605, which is an error of less than one percent.

So, where did Ken find Pi in the Bible? Pi as a mathematical constant is not there but it is there by inference. When King Solomon built his temple in Jerusalem it included a large circular basin for the priests to wash in. Its measurements are included in the description in the Bible:

> "He made the Sea of cast metal, circular in shape, measuring ten cubits (4.572 meters, 15 feet) from rim to rim and five cubits high (2.286 meters, 7½ feet). It took a line of thirty cubits (13.716 m, 45 feet) to measure around it. … It was a handbreadth (75 millimeters, 3 inches) in thickness, and

---

[4] The Rhind Papyrus, dating from around 1650 BCE, is a kind of instruction manual in arithmetic and geometry, https://www.storyofmathematics.com/egyptian.html
[5] wikipedia.org/wiki/Rhind_Mathematical_Papyrus

its rim was like the rim of a cup, like a lily blossom." (1 Kings 7:23-26)

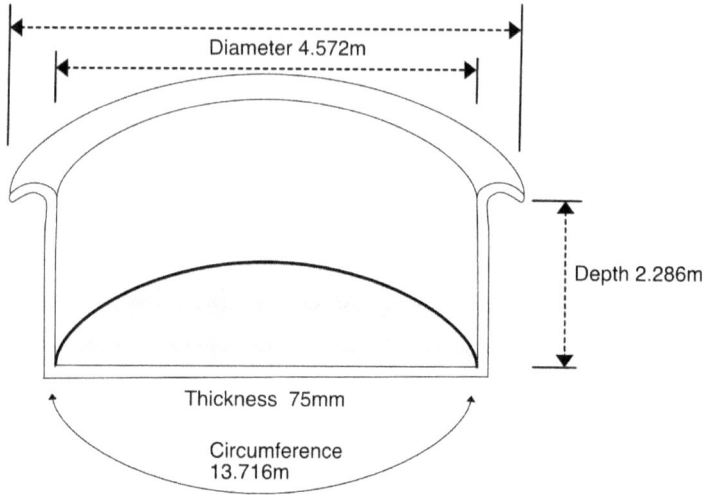

**Figure 5.3** *Cut away view of sea (not to scale)*

If we assume the dimensions are for the outside of the Sea (Figure 5.3) then Pi is the approximate length of the circumference (13.716 meters, 45 feet) divided by the diameter (4.572 meters, 15 feet) resulting in a value for Pi of 3. But the rim is flared out and the walls are 75 millimeters (3 inches) thick. So where on the rim were the measurements made?

If we assume that the measurement of the diameter is for the inside then the approximate length of the circumference is 14.3561 meters (47.1 feet), giving a measurement error of 4.45%. We don't know where on the basin the measurements were made or how they were made. A 5% measurement error of the circumference of a cylinder with the rim flared out to look like a water lily blossom is probably reasonable.

# MATHEMATICS

Two issues complicate this discussion further. First the measurements were made in cubits. The length of a cubit varied from culture to culture. In ancient Egypt, the length varied from 523.5 to 529.2 millimeters (20.61 to 20.83 inches), a variation of 1.06%. As Pi is the ratio of two measurements the length of a cubit doesn't matter when the same cubit is used in both measurements. That is, they are made by the same person with the same measuring line.

The second issue is that the measurement used for the circumference is the length of the line used to measure it: "It took a line of thirty cubits (13.716 meters, 45 feet) to measure around it." (1 Kings 7:23). So, the measurement was approximate.

A few years later Ken and I both attended the funeral of the son of a colleague. It was a tragic event with the young man committing suicide. Ken came into my office and asked,

> "Do you believe the verse you have in your email signature?"
> The verse was:

> "For God so loved the world that he gave his one and only Son, that whoever believes in him shall not perish but have eternal life." (John 3:16).

> "Yes," I replied.

> "So, you believe that if he didn't believe in Jesus, he has perished, I can't accept that," he said and left.

Sometime later I was told that during his battle with mental health the young man had expressed faith in Jesus and joined a Bible study group. The person who told me this believes that the young man has received eternal life. Issues that this story may raise are picked up in Chapter 10.

## MATH'S

Scientists use mathematics to encode the laws of science. Makers use mathematics to describe the objects they are making, and to model the systems they want to control. Maths is very useful because it is accurate. Some people say that the beauty of mathematics is evidence for the existence of God. If we can put our faith in beautiful equations, then why can't we put our faith in the God who created them?

When faced with a problem during making we can go back to first principles where our hand maiden mathematics is waiting. Scientists use equations to model theories and to describe the physical world. Engineers use mathematics to design objects from pencils for writing notes to expressways for cars to travel on. Virtually everyday makers use models, logic, statistics, and frames of reference in their making.

It is ironical that, while we use mathematics regularly, Wikipedia says it has no generally accepted definition.[6] This statement is confirmed by the definitions found in dictionaries, which vary considerably. The *Wordweb on-line dictionary* has a theoretical definition:

> "Mathematics is a science (or group of related sciences) dealing with the logic of quantity and shape and arrangement."

The *Macquarie Dictionary* has a more practical definition:

> "Mathematics is the science that treats the measurement, properties and relation of quantities, including arithmetic, geometry, algebra, etc."

---

[6] wikipedia.org/wiki/Mathematics

### MATHEMATICS

Sir Roger Penrose, Emeritus Professor of Mathematics at the University of Oxford, says there are two aspects to mathematics: its beauty and its precision. The mathematics that doesn't appear to have relevance to the physical world is studied for its beauty.[7] The mathematics that does have relevance to the physical world, such as Einstein's equations, is incredibly precise. Math's facts are always true, waiting somewhere for us to discover them, quite independent of any role they may have in physics.

## MODELS

The area of mathematics that I have used most during my career is the modeling of machines in-order to develop controllers for them. These models have varied from the simple model of steel extension below, to a non-linear model of galvanizing[8] (coating of steel strip with zinc), to empirical models of echolocation,[9] and dynamic models of drones (Figure 5.1).[10]

A simple example of how a mathematical model is used in practice is the measurement of the extension of steel strip as it passes through a four high reversing mill (Figure 5.4) used as a temper mill.[11] The coil of steel strip is loaded onto one reel (right reel for example) (Figure 5.5). Then the strip passes over the right deflector roll, through the work rolls, out the left side, and over the left deflector roll to be coiled up again on the left reel.

---

[7] youtube.com/watch?v=ujvS2K06dg4
[8] M<sup>c</sup>Kerrow, P.J. 1983. 'Computer Controlled Galvanizing', Computers in Industry, North-Holland, Vol 4 No 1, March, p 19-30.
[9] M<sup>c</sup>Kerrow, P.J. and Kristiansen, B.E. 2006. 'Classifying surface roughness with CTFM ultrasonic sensing', IEEE Sensors Journal, Vol. 6. No. 5., October, pp 1267-1279.
[10] M<sup>c</sup>Kerrow, P.J. 2004. Modelling the Draganflyer four-rotor helicopter, Proceedings ICRA'04, New Orleans, April, pp 3596-3601.
[11] H.E. McGannon, ed, The Making, Shaping and Treating of Steel, Eighth Edition, United States Steel, 1964. P 928

**Figure 5.4** *Four high reversing mill. View right to left: right reel, deflector roll and entrance to mill work rolls*

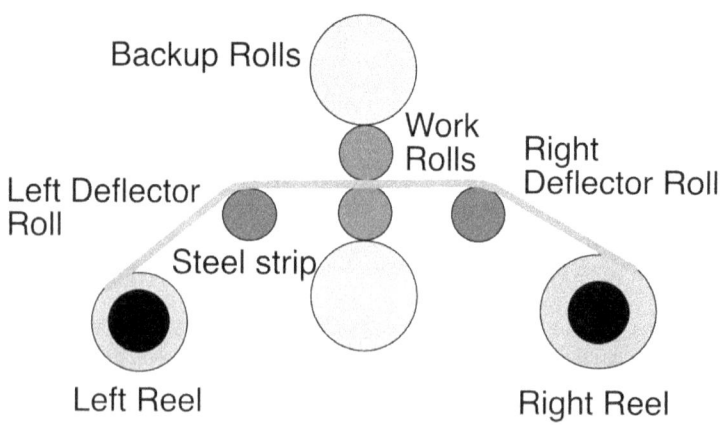

**Figure 5.5** *Setup of four high reversing mill*

## MATHEMATICS

The strip is driven forward by the work rolls. The backup rolls control pressure along the work rolls to give an even extension across the strip. Each reel controls tension between it and the mill. This combination of work roll pressure and strip tension results in extension of the strip. The mill runs at high-speed requiring automatic measurement (Figure 5.6) and control of extension.

In a previous process, when the steel strip was cold rolled from about 6 mm thick to about 1mm thick, it lost its ductility. To restore their ductility coils of strip are annealed in box furnaces. After annealing, the strip is cold-worked in a temper mill to temper the strip to the desired stiffness. In addition to developing the required mechanical properties, temper rolling restores the flatness of the annealed strip, and imparts the desired surface finish.

**Figure 5.6** *Extension Meter running test of 45.4% extension*

The reduction in strip thickness caused by temper rolling increases the length by a small percentage, referred to as extension. Measurement of extension is used as the criteria for controlling the reduction in thickness.

Percentage Extension = increase-in-Length divided by original-Length *100.

In symbolic form: %E = ∂L / L * 100.

At that time, we were building electronics with gate level chips to implement models. Today, we would use an Arduino microcontroller to make this instrument. To measure extension, we mounted pulse generators on the deflector rolls. These idling rolls are turned by the tension in the strip as it passes over them, so measurement of their revolutions is equivalent to measuring the linear velocity of the strip.

As is often the case, the engineer must reformulate the theoretical model provided by the mathematicians to a model suitable for implementation. The reformulated model used in the measurement of extension is:

Percentage Extension = (Extended-length - Length) divided by Length *100

where Extended-length = Length + Increase-in-Length

In symbolic form: %E = (EL - L) / L * 100

where EL = L + ∂L

When L = 1000,

%E = ((1000 + ∂L) - 1000) / 1000 * 100

The length of the strip before extension is measured with the pulse generator on the incoming side (right in this example). When the incoming count reaches 1000 the count of the pulses from the pulse generator on the outgoing side is read and both counters are reset. The difference between the outgoing count and the incoming count (1000) is the extension.

## MATHEMATICS

Percentage extension is presented to the mill operator by displaying the outgoing count with a 3-digit display. The subtraction is achieved by ignoring the first digit and a decimal point is placed between the third and fourth digits. For example, when the outgoing count is 1151 (incoming count of 1000 + 151) the display reads 15.1% extension.

Models are abstractions. They describe the real world from one point of view. They allow us to understand and control objects in the world. For example, this book can be described as molecules of cellulose and atoms of carbon by a chemist, or text by a printer, or as a stimulating story of making by a reader. Each description is an abstraction. All three are different and at one level all three can be considered to be true.

Mathematical models are one representation of a system. They describe the physical world with symbols and numbers to some level of accuracy. For example, Newton's second law,

force = mass times acceleration ($f=ma$),

tells us about the force with which an apple hits the ground, but it can't tell us whether the apple bounced or went thud. We need additional equations to model that. A scientific model is only one abstraction of reality and thus only captures part of it. In Chapter 9, we will compare the use of models with the use of neural networks in AI systems.

As models become more complex, the more likely they are to have minor errors. When transforming a science model into an engineering model, the maker should determine which parameters are first order, and hence of most importance. By contrast, some parameters are second order and as they have very little impact on the accuracy of the output they can be ignored.[12] Some parameters are easy to measure, and others must be estimated from available measurements.

---

[12] Modelling errors - skip to 2:42 to see errors in derivatives
youtube.com/watch?v=S0_qX4VJhMQ

When working with models and with the technology to measure their parameters, I humbly admit that God thought about them first. On many occasions, I have prayed to find a bug in code, or to understand how to manipulate a model, or to determine what is causing electronics to fail. I believe these prayers have been answered, even if only to calm me down to think more clearly.

## LOGIC

When we are unable to model a physical process by direct observation, we may be able to use logic to draw a conclusion based on circumstantial evidence.

> A high-school student told me that he had decided to believe in God. He said, "I was reading a science fiction book when the main character decided to believe in God because that would give him the best quality of life."

In the book that the student was reading, the main character's reasoning was a science fiction version of Pascal's wager.[13] Pascal was a French scientist and philosopher. The SI unit for pressure is named after him in recognition of his scientific research.[14] Most computer science students have done an assignment to write code to generate Pascal's triangle.[15] Pascal believed that it is not possible to prove or disprove that God exists. Therefore, he suggested, it is better to bet that God exists.

Even though the existence of God cannot be determined through reason, Pascal suggested that people gamble with their lives by not believing.

---

[13] simple.wikipedia.org/wiki/Pascal%27s_Wager
[14] wikipedia.org/wiki/International_System_of_Units
[15] mathsisfun.com/pascals-triangle.html

## MATHEMATICS

His wager involved a logical proposition involving two ideas: belief in God and existence of God. Logically, from a Christian viewpoint, there are four possible outcomes. They are:

1. You believe in Jesus, and He exists, so you will receive eternal life.
2. You don't believe in Jesus, and He exists, so you won't receive eternal life.
3. You believe in Jesus, but He doesn't exist, so you won't receive eternal life.
4. You don't believe in Jesus, and He doesn't exist, so it makes no difference.

These statements can be expressed with a simple logic formula, a Boolean equation,

(Receiving eternal life) = (you Believe in Jesus) AND (Jesus Exists)

Which expressed in symbols is: R = B AND E

Or they can be expressed as an addition where true = +1 and false = -1 the result of the four statements is +2, 0, 0, -2.

Pascal suggests that the first statement is the most important because it results in the maximum gain or loss. So, if you are a gambler then you will bet your life on the first statement because it has the best odds, and you will live in a way that shows you believe in God.

This is cold hard logic where everything is black or white. It captures the logic of Jesus' teaching but doesn't capture the love of God expressed by Jesus.

> "For God so loved the world that he gave his one and only Son, that whoever believes in him shall not perish but have eternal life. For God did not send his Son into the world to

condemn the world, but to save the world through him." (John 3:16-17)

Counter arguments are mainly based on the claim that the two ideas are not black and white, but somewhat fuzzy. If you are an atheist, then your beliefs are described by the fourth statement. If your beliefs are founded on the logic that I can't see God therefore he doesn't exist, then you may believe that Pascal assumes logic where there is no logic. What are you betting your life on?

## BEAUTY

For some people, the beauty of mathematical equations is sufficient reason to bet their life on belief in a maker. Leonhard Euler is thought to be the greatest mathematician of the 18th century because of his vast contribution to mathematics.[16] Euler's formulae is named after him.

$e^{ix} = cos\ x + i\ sin\ x$

Euler's formula becomes Euler's identity when $x = \pi$

$e^{i\pi} + 1 = 0$

It combines constants from four areas of mathematics: arithmetic, calculus, imaginary numbers, and geometry - using three basic arithmetic operations: addition, multiplication, and exponentiation. Where:

1. 0 and 1 are the additive identity and the multiplicative identity respectively - from arithmetic,
2. e (2.718…) is Euler's number, the base of natural logarithms - from calculus,
3. i ($i^2 = -1$) is the imaginary unit - from imaginary numbers, and

---

[16] wikipedia.org/wiki/Leonhard_Euler

# MATHEMATICS

4. π (pi = 3.141…) is the ratio of the circumference of a circle to its diameter - from geometry.

There is no logical reason why this equation should be so. Benjamin Peirce, a 19th-century American philosopher, mathematician, and professor at Harvard University, proved Euler's identity during a lecture and then stated that the identity:

> "… is absolutely paradoxical; we cannot understand it, and we don't know what it means, but we have proved it, and therefore we know it must be the truth."[17]

Euler's number and pi are both irrational numbers that can't be reduced to simple fractions. The digits to the right of their decimal points go on forever without repeating.

Many processes are described with exponential functions of the form $y=e^x$. The slope of $y=e^x$ at any point x is also $e^x$, and the area under the curve from negative infinity up to x is also $e^x$.[18] No other curve has this property.

Another set of equations that people consider to be beautiful are Maxwell's four equations, which form the basis of electrical and optical engineering.[19] In a poll of the most prominent physicists by *Physics World Magazine* (December 1999) Scottish mathematician James Clerk Maxwell was voted the third greatest physicist of all time, behind only Newton and Einstein. Maxwell was a Christian who desired to obey the will of God by serving his own generation.[20]

Some people believe that Euler's identity is the best empirical evidence we have for the existence of God. It has been called the *God Equation*. It is

---

[17] wikipedia.org/wiki/Euler%27s_formula
[18] popularmechanics.com/science/math/a24383/mathematical-constant-e/
[19] wikipedia.org/wiki/Maxwell%27s_equations
[20] wikipedia.org/wiki/James_Clerk_Maxwell#Personal_life

one way that nature proclaims the glory of God, confirming the truth of the Bible.

> "The heavens declare the glory of God;
> the skies proclaim the work of his hands.
> Day after day they pour forth speech;
> night after night they reveal knowledge."
> (Psalm 19:1-2)

Euler believed that such a simple relationship between the five most important numbers in mathematics was too unlikely to be a coincidence. It is the most beautiful equation because of this profound relationship. Is the beauty of this equation evidence for the existence of God or is it just a result of the chance that formed the universe?

## STATISTICS

Some problems cannot be modeled with equations or reasoned about with logic. They require the collection and interpretation of data with statistics. Probability theory is used to estimate the most likely result using inductive reasoning, which forms a general conclusion from a set of measurements. Inductive arguments lead to the most probable explanation for the observed data. The stronger the argument, the higher the probability associated with the result. The conclusions are highly likely but not certain.

# MATHEMATICS

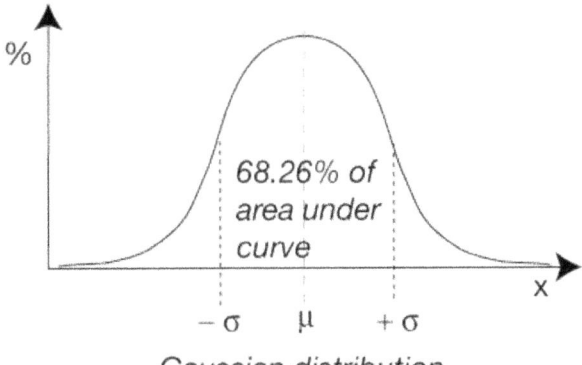

Gaussian distribution

**Figure 5.7** *Statistical Distribution*

Statistical analysis assumes that the input data fits a gaussian distribution, commonly known as a bell curve (Figure 5.7). The results are presented as a mean (estimated value) and standard deviation (a measure of how certain the mean is). 68.26% of the data is within one standard deviation and 95.45% within two standard deviations of the mean. The more probable the result, the smaller the standard deviation and the narrower and higher the curve. A result that is certain graphs as a vertical line.

Rob Hyndman, Professor of Statistics at Monash University, suggests that inductive reasoning is suited to evaluating the evidence for the existence of God.

> "This is precisely the type of reasoning that is necessary when considering the evidence for God and the Bible. We cannot deduce that God exists by following a series of logical statements. But we can consider the inductive argument — is what we observe best explained by a supernatural God, or is there a more probable explanation?" - Rob Hyndman, 2015.[21]

---

[21] robjhyndman.com/unbelievable/

**Figure 5.8** *Ariane Sherine and Richard Dawkins at the Atheist Bus Campaign, Photo Zoe Margolis, 2009, Wikimedia commons*

People who believe there are reasons for believing in Jesus weigh up evidence to confirm their faith. Looking at evidence convinced them that God exists and in response they choose to believe in Jesus. But ultimately, it is the presence of the Holy Spirit in their lives that confirms the existence of God. When they expressed their belief in Jesus to God in prayer, He sent His Holy Spirit to live in them. The Holy Spirit is the third person in the trinity with the responsibilities of confirming the existence of God and conducting our relationship with him.

In 2009, Ariane Sherine proclaimed to the world that she does not believe in God by displaying a slogan on a London bus (Figure 5.8): "There's probably no god. Now stop worrying and enjoy your life."[22] The use of the word "probably" indicates that she is not completely sure that there is no god. She has left room for doubt. This is an old philosophy (see

---

[22] commons.wikimedia.org/wiki/File:Ariane_Sherine_and_Richard_Dawkins_at_the_Atheist_Bus_Campaign_launch.jpg

## MATHEMATICS

Ecclesiastes 8:15) that the best you can hope for, if you don't believe in Jesus, is to enjoy life. We can be certain that God does not doubt his own existence. But what about you, can you be certain that God exists?

In the Old Testament they were so sure that God controlled statistics that the priest carried the Urim and Thummim with him to determine the LORD's will for his people whenever he went before the LORD. We don't know what the Urim and Thummim were, but we think they were stones with carved images on, them much like dice.[23]

> "The lot is cast into the lap,
> but its every decision is from the LORD."
> (Proverbs 16:33)

### CHANCE OF LIFE

An area of research, that is collecting huge amounts of data, that has to be analyzed with statistics is the search for exoplanets that may support life. Life exists on earth in some very hostile environments, so it may exist on another planet. "Scientists are having a hard time agreeing on when, where and - most importantly - how life first emerged on earth," - wrote John Horgan in a 1991 Scientific American article.[24]

In 2013, Russian billionaire, Yuri Milner, donated $100 million to fund the search for alien life. In support of this research the late Stephen Hawking, Professor of Cosmology, University of Cambridge said: "We believe that life arose spontaneously on earth, so in an infinite universe there must be other occurrences of life."[25]

---

[23] Exodus 28:30
[24] Horgan, J. 1991. In the beginning, Scientific American, February, pp100-109
[25] nbcnews.com/tech/tech-news/stephen-hawking-yuri-milner-back-100m-search-alien-life-n395046

The search for life on other planets is motivated by the difficulty of finding evidence that life originated on earth. Some scientists have proposed that life originated on another planet. Their thinking is that if evolution is the process by which life developed on earth, then it is likely that it also occurred on other planets. Finding that life is seen as evidence that we evolved by chance.

The physicist Enrico Fermi posed a famous question, known as the Fermi paradox, while at lunch with colleagues: "Where is everybody?" If all that is required for life to start on a planet is the right environment, then, given that there are four hundred billion stars in the Milky Way galaxy, why haven't we detected any of them?

Evolution is a two-step process: mutation followed by natural selection. Mutations are chance events, but their survival is dependent on the environment. An analogy for evolution, based on a column on 'Evolution Myths' by Michael Le Page in New Scientist on 16 April 2008 is:

> "The chances that life just occurred are about as unlikely as a cyclone blowing through a million junkyards. Then painstakingly testing the wreckage left in each one to find the most flight worthy, making a million exact copies of that junkyard, unleashing another million tornadoes, running another series of exhaustive tests, and so on, until you produce some kind of machine, no matter how crude, capable of flying at least a few yards."[26]

The chance of life on earth just occurring is infinitesimal. Each stage in the process of making a human involves selection of working designs for atoms, molecules, DNA, skeletons, body and for the most complex object

---

[26] newscientist.com/article/dn13698-evolution-myths-evolution-is-random/#ixzz7316mGMfl

in the universe - the human brain. An unexpected result that has come from this research is that parameters that measure the conditions required for life on earth are finely tuned. A small change to any one of them has a significant impact on the chance of life.

## FINE-TUNED UNIVERSE

Mathematical equations are a description of what is. A small change in any one of the constants in an equation changes the physics, while a change in the value of a variable, within limits, changes the possibility of something occurring. For example, in 2021, we experienced chaotic weather events due to a small rise in temperature causing climate change. Ocean temperature has increased at an average rate of 0.18° Centigrade per decade since 1981, for a total of 1.2° Centigrade since the start of the industrial revolution.[27]

To be habitable over the long term a planet must be in the habitable zone around its sun and avoid circumstances that cause it to lose its water and its atmosphere.[28] The more variables that must be satisfied the smaller the chance of a planet being habitable.

In a discussion of the pros and cons of a fine-tuned universe, Richards describes twenty-one widely accepted examples of fine-tuning for the existence of life.[29] These features must fall within a very narrow range of possible values for chemical-based life to be possible. Twelve of these are classed as local features of habitable planets, such as a planet's distance from its sun.

> "… given a large enough universe, perhaps you could get these local conditions at least once just by chance (though

---

[27] climate.gov/news-features/understanding-climate/climate-change-global-temperature
[28] ui.adsabs.harvard.edu/abs/2017AAS...22911603M/abstract
[29] discovery.org/m/securepdfs/2018/12/List-of-Fine-Tuning-Parameters-Jay-Richards.pdf

it would be "chance" tightly constrained by cosmic fine-tuning)." - Jay Richards, Distinguished Fellow of the Institute for Faith, Work, & Economics, 2018.

Changes in some parameters result in changes in other parameters. For example, the polarity of the water molecule is the result of features of subatomic particles. If it were greater or smaller, its heat of diffusion and vaporization would make it unfit for life as we know it.

"The remarkable fact is that the values of these numbers [the constants of physics] seem to have been very finely adjusted to make possible the development of life." - Stephen Hawking, 2011.[30]

Life on earth is possible because the earth is at the right distance from the sun to be warm, has a moon to stabilize its orbit, is tilted on its axis to evenly spread the heat from the sun, has enough water to support life, rotates at the speed needed to generate a magnetic field that protects it from radiation, etc. Contemplating this statement can only lead to wonder and a feeling of being created for a special reason. Could that reason be to know God?

Atheists believe in evolution by chance. The evolution of the earth as we know it is an infinitesimal chance. To make it possible for the evolution of one universe like ours to occur, scientists have invented a theory of an infinite number of parallel universes, called a multiverse. If there are other universes, can there be life there too? Or is the physics different enough to preclude life?[31]

---

[30] Stephen Hawking, 2011. A Brief History of Time, p. 125, Bantam
[31] universetoday.com/139241/if-there-is-a-multiverse-can-there-be-life-there-too/

Their logic is that the chance of life on earth is increased from one-in-infinity to one-in-one by having an infinite number of universes. The problem with this logic is: which universe do we choose to belong to? We are back to our infinitely impossible chance.

Does the requirement to fine-tune many constants make it impossible for life on earth to have just occurred or did it occur because all these parameters and variables were just right? Was earth created by an infinitely powerful God or is it the result of an infinitesimal chance?

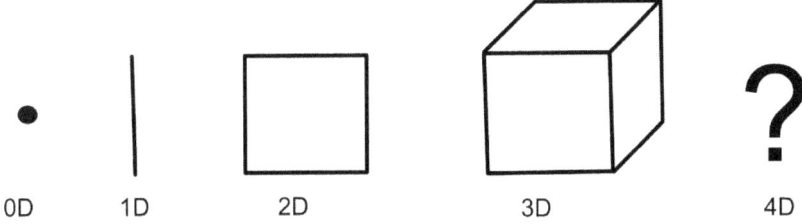

**Figure 5.9** *2D representation of a point, a line, a square, a cube and a tesseract*

## PLANIVERSE

The logic, models, and statistics used by makers exist in space-time. We are firmly ensconced in three spatial dimensions. I have heard it suggested on several occasions that God is a higher dimensional being and that eternity exists in the fourth and higher dimensions.

To better understand space-time, some researchers are seeking to determine what happens when we scale up to a higher dimensional system. Some start this investigation by scaling down to a two-dimensional world. Every day we see two-dimensional representations of three-dimensional objects when we look at drawings, paintings, and photographs (Figure 5.9).

Figure 5.10 *Arde. A 2D world where beings wait under a bridge for other beings pass them. cs.stanford.edu*

Emeritus Professor Thomas Banchoff ran a course at Brown University titled: *Beyond the Third Dimension: Geometry, Computer Graphics, and Higher Dimensions*, reflecting the need for graphic illustrators to be trained to think beyond the 2D rectangle.[32]

He raised the issues with the example of an amoeba living in the narrow region between the microscope slide and its cover. When we observe it from above, through a microscope, we see what looks like a 2D creature. We can see it forming temporary outgrowths for feeding and locomotion. Also, we can see its insides and the cell membrane that surrounds it, protecting the amoeba from the world it lives in.

We can surprise the amoeba by poking it from above, introducing the third dimension into its 2D life. Our experience and the amoeba's experience of the same world are totally different. In 1884, Edwin Abbott wrote a book that explored the fictional 2D world of *Flatland*.[33] Flatland is a 2D horizontal plane, like the microscope slide. It can be used as a metaphor of the relationship between the physical and the spiritual. The 2D world represents the physical and the third dimension - the spiritual.

---

[32] Banchoff, T.F. Beyond the Third Dimension: Geometry, Computer Graphics and Higher Dimensions, Scientific American Library (20 September 1990) math.brown.edu/tbanchof/Beyond3d.new/chapter3/questions.html

[33] Edwin A. Abbott, 1884. Flatland: A Romance of Many Dimensions

## MATHEMATICS

Another book, *Planiverse* is a story that describes a different 2D space.[34] The geometry of this world is a circle with the inhabitants living on the rim. They are flat in the same dimensions that a circle is flat. To explore this world, A.K. Dewdney and his computer science students simulate this world and its complex ecosystem.

To their surprise, their simulation accidentally enables them to communicate with Arde, an apparently actual 2D world. They contact Yendred, a highly philosophical Ardean. Yendred leads them on a journey around Arde in search of God.

On the way they see how many geometric problems are solved to enable the beings to move around freely, such as: how do beings heading in one direction pass beings heading in the other? The answer is shown in Figure 5.10 where the group going one way step down into a pit and the group going the other way walk across a rope stretched over the pit.[35]

A being like Yendred is unable to go outside its 2D world to the 3D world where God is. Their science cannot observe a 3D object. But that doesn't mean it doesn't exist. Their 2D world could be a slice through a 3D object but they couldn't observe that. They could develop a mathematical description of 3D but that would remain a theory without scientific proof.

Unless a 3D object chooses to reveal itself by moving into the 2D world its existence remains unknown. Imagine a sphere moving through the sky of the Planiverse. It would start as a dot, then appear to form a line, which gets longer, then shorter, and back to a dot which disappears. We can imagine it because we are 3D beings.

Can you imagine what an object with four physical dimensions (4D shape) would look like in our 3D sky? Several YouTube videos attempt to

---

[34] A.K. Dewdney, 2000. The Planiverse, Computer Contact with a Two-Dimensional World, Springer-Verlag New York Inc
[35] cs.stanford.edu/people/eroberts/courses/soco/projects/2005-06/planiverse/images/traffic.jpg

show how to draw a 2D representation of a tesseract, the 4D analogue of the cube.[36]

Similarly, God is outside of space and time, He created both. He can see everything in 3D space because He is in eternity. We cannot, by our own efforts, go to where God is in eternity. We cannot observe him in three dimensions of space and half a dimension of time. But that doesn't mean He doesn't exist. If part of us, our souls, is in eternity we may not be aware of it, but God can communicate with us through it.

The mathematics of higher dimensions tells us that science can neither prove nor disprove the existence of God. However, we can observe God if He chooses to reveal himself by coming into space-time. The apostle John described God's revelation of Himself in our world with the following words.

> "The Word became flesh and made his dwelling among us. We have seen his glory, the glory of the one and only Son, who came from the Father, full of grace and truth." John 1:14

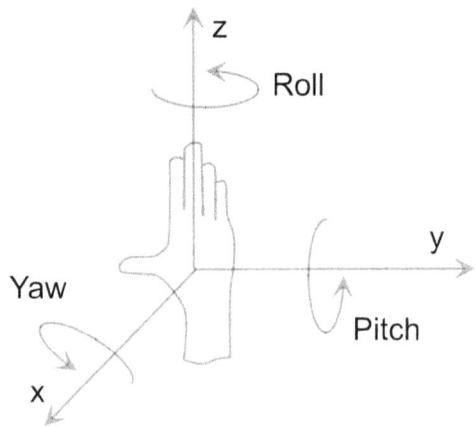

**Figure 5.11** *3D coordinate frame showing six degrees of freedom*

---

[36] https://en.wikipedia.org/wiki/Tesseract

## FRAMES OF REFERENCE

Frames of reference help us to locate ourselves in the world. A frame of reference can be a real object, such as the surrounding environment, or a map, or GPS coordinates. Also, it can be a mathematical object that is used when calculating the location of objects, such as a robot's hand, or it can be an imaginary object in a story. Because we are in 3D space, we can decompose any location into six separate coordinates, and decompose any motion into six degrees of freedom (Figure 5.11).[37]

For centuries, sailors have navigated using the stars. For example, the people of *Puluwat Atoll* in the *Caroline Islands* navigate over a range greater than 1,000 kilometers, in their 8-meter sailing canoes, through open seas.[38] Their journeys are usually broken down into a series of island hops. However, they regularly travel 100 to 200 kilometers across the Pacific and arrive exactly at their destination, demonstrating their considerable navigation skills.

The navigator starts his voyage by imagining the position of his destination relative to the position of the island that he is leaving. As he sails along, he constantly adjusts his directions according to his awareness of his current position. His decisions are improvised continually by checking relative positions of landmarks (reefs, atolls, trees, etc.), sun, stars, wave direction, wind direction, cloud patterns, etc.

He navigates with reference to where he started, where he is going, and the space between his destination and his current location. He has difficulty explaining his navigation in words. However, if asked where he is he can tell you relative to all the surrounding islands. His frame of reference is the surrounding environment.

---

[37] M<sup>c</sup>Kerrow, P.J. 1991. Introduction to Robotics, Addison-Wesley
[38] Gladwin, T. 1970. East is a Big Bird - Navigation and Logic on Puluwat Atoll, Harvard University Press, Cambridge.

## FAITH OF A MAKER

In contrast, a European navigator develops a plan that can be written in terms of directions, locations (degrees of longitude and latitude), and estimated times of arrival at locations on a map, before setting sail. Once the plan is complete, the seafaring officer has only to carry it out step by step to be assured of arriving on time at the planned destination.

The European navigator uses compass, sextant, maps, GPS etc. to check his location, and can describe exactly how he got to his current location. However, if asked where he is he usually points to a spot on the map but has difficulty telling you where he is in relation to surrounding islands. His frame of reference is a coordinate on a map.

Similarly, a Christian uses the bible to map the path of his life and to navigate through changing circumstances. His frame of reference is the door into eternity, that is his destination.

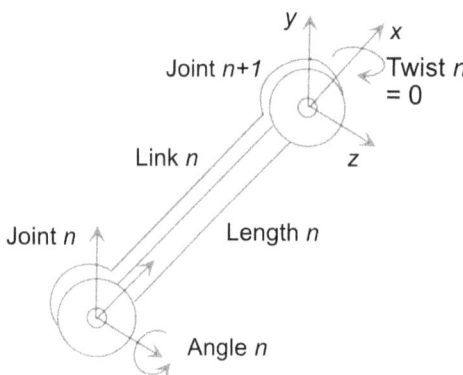

*Figure* 5.12 *Frames on a simple robot linkage*

To control a robot arm to pick up objects within its 3D workspace we model its links and joints (Figure 5.12).[39] From this model we calculate the

---

[39] McKerrow, P.J. 1991. Introduction to Robotics, Addison-Wesley

motions required to bring the hand to the object. The frame of reference for the arm is located within the base of the arm. The frame of reference for the operation of picking up an object is located within the workspace. Mathematical equations are used to describe the relationship between the object and the linkages in the robot arm.

The human brain unconsciously calculates frames of reference.[40] We do not know how they are described or stored, but we do know they exist. Three important frames are located within our feet and midway between our eyes. When we walk, our head doesn't bob up and down or sway from side to side. Instead, our brain controls the motion of our limbs so that the midpoint between our eyes remains at a fixed distance above the ground and our gaze remains in a fixed direction.

As a roboticist, the more I study the human body, the more I am moved to worship. Joseph Engleberger, Father of robotics wrote: "You end up with a tremendous respect for a human being if you're a roboticist " - (M$^c$Kerrow, 1991)

## SPACE

In maths, a frame of reference is a set of coordinates that establish our position. In life, a frame of reference is a system of axioms that give our behavior meaning. When we leave the earth's surface and travel through space to Mars our frame of reference changes from being centered in the earth, to being centered in the space craft, to being centered in Mars.

Private companies are developing a new generation of spaceships as they attempt to make space travel possible for the rich. Launching a space craft into orbit and returning involves complicated mathematics to cal-

---

[40] Berthoz, A. 2000. The Brain's Sense of Movement, Harvard College

culate both the trajectories and when to fire the rockets to achieve those trajectories.

The movie *Hidden Figures* portrays the work of Katherine Johnson and a team of female African American mathematicians.[41] They analyzed test flight data and helped calculate the trajectory for the first American manned space flight by Alan Shepard in 1961.

American astronauts have been awed by the beauty of earth when seen from space. John Glen, the first American to orbit the earth, circling it three times in 1962 said, "To look out at this kind of creation and not believe in God is to me impossible."

The Overview effect is a phenomenon that happens to astronauts when they see the earth from space. The emotions brought about by their change in frame of reference are very strong. Suddenly, the planet that has been their whole world becomes a tiny dot. As their perspective shifts, astronauts are reminded of their insignificance in relation to the magnitude of the cosmos.

Frank Borman was commander of the first space crew to travel beyond the earth's orbit. Looking down on the earth from 250,000 miles away, Borman radioed back a message. He quoted the first verse in the Bible: "In the beginning, God created the heavens and the earth."

As he later explained, "I had an enormous feeling that there had to be a power greater than any of us - that there was a God, that there was indeed a beginning."

There was no overview of earth until people flew in space. Apollo Astronaut, Neil Armstrong, reflected on his smallness.

> "It suddenly struck me that that tiny pea, pretty and blue, was the earth. I put up my thumb and shut one eye, and

---

[41] imdb.com/title/tt4846340/

my thumb blotted out the planet earth. I didn't feel like a giant. I felt very, very small." - Neil Armstrong.

William Shatner is famous for playing Captain Kirk of the starship Enterprise in the *Star Trek* television series and movies. In 2021, at age 90, he became the oldest person to fly in space when he flew passed the Karman line onboard a Blue Origin space shuttle. At one hundred kilometers above the earth's surface, the Karman line is deemed to be the boundary between earth's atmosphere and outer space. When he looked back at the retreating earth he could see the majestic colors of life.

> "But when I looked in the opposite direction, into space, there was no mystery, no majestic awe to behold … all I saw was death. I saw a cold, dark, black emptiness. I turned back toward the light of home. I could see the curvature of earth, the beige of the desert, the white of the clouds and the blue of the sky. It was life." - William Shatner.[42]

Our reference point is the surface of the earth. What do you feel when you look at the night sky? Do you feel very, very small like Neil Armstrong, or death like William Shatner, or filled with awe like David, the writer of Psalm 8?

> "When I consider your heavens,
> the work of your fingers,
> the moon and the stars,
> which you have set in place,
> what is mankind that you are mindful of them,
> human beings that you care for them?"
> (Psalm 8:3,4)

---

[42] popularmechanics.com/space/a41691361/william-shatner-overview-effect/

## HAND MAIDEN

We have seen that Makers use mathematics to describe the objects they are making, and to model the systems they want to control. When faced with a problem during making, they can go back to first principles where their hand maiden mathematics is waiting. In the next chapter we will see that Makers often encode their axioms in mathematical equations. Does the beauty of some mathematical equations convince you that God exists?

# 6

# AXIOMS

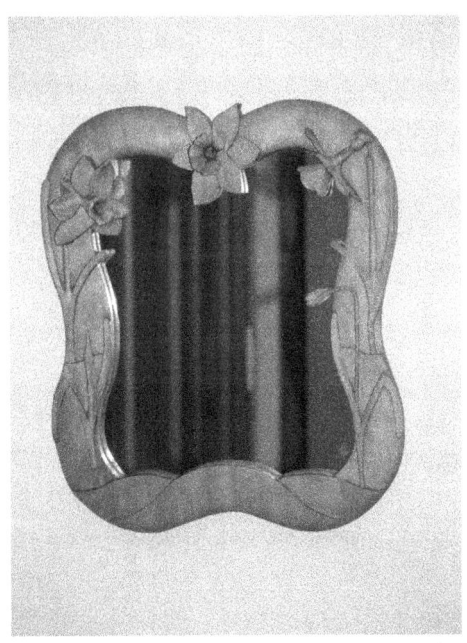

**Figure 6.1** *Daffodil Mirror. Carved from Huon Pine by the author.*

"I do not believe that science can disprove the existence of God; I think that is impossible. And if it is impossible, is not a belief in science and in a God — an ordinary God of religion — a consistent possibility? Yes, it is consistent. Despite the fact that I said that more than half of the scientists don't believe in God, many scientists do believe in both science and God, in a perfectly consistent way. But this consistency, although possible, is not easy to attain, and I would like to try to discuss two things: Why it is not easy to attain, and whether it is worth attempting to attain it."_- Caltech Professor Richard Feynman, 2015.— joint winner of the Nobel Prize in Physics in 1965.[1]

"I have my own values, what is right for me, and if I do something to break one, I try harder to do what is right next time. I don't need a religion to tell me what to do. My conscience guides me." - Physics Major.

> "The circle was a circle
> until I walked around the corner.
> The square to stay a square
> Until she walked around my own." -
> Joel McKerrow, Poet, 2019.[2]

## STUTTERING

"I'm not going back next week," I said as we drove home.

---

[1] brainpickings.org/2015/05/11/richard-feynman-science-religion/
[2] McKerrow, J. 2019. Woven, Acorn press, p 110.

# AXIOMS

Ann, my wife, replied, "I wondered how you would react to that announcement."

We had been attending a course in pastoral care. The lecturer had announced that next week we would do an exercise to help us feel what it is like to be disabled. The exercise would involve everyone in the group stuttering.

I wanted to shrink through the floor. I had spent the first seventeen years of my life stuttering. The thought of a room full of people stuttering brought back the pain of many cruel experiences. I didn't want to be there. I had not thought of stuttering as a disability until this announcement. I think that I just thought of it as a problem I had to live with.

Stuttering sapped my confidence. It took away my social esteem. I was the bright kid with red hair who stuttered and wore a hat. I couldn't speak without stuttering. Other kids teased me. I became the object of their cruelty. The more they teased me the more I stuttered.

No one knew how to cure it. School teachers tried to help me read. One teacher got me to blow ping-pong balls across a table to see if I had air flow problems. Often, I was embarrassed when I tried to say something. It was as if the words were stuck in my throat and wouldn't come out. The harder I tried the more stuck they got.

When I was sixteen, in the final year of high school, I applied for a scholarship to become a schoolteacher. The principal asked me to go into the education office in Lismore NSW for a test of my speaking. I failed. The inspector said:

"You would be a nervous wreck in a few months in a classroom, so I cannot accept your application."

When I finished high school, I moved to Wollongong to study engineering. Stuttering is not a problem when you are working with machines.

After attending church one Sunday evening I returned to the dormitory where I was living. A group of us sat in the lounge and watched a Billy Graham crusade on television.

Another university student asked me what I believed. We sat and talked for three quarters of an hour. When I returned to my room, I realized that I had just talked for half an hour without stuttering. I felt elated. Many years later I recalled this story to a Christian friend who lived in the same dormitory. He said,

> "We weren't worried by your stuttering. You never stuttered when you prayed."

I had not realized that. God had done what the doctors couldn't. Over the next few months my speech improved to the point where I bought a book titled: *Learning to speak effectively* by J.W. Cox.[3] In those sixty pages I learned techniques for speaking, including breathing control, voice projection, and overcoming stage fright.

My confidence in God grew, and with it, my confidence in speaking. However, the mental hurt takes longer to heal than the physical problem. I went back to the pastoral care course. Ann told the lecturer about my reaction to the stuttering exercise, and he cancelled it. It was many years before I could have a conversation with another person who stammered without a strong emotional response.

From a seventeen-year-old who couldn't apply for a teaching scholarship, I grew to become a university professor who has spoken at international conferences without stuttering. I feel very thankful to God for the confidence to speak clearly. When I read over this story, I said to Ann:

---

[3] Cox, J.W. 1966. Learning to speak effectively", Hodder.

"I feel like crying."

She replied, "I'm surprised you were able to write it."

## ASSUMPTIONS

We all make assumptions, assumptions that combine to form our world view, assumptions that provide our frame of reference when making decisions. What we do is based on what we think, what we think is based on what we believe, and what we believe is based on our assumptions. An assumption is a statement that we assume is true and from which we can draw conclusions using the rules of logic. It is a saying that is widely accepted on its own merits.

My view of the world is based on several assumptions. One of my assumptions was: stuttering was a problem that I had to live with. God came into my world and showed me that my assumption was wrong. My assumptions influence the whole of my life by providing a framework in which I can think about questions like: "Should I make this object?"

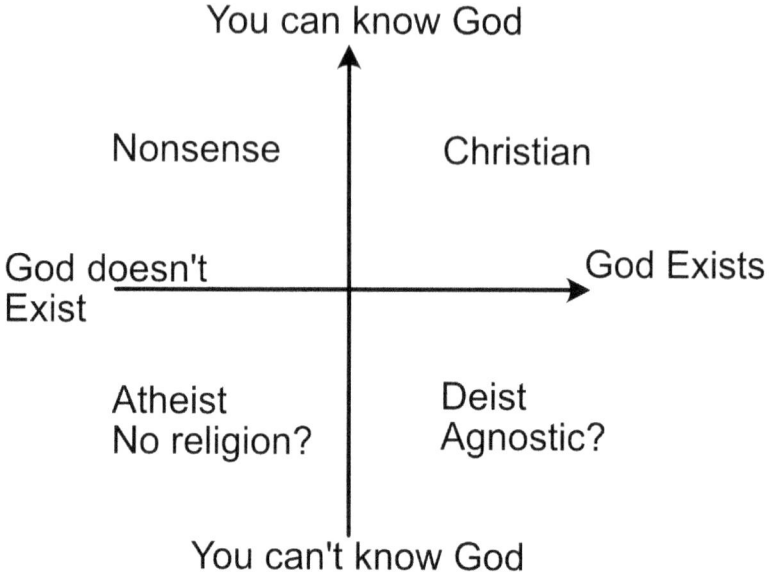

**Figure 6.2** *Simplistic model of Christian beliefs*

A simplistic model of Christian belief is based on the two assumptions shown in Figure 6.2. The horizontal axis is the assumption that God exists, ranging from dis-belief to certainty. The vertical axis is the assumption that a human can have a personal relationship with God, ranging from total separation to delightful intimacy. The four quadrants represent a relational view of some of the belief systems found in Western society.

In the first quadrant, a Christian is someone who believes that God exists, and that he has a personal relationship with Him. In the third quadrant, an Atheist has the two opposite assumptions, believing that God doesn't exist, and you can't know him. Survey forms give the option of selecting 'no-religion'. When a person checks no-religion they often mean that they don't practice a religion. It says nothing about whether they believe God exists or not. Many no-religion people believe that God is not relevant.

In the second quadrant, a Deist believes that God created the universe and then abandoned it, so they cannot know him. An Agnostic believes that God exists, but they cannot have true knowledge about him, so it is questionable whether they can know him. The model is simplistic because it doesn't quite capture the agnostic. It doesn't include a third assumption of knowledge about God. There is a difference between knowing God and knowledge about God. Jehovah's Witnesses' teaching that they can know about God conflicts with Christian teaching that you can know God.

The fourth quadrant I have called the nonsense belief because it says that you believe in a God that doesn't exist. I thought that this belief was a logical absurdity that no-one would believe until I heard a neo-orthodox minister preach. He said, "The Bible isn't true, but we believe it anyway."

I was flabbergasted, I did not expect such a statement from a man who professed to be a Christian minister. Neo-orthodox theology is a reaction against liberal theology, which emphasizes reason and experience over the authority of the Bible, because liberal theology provided no basis for pastoral care. Neo-orthodox theology has difficulty accepting that the Bible is the World of God.

Many religions have internal inconsistencies between their assumptions. Most religions have external inconsistencies with other religions as well. For example, Islam and Christianity are both monotheistic religions, but their descriptions of God are contradictory. You can claim that one of the sets of assumptions in the model is the basis of your faith, or lack of faith, but how do you know it is true? You don't, that is why they are called assumptions.

Before we look at three world views that derive from this model, we will explore the axioms of mathematics and science; their origins, their problems, and, how they form the basis of a world view.

## AXIOMS OF MATHEMATICS

Axiom is the mathematical term for an assumption. An axiom is a proposition that is not able to be proved or disproved; its truth is assumed to be self-evident. It serves as a premise or starting point for further reasoning and argument. A proposition is a statement that affirms or denies something and is either true or false.

A mathematician builds a system of equations (a mathematics) by creating a set of axioms and then building a set of postulates on top of those axioms. Not being able to prove a postulate using this base set of axioms excludes the postulate but does not indicate that the postulate is not true. Proof exists with reference to a set of axioms. Truth is a higher-level concept that is not dependent on your axioms.

In 300 BC Euclid compiled and systematized all that was known about plane and solid geometry. He began with very simple concepts as axioms and gradually built his system of geometry on top of them. The first four of his axioms are:

1. A straight-line segment can be drawn joining any two points.
2. Any straight-line segment can be extended indefinitely in a straight line.
3. Given any straight-line segment, a circle can be drawn having the segment as the radius and one end point as the center.
4. All right angles are congruent - they coincide when laid on top of one another.

He had a fifth axiom, that defined parallel lines, but he did not need it in the first 28 of his postulates. Many people tried to prove or disprove the 5th axiom but have been unable to. Instead, they found that by changing the 5th axiom they invented a new mathematics. Euclid's axiom for parallel lines is based on observing lines on a plane; they go on forever and never intersect. However, if you observe lines on a sphere, lines that are parallel at the equator intersect at the poles, forming the basis of spherical mathematics.

In 1920, English mathematicians Alfred North Whitehead and Bertrand Russell wrote *The Principia Mathematica*, a three-volume work on the foundations of mathematics.[4] In it they attempted to show that mathematics is based on a complete set of axioms and provide a proof that these axioms are consistent.

They were unable to achieve this goal of a closed system where mathematics is proved by reference to itself. In fact, it is impossible to find a complete and consistent set of axioms for all of mathematics. An example of the problems involved in a supposedly closed system is strange loops. Consider this statement of the liar paradox: *This statement is false*. It cannot be resolved into true or false with the information contained in the statement.

In 1931, Austrian mathematician Kurt Gödel showed that a consistent set of axioms can produce inconsistent results.[5] His incompleteness theorem demonstrates that no set of axioms, that include arithmetic, can be both free of contradictions and be able to prove every true statement.[6] Thus it is not possible to produce a closed system that refers only to itself. That is, you cannot prove your axioms are true from within your axiomatic system. That can only be done at a higher level.

The communication of truth from a higher to a lower level is called revelation. Thus, the Bible talks about God, who is in eternity, revealing truth to people, who are in space-time. Unlike people who reject the idea of

---

[4] wikipedia.org/wiki/Alfred_North_Whitehead
[5] wikipedia.org/wiki/Gödel's_incompleteness_theorems
[6] edition.pagesuite.com/popovers/dynamic_article_popover.aspx?artguid=f9210139-d0c7-43be-98dc-fd2faf1d7485

truth, the Christian believes in revealed truth, which we can know by faith, and observed truth, which we can know by observation. Faith is credible because God has revealed truth.

One outcome of Godel's work is that there are mathematical theorems that can't be proven. A few years later, Alan Turing developed the Turing test: a theoretical computer that could mimic the operation of any machine.[7] But it cannot predict whether a program will finish its task and halt. This is known as the halting problem.

So, we have the number Pi with an infinite number of non-repeating digits, and we are unable to predict whether a program will halt, and we cannot prove that a set of axioms is correct and complete. Gregory Chaitin, an emeritus researcher at IBM's Thomas J. Watson Research Center in New York, claims that the core of mathematics is full of holes.[8] "There are a lot of mathematical facts, but very few are related to each other. So, Euler's identity is a rarity."[9] Chaitin found another strange problem: a number that is definable but can't be calculated that he called Omega ($\Omega$). Chaitin's constant $\Omega$ is an expression of the probability that a random program will halt.

Mathematics is the main language that science uses to express its theories. Chaitin's theories imply that there can never be a reliable *Theory of everything*. Steven Weinberg, Nobel laureate in physics agrees: "We will never be sure that our final theory is mathematically consistent." - Steven Weinberg, 1993.[10]

---

[7] wikipedia.org/wiki/Turing_test
[8] Chaitin, G. 2001, The Omega Man, New Scientist, 16 March, p 1-5
[9] youtu.be/HeQX2HjkcNo
[10] Steven Weinberg, 1993. Dreams of a final theory, Vintage Arrow

## WORLD VIEW

Kay and Jane didn't believe in God.[11] Their parents were Atheists who had taught them that God probably doesn't exist. Jane had a baby daughter. Sadly, her baby became very sick and died. During her grief, Jane questioned everything she had been taught. She realized that she had no answer to death. A Christian friend told her about Jesus and Jane decided to follow Him.

> Kay didn't understand. "Why would my sister believe in God because her baby died?" she asked.

If we look at this story in the light of *The model of Christian belief* in Figure 6.2, we see why it is hard for an atheist to believe in Jesus. The atheism that Kay and Jane had been taught was based on the assumptions that God doesn't exist, and you can't know Him (Quadrant 3 in Figure 6.2).

To become a follower of Jesus, Jane had to completely change her world view. It took a traumatic event in her life to move Jane to change her axioms from God doesn't exist and you can't know Him to God does exist and you can know Him. Kay couldn't understand Jane's change in belief because her world view was based on a different set of axioms.

Each of us has a world view. It is the set of assumptions that we base our thinking about life on. We interpret the available evidence in the light of what we already believe. This is called 'confirmation bias.'[12] Our interpretations are biased in order to confirm and support our beliefs.

Can we draw the conclusion from this that, in the realm of belief, people value opinions more than facts? For example, during the second World War the United States Government contracted the late Peter Drucker to

---

[11] True story, names changed
[12] robjhyndman.com/unbelievable/

work out why some managers were effective at getting things done and some were not. His conclusions were published in a book: *The Effective Executive.*[13]

As part of the traineeship program at John Lysaght Australia Limited (JLA), I went to a management course based on a set of films by Drucker. One of the principles it taught was:

> "Effective managers don't make decisions based on facts.
> They make decisions based on opinions about facts."

The uptake of misinformation about vaccines from social media during the recent pandemic would appear to support the idea that people value opinions more than facts. Our axioms are the pillars of our world view. Our beliefs are opinions based on those axioms. If your world view assumes that God does not exist, then your opinion will be that any evidence for His existence is false and should be disregarded. Evidence is not sufficient to change your belief unless you change your world view.

If you try to separate your beliefs from your world view, you lose the reason for your beliefs and live an inconsistent life. In Australia, politicians promote *Australian values* in an attempt to keep the social results of thinking in a Christian world view while rejecting God and the Bible from which those values came. Their attempts are failing because people no longer have a reason to act in ethical and moral ways based on Christian axioms. They have to find a new set of axioms to provide a basis for their beliefs and get the population to accept those axioms.

The organization WorldviewU runs workshops to teach people to communicate and interact with people from other cultures by understanding

---

[13] Peter F Drucker, 2006. Effective Executive: The Definitive Guide to Getting the Right Things Done, Harper Business; Revised edition.

their world views. They suggest that your world view addresses life's biggest questions, including:[14]

- How did we get here? This question addresses origins.
- Why are we here? This question addresses meaning.
- Where are we going? This question addresses the future and the afterlife.
- Who's in charge? This question addresses the existence of a supreme being.
- What is true? This question is about the nature of truth and whether it is objective or subjective. If truth is objective, what is it based on (what is the source of truth)?
- What is right and what is wrong? This question deals with morality. Are right and wrong based on an objective set of moral standards, or are they based on a person's or group's feelings, desires, or standards that fit their time and place?

We will examine four world views in the following sections. To understand your personal world view, write down your answers to the above questions. What must change for you to have a world view based on the axioms that God exists and You can know God, as shown for the Christian world view in Figure 6.2?

## AXIOMS OF SCIENCE

A Christian world view (Quadrant 1 in Figure 6.2) gave rise to modern science in 17th century Europe. The 17th century scientists believed in the Christian God who is thoughtful, purposeful, and ordered. Consequently,

---

[14] worldviewu.org/world views-definition

nature must also be ordered and, therefore, able to be studied in an ordered manner. The late Frank Rhodes, Professor of Geology at the University of Wales, Swansea, and President of Cornell University, claimed that the basic presuppositions of science were developed from the belief that the universe was created by a God who is ordered and compassionate.[15] They include:

- a belief in an orderly, regular, rational universe,
- A belief that this orderliness of the natural world is intelligible to the scientist,
- A belief in the reliability of human reason,
- A belief in the broad principle of causality, and
- A belief in the personal integrity of the scientist.[16]

The method of inductive reasoning and empirical enquiry is based on these axioms, giving us the processes of observation, experimentation, and hypothesis formulation that are fundamental to scientific enquiry. Hypothesis formulation involves the abstraction of certain elements from the total range of human experience. Thus, the scientific method is only one of a set of methods for describing the world we live in.

The scientists who do not believe in God are left in the position of having a set of axioms, which are based on a world view that they do not accept. Some people claim that evolution is an axiom because they use it as a valid research framework. Others suggest that the practice of science is sufficient to validate its axioms. But you cannot validate the truth of your axioms from within your axiomatic system.

---

[15] Rhodes, F. 1965. Christianity in a Mechanistic Universe, in MacKay, D. Christianity in a Mechanistic universe and other Essays, IVP, p 11-48
[16] McKerrow, P.J. 1991. Introduction to Robotics, Addison-Wesley. P 14

The importance of axioms is demonstrated by the cosmological principle which contains the accepted axioms in cosmology.[17] It assumes that nothing distinguishes the position of the Milky Way galaxy from any other place in the universe. It is based on two assumptions. First, averaged over large enough scales, the universe is homogeneous: having the same properties in all locations. Second, the universe is isotropic: it appears to have the same properties when viewed in different directions at any location.

These simplifying assumptions were introduced to make it possible to solve Einstein's equations. The big bang theory is based on his equations by dropping the assumption that the universe is unchanging. When distant supernovae were discovered to be racing away from us, dark energy was introduced to accommodate the cosmological principle.

These two assumptions were challenged in 1999 when a team from the University of New South Wales claimed to have detected a variation in the fine-structure constant $\alpha$.[18] The results of their measurements indicated that $\alpha$ has varied over time and varies with the direction you look away from the earth.[19] That is, it is not constant, contradicting the cosmological principle. In lay language, the fine structure constant is the length of the circumference of an electron divided by the wavelength of the electron.

There are several ways of measuring $\alpha$ and it has several physical interpretations. One is that it determines the strength of the interaction between electrons and photons. Thus, any change in it has a dramatic impact on our model of an atom. Many researchers questioned these results, but in 2020, the Australian team claimed they had verified their previous results. These and other results raise questions about the truth of the cosmological principle and the existence of dark matter.

---

[17] Chown, M. 2008, Our special place, NewScientist, 15 November, p32
[18] Brooks, M. 2010, Operation alpha, New Scientist, 21 October p 33-35
[19] wikipedia.org/wiki/Fine-structure_constant

In a paper in Zygon (Wiley Journal of Religion and Science) Matthew Orr, Instructor in Biology, University of Oregon, made the following comments about a scientific world view:

> "A scientific world view consists strictly of axioms and propositions that can be verified or falsified by experiment or observation. Such a world view, based solely on ideas that can be tested with empirical observation, conforms to the highest levels of objectivity but is severely limited in utility.
>
> The limits arise for two reasons. First, many falsifiable ideas cannot be tested adequately until their repercussions already have been felt. Second, the reach of science is limited, and ethics, which compose an inevitable part of any useful world view, are largely unfalsifiable."[20]

## ATHEISTIC WORLD VIEW

Atheism is the denial of the existence of God (Quadrant 3 in Figure 6.2). Although some atheists deny that atheism is a world view, many atheists share several beliefs such as naturalism, evolution, and abiogenesis. Naturalism is the doctrine that the world can be understood in scientific terms without recourse to spiritual or supernatural explanations. Abiogenesis is a hypothetical organic phenomenon by which living organisms are created from nonliving matter. Atheism rejects the possibility of supernatural phenomena.

---

[20] Matthew Orr, 2006. What is a scientific world view and how does it bear on the interplay of science and religion, Zygon (Wiley Journal of Religion and Science), 16 June. onlinelibrary.wiley.com/doi/abs/10.1111/j.1467-9744.2005.00748.x

Atheists like evolution because it appears, in their eyes, to do away with the need for a Creator. They claim that evolution makes atheism intellectually credible. Their assumptions do not allow them to consider the possibility of a Creator. Their beliefs are based on human thought within the context of their axioms. Stephen Hawking hoped that evolution is correct:

> "Before we understood science, it was natural to believe that God created the universe. But now science offers a more convincing explanation. What I meant by 'we would know the mind of God' is, we would know everything that God would know, if there were a God, which there isn't. I'm an atheist." - Stephen Hawking, 2013.[21]

A Christian world view should be a very rich and comprehensive world view that gives meaning to life: a world view that makes connections between all disciplines because Christians believe in a God of order. The most whimsical of things that God has created are ordered. Look at the petals on any flower, they vary in shape, color, and perfume and, while often whimsical in design they join together to form a display of great beauty. The Bible presents God as creator of the foundation of everything.

> "My own hand laid the foundations of the earth,
> and my right hand spread out the heavens;
> when I summon them,
> they all stand up together."
> (Isaiah 48:13).

---

[21] nbcnews.com/science/space/im-atheist-stephen-hawking-god-space-travel-n210076

In contrast, an atheistic world view that is based on a belief that everything is a result of chance will be a very impoverished world view because chance provides no reason to connect ideas, things, or disciplines.

## SECULAR WORLD VIEW

The secular world view (Quadrant 3 in Figure 6.2) is a religious world view in which, at its center, people are worshiped. Secularism is a view of the world that encompasses materialism, faith in science, and the worship of nature. Therefore, the secularist sees no place for the supernatural. They assume that people can figure out what is best for society without reference to a belief system. As a result, they lobby for the exclusion of religion from government and education.

> "We need only ensure that our schools teach only secular knowledge ... If we could achieve this, God would indeed be shortly due for a funeral service." - Richard Bozarth, 1977.[22]

They measure the worth of anything by its benefit to human beings. All of life centers on human beings. The pinnacle of secular worship is the Olympic Games. They show what people can do when they work together. The athletes are treated like gods. Some secularists are atheists, others are agnostics (Figure 6.2).

The state is given sovereignty, which is entirely rational because they consider that there is no higher power to be taken into consideration, no god to execute justice. People are seen as the final word in ethics. The state is seen as the only source for *legal truth*. Crime is often seen as the fault of

---

[22] Richard Bozarth, The American Atheist, 1977

the social order, not due to an individual's inclination to sin. Often secularists are intolerant toward people with a different world view.

When public education was established in Australia, the curriculum was divided into religious subjects and secular subjects.[23] In many areas, religious subjects were taught by volunteers from the churches and the government employed people to teach secular subjects.

Originally, public schools were to teach secular subjects within a Christian world view. Such was the influence of Christianity on Australian society that this principle underlay public education for over a century. Today, this heritage continues to provide a justification for Christian involvement in all levels of public education. Even a prominent atheist supports teaching the Bible:

> "The Bible should be taught, but emphatically not as reality. It is fiction, myth, poetry, anything but reality. As such it needs to be taught because it underlies so much of our literature and our culture." - Richard Dawkins, 2011.[24]

## TRINITY

A Christian world view (Quadrant 1 in Figure 6.2) claims that God exits, not because it can be proven in space-time but because Jesus came into space-time from eternity to reveal God to us. This is the basis for claiming revelation as a source of truth. A source that is complete and consistent. Also, it shows that the claim of people to be self-sufficient and therefore, they don't need a relationship with God is false.

---

[23] Education: State or Church, 1971, Australia's Heritage, Volume 11. Hamlyn House, Sydney, p 1231-1233
[24] Richard Dawkins interested in setting up 'atheist free school' - Telegraph 7/02/11

Christians believe that God is three persons in one God: Father, Son, and Holy Spirit. This belief is one of the axioms that describes the character of an infinitely powerful God. Four of them are:

1. God exists in eternity,
2. God is three persons - a trinity,
3. God created people in His own image – able to relate to Him, and
4. God acts in love in space-time.

God's actions in space-time include both the creation of space-time and His revelation of Himself to human beings. Jesus came from eternity into space-time to tell people about the *Kingdom of Heaven*. At the start of Jesus' teaching ministry, all three persons of God were involved in His baptism. The Holy Spirit commissioned Him. The Father praised Him and Jesus began to reveal the Kingdom of Heaven to people.

> "At that time Jesus came from Nazareth in Galilee and was baptized by John in the Jordan. Just as Jesus was coming up out of the water, he saw heaven being torn open and the Spirit descending on him like a dove. And a voice came from heaven: "You are my Son, whom I love; with you I am well pleased." Mark 1:9-11.

God's creation of people in His image defines for us what it means to be human. We know what it is to love others because God loves us. God's name expresses the trinity: Father, Son, and Holy Spirit. Christians believe in one God who is three persons. At the end of His teaching Jesus used the name of God when He commissioned His disciples to take over His work of revelation.

# AXIOMS

"Then Jesus came to them and said, "All authority in heaven and on earth has been given to me. Therefore, go and make disciples of all nations, baptizing them in the name of the Father and of the Son and of the Holy Spirit, and teaching them to obey everything I have commanded you. And surely I am with you always, to the very end of the age." Matthew 28:18-19.

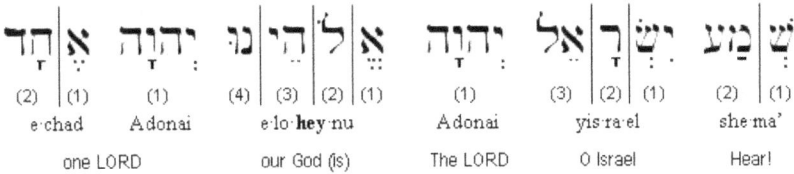

Hear, O Israel: The LORD our God, the LORD is one. (Deut 6:4)

**Figure 6.3** *Hebrew script for Deuteronomy 6:4*

Jews believe that: *The LORD is our God, the LORD alone* (Figure 6.3).[25] It was revealed to them that there is only one God. So, the idea that the Lord is three persons was new to the disciples of Jesus. Yet, John, the apostle, writes about Jesus being present at creation as the word of God who became human.

> "In the beginning was the Word,
> and the Word was with God,
> and the Word was God.
> He was with God in the beginning.
> Through him all things were made;

---

[25] hebrew4christians.com/Scripture/Torah/The_Shema/the_shema.html

without him nothing was made that has been made."
(John 1:1-3)

Jesus told his disciples that he would ask the Father to send the Holy Spirit. When you believe in Jesus, the Holy Spirit comes to live in you and teach you God's ways. The Holy Spirit guides you to obey Jesus' commandments and prays to the Father for you. This relationship between the Holy Spirit and people is the deepest relationship we can have.

> "If you love me, keep my commands. And I will ask the Father, and he will give you another advocate to help you and be with you forever— the Spirit of truth. The world cannot accept him, because it neither sees him nor knows him. But you know him, for he lives with you and will be in you." (John 14:15-17).

From the trinity comes the Christian concept of relationships between beings: God, angels, and humans. This relationship finds its ultimate expression in God's love for us. It overflows in our love for others. When a Christian shows love to someone they reflect the character of God, just like a mirror (Figure 6.1).

> "The deepest longing of the human heart is to know and enjoy the glory of God. We were made for this." - John Piper.[26]

---

[26] azquotes.com/author/11695-John_Piper

# AXIOMS

## TRUTH

Can we know that the Christian world view is true? Proof, evidence, and truth are different concepts. Proof exists within a set of axioms. Truth is more general, and if something is true, then it is true irrespective of your axioms. When we say we have evidence to prove something we are saying that the evidence we have is consistent with the set of axioms in which we make and analyze the evidence. While a piece of evidence may be used to prove a statement within one set of axioms it can't be used to show that the statement is true because you cannot prove that your axioms are true.

If something is true, then it is true at all levels, irrespective of your axioms. It is possible to prove a false proposition by your choice of axioms. Also, it is possible to prove that a true proposition is false by your choice of axioms.

For example, if one of your axioms is that God does not exist then it is not possible to prove that God does exist within your axiomatic system. Unless you change your axioms to allow for the possibility that God exists, you cannot prove that God exists even if it is true that God exists.

C.S. Lewis, Lay Theologian and Professor of English Literature at Oxford and Cambridge Universities, wrote the Narnia series of children's books to use myth to communicate truth. He was a convinced atheist until his friends showed him that Christianity was a relationship not a doctrinal system consisting entirely of axioms.

> Tolkien and Dyson showed him (see Lewis' letter of 18 October 1931) that doctrines are not the main thing about Christianity. Doctrines are translations into our concepts and ideas of that which God has already expressed in 'a language more adequate'.

The more adequate language was the actual incarnation, crucifixion, and resurrection of Christ. The primary language of Christianity is not doctrinal — not propositional or systematic — but historical: a lived language, the factual story of someone being born, dying, and living again in a new, ineffably transformed way.

"…When Lewis understood that Christianity too was to be approached first as a sequence of historical events and only secondarily as a doctrinal system, it was a huge breakthrough for him. Christianity, he began to see, was "the true myth" whereas pagan myths were merely "men's myths." - Michael Ward.[27]

We consider the physical creation to be true because we can see, touch, feel, taste, and hear it. Also, we consider the Bible to be true because God inspired men to write it. Both are true because God created them. In contrast, theology and science will contain errors because they are created by people. Laws that we consider to be true from our experience of living in space-time may prove to be false when we move outside of space-time into eternity. Logic has shown us that the truth about God is more powerful than the proof of His existence.

When a group of people make a society, they consciously express the rules of that society in their laws. These rules are based on a set of axioms, often unconsciously.

---

[27] patheos.com/topics/religion-and-myth/cs-lewis-on-christianity-as-the-true-myth-michael-ward-03-09-2016

## YOUR AXIOMS

What you think is based on what you believe and what you believe is derived from your axioms. When you are asked, "Why are you making this object?" or "Do you believe in Jesus?" the answer you give is based on your axioms. It is a worthwhile exercise to explore the truth of your belief system by asking, "What are my axioms?" "What is my world view?" and "How do my axioms influence the amount of time I spend making?"

# 7

# TIME

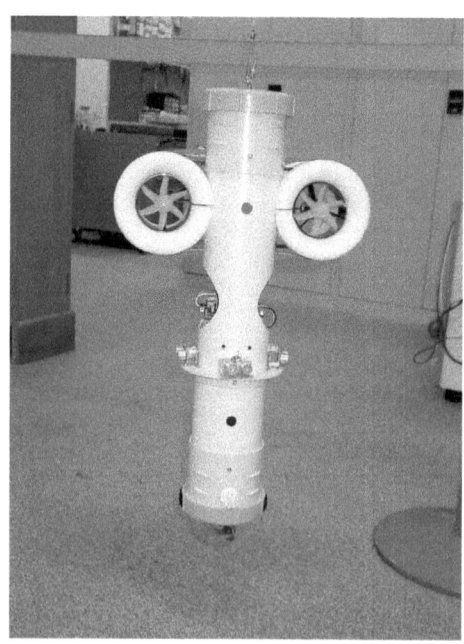

**Figure 7.1** *Swinging robot*

# TIME

"Time is what prevents everything from happening at once". Albert Einstein, physicist.

"… the order of experiences in time obtained by acoustical means can differ from the temporal order gained visually, so that one cannot simply identify the time sequence of events with the time sequence of experiences." - Albert Einstein, 1920.[1]

"There is a time for everything,
and a season for every activity under the heavens:
a time to be born and a time to die,
a time to plant and a time to uproot,
a time to kill and a time to heal,
a time to tear down and a time to build, …"
(Ecclesiastes 3:1-3)

"He made the moon to mark the seasons,
and the sun knows when to go down.
You bring darkness, it becomes night,
and all the beasts of the forest prowl."
(Psalm 104:19-20)

"Time feels so natural to us that it is easy to forget just how stunningly peculiar it is." - New Scientist, 2011.[2]

---

[1] Einstein, A. 1920. Relativity, reprinted 1964. Methuen, p 140.
[2] Special Issue, Time the most mysterious dimension of all, New Scientist, 8 October 2011.

## LITTLE BLUE BOAT

Back and forth, back, and forth, Dad rowed. The rhythm of the oars dipping into the water giving a sense of time. I sat in the back of the boat. Back and forth, back, and forth between bridge pylons. The repeated turning of the boat accentuated my sense of time. Mum sat in the front, three of us in a rowboat. Back and forth under the bridge. Back and forth out of the rain, going nowhere.

Dad loved to build things. He had no formal training, just his natural skills. He wanted a boat, so he bought a boat kit: a set of plans, some sheets of ply for the hull, a bundle of timbers for the frame and lots of copper rivets. I watched him build it and heard him swear when he made a mistake.

The day after he finished the little blue boat was exciting; we were going to launch it. We loaded it in the back of our utility and drove to the Brunswick River in NSW. No sooner had we put out on the water than a thunderstorm broke. The rain came down in buckets and we rowed back and forth under the bridge trying to stay dry, hoping the rain would stop.

After a couple of years rowing got hard, so Dad bought an outboard motor. Not the shiny motors we see on boats today. It was a lawn mower motor with a driveshaft and propeller attached. It stuck out the back of the boat at about 30° below horizontal. I doubt it was very safe, but it powered the boat for several years.

For reasons unknown to me, Dad decided that the boat needed an inboard motor. So, he installed a bigger keel in the boat and made the outboard motor into an inboard motor. He drilled a hole in the keel and inserted the driveshaft into it. Then he attached the propeller to the end of the driveshaft that was to go into the water. He attached the motor to a stand inside the boat and the motor shaft to the driveshaft. Finally, he wrapped the exhaust pipe in asbestos so that no one would get burnt on it.

# TIME

We went for many fishing trips in that boat. One day, a storm blew up. As we motored down the Clarence River the waves grew larger and larger. Up and down rocked the boat with the surge of the waves. I was afraid. Water splashed into the boat. A large tugboat came up the river, slowing down as it passed so that its wake did not add to the waves. We reached the beach where we anchored the boat. It rose and fell with the swell and washed back and forth as the waves ran up the sand.

One night, we were sitting in the boat fishing. When I pulled my line in the water began to glow. We watched in fascination as water drops emitted a silver glow as they fell into the water. We splashed the water with our hands, sending trails of silver through the air. A fish swam by, glowing with each sweep of its tail. Time seemed to stop as we were immersed in one of the most beautiful sights I have ever seen. The water was alive with bioluminescent algae. It was magical.

The lawn mower motor wore out and Dad pulled the large keel out and made it back into a rowboat. He bought a proper outboard motor, but it was not very reliable. My cousin took the boat out for a cruise, she turned too fast and dropped the motor in the water. Dad was not happy. His expression of his unhappiness turned the air blue. Then he dived into the river to retrieve the motor. After that it was on and off the boat regularly because it was even less reliable. Dad bought a bigger boat and sold the little blue boat to a workmate. I doubt that the little blue boat still exists.

## WHAT IS TIME?

Time is an axiom in our model of space-time, an axiom that influences our making. One axiom of the theory of evolution in space-time is that creation of the universe took billions of years, which contradicts the Bible's axiom of creation in six days. Christians feel a tension between the two!

Engineers can measure time, but scientists have not been able to define it. We think of time as the interval between two events. Often, the repetition of an event forms a rhythm. A rhythm is an abstract concept related to the flow of time.

For example, when we rowed the little blue boat, we developed a rhythm with each stroke of the oars. Our bodies created this rhythm, and our brains perceived it. The rhythm of rowing the little blue boat produced a different sense of time than the urgency of getting it under the bridge before the storm broke. Some rhythms are created by the motion of machines. For example, when we made a robot to swing on the end of a tether, it often went into a repeating cycle that flowed in time (Figure 7.1).[3]

The flow of time is defined by the sequence in which the events occur, like a piece of music where one note flows after another as we listen.[4] The same event is thought of as being in the future before it happens, in the now as it is happening, and in the past after it has happened. Time to future events is continually decreasing. Time in the now is fleeting and time to past events is continually increasing.

For example, our bodies have biological clocks that regulate the timing of circadian rhythms. Circadian rhythms are physical, mental, and behavioral changes in our bodies that follow a daily cycle.[5] These rhythms are loosely synchronized with the rising and setting of the sun. These internal clocks seriously struggle when we are isolated from the sun for a long time - for example in a cave.[6] The importance of the sun as a marker of time is recognized at the start of the Bible. And God said,

---

[3] McKerrow, P.J. 2007. The design of a tethered aerial robot, Proceedings ICRA'07, Rome, April, pp 355-360.
[4] youtube.com/watch?v=5vzymaIabWI
[5] nigms.nih.gov/education/Documents/CircadianRhythms.pdf
[6] insidehook.com/daily_brief/science/french-cave-deep-time-experiment

> "Let there be lights in the vault of the sky to separate the day from the night,
> and let them serve as signs to mark sacred times, and days and years,
> and let them be lights in the vault of the sky to give light on the earth."
> (Genesis 1:14-15)

Our measurement of time is based on the rising and setting of the sun, which occurs due to the rotation of the earth. So, is our sense of time different on another planet? If SpaceX achieves their goal of making a habitable building on Mars we may find out, although the rotation of Mars is very similar to that of earth: 24.6 earth hours for a day on Mars compared to 23.9 earth hours for a day on earth. A year on Mars is 687 earth days.[7]

Among scientists there is little agreement about what time is.[8] "We can recognize time, but we do not understand it," wrote New Scientist writer, Julian Barbour, in 2011. In his television documentary titled *What is time?* Science commentator Professor Brian Cox admits that we do not understand time and seeks to help the viewer experience it.[9] His presentation is almost worship, as he stands in awe of the nature of time, but he does not take the step of acknowledging the creator of time. To him, the existence of time is a great mystery.

The laws of physics: Newton's laws of motion, Einstein's General Relativity, and quantum theory, do not require us to know the nature of time for us to use them. For example, Newton's second law (force = mass times acceleration) is not about how a body moves in time but how one

---

[7] solarsystem.nasa.gov/planets/mars/in-depth/
[8] Clark, S. The origin of time, Special Issue, Time the most mysterious dimension of all, New Scientist, 8 October 2011, pp 38-39.
[9] Brian Cox's Adventures In Space And Time, 2021, Episode 4 What Is Time? iview.abc.net.au/video/ZW3043A004S00

body moves relative to another, even though time is included in the measurement of acceleration.

Our experience of time is that it can only go forward, not backward. So, we perceive an arrow in time that makes the time dimension of space-time half a dimension. But the direction of time does not show up in the equations of physics. The laws work whether time is going forward or backward.

We have invented clocks to measure time. A clock needs a moving part to estimate the passing of time. This links time to change - that is to a sequence of events separated by intervals. So, is time a real fundamental property of the universe, like space, or is it a perception of change created in our brains?

Whether time is a real physical quantity or a perception of change the Bible claims that God created time. "He has made everything beautiful in its time. He has also set eternity in the human heart; yet no one can fathom what God has done from beginning to end" (Ecclesiastes 3:11). It took an infinitely powerful God to create time as part of space-time. This puts God outside of space-time. He can enter and control space-time from eternity at any instant in time.

The Bible is often criticized for Genesis 1 presenting the story of creation as occurring in six days when science claims it took about 13.772 billion years. One of the outcomes of creation by God is that space-time exists within eternity, and time in eternity is different to time on the earth. The Apostle Peter wrote: "With the Lord a day is like a thousand years, and a thousand years are like a day." (2 Peter 3:8).

A day on earth is like a thousand years in eternity. Or could we say that a day in eternity is like two billion years on earth? Our answer depends on whether we take the Bible passage literally or metaphorically. The point is that God could create the universe as we know it in six days in eternity and make it look like it took 13.7 billion years of earth time in space-time or vice versa.

# TIME

## MODEL OF SPACE-TIME

I use a mental model to think about the relationship between space-time and eternity (Figure 7.2). Consider space-time to be an ellipsoidal (shape of an egg) region inside eternity. Everything that occurs in space-time is observable from eternity, like viewing a 2D object in a 3D space. The long axis of the egg represents time. The other axes represent 3D space.

A slice through the egg at right angles to the time axis represents the current time and space. The future is to the right of the current slice. The past is to the left. The position of the current slice is continually moving to the right into the future. God can look at any point along the time axis and see the associated slice.

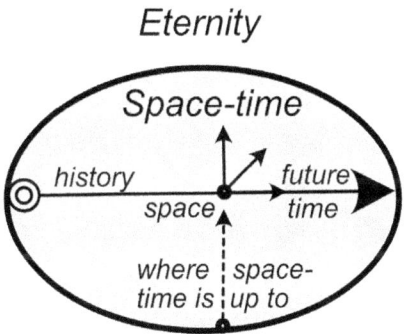

**Figure 7.2** *Ellipsoidal model of space-time in Eternity*

Because He is outside of space-time, He can observe any time in earth's history; past, present, and future. When He wants to know where earth time is up to, He looks at the current slice. God can reveal himself in space-time by acting in the current slice. Also, He can observe the future, but He does not determine the future. The future is determined by our choices in the current slice.

I hope this model helps you understand the relationship between eternity and space-time.

## INSTANTANEOUS OR PROCESS

In the ellipsoidal model of space-time in Figure 7.2 the world inside space-time processes into the future at each time step. Starting in my 69th year I spent two years building a Peeler Skiff wooden motorboat using the stitch and glue method. Over time I settled into a construction process.[10] I learned that building a boat is a series of steps - each step is a problem to be solved. Each step moved me forward in time.

**Figure 7.3** *Making rear seat for Peeler Skiff using puzzle joints*

---

[10] clcboats.com/shop/boats/powerboats/peeler-outboard-power-skiff.html

When I finished one step I would move on to the next step and the next problem. I found that solving each construction step required a process. The process started with the current state of the boat and finished with the achievement of the construction step.

For example, the rear seat was made by butting three pieces of ply together with three puzzle joints and permanently gluing them with epoxy (Figure 7.3). In addition, the edges of the seat were doubled in thickness with five narrow strips of ply. First of all, eight pieces of ply were cut out and their edges sanded before they were glued.

Epoxy glue is made by mixing a hardener with an epoxy resin. Gluing with epoxy required a clean and efficient process to measure the two parts of the epoxy and stir them together to initiate the chemical reaction to cure the epoxy. Then the rapidly curing glue was applied to the joints. This glue up had to be done quickly before the epoxy cured.

In the step to make the rear seat, all the pieces could not be glued in one go. I had to glue the puzzle joints first. But the edge of the ply soaks up the epoxy at a much faster rate than the face of the ply, so I had to apply two coats to each edge to reduce the chance of a dry joint. The first coat soaks into the edge. The second coat fills any gaps in the joint. Then I had to push the joint together, often with taps from a mallet. Finally, I removed the excess glue.

I built this boat step by step using a sequence of processes. Did God create plants, animals, and people instantaneously as complete objects, or did he use processes over time? Our experience of making things is that making takes time. We cannot make things instantaneously, but I believe an infinitely powerful God can, as recorded in the following description.

"Then God said,
"Let the land produce vegetation:

> seed-bearing plants and trees on the land
> that bear fruit with seed in it,
> according to their various kinds.
> And it was so…"
> (Genesis 1:11)

Genesis 1:11 not only describes a process of creation but a continual process of re-creation. The author wrote it to counteract the idolatry that was prevalent in the surrounding nations. He wanted the people of Israel to worship the one true and living God not the dead gods made of wood and brass. Praying to blocks of wood will not bring the rain required to grow crops.

The agricultural cycle described by this verse takes time. Hence, if we consider Genesis 1 to be a poem then one day may represent the time for the first plants to grow to maturity. The seeds were created instantaneously but it takes time for them to sprout and produce fruit to reproduce new seeds. God built the process of growing from seeds into nature.

> 'He also said, "This is what the kingdom of God is like. A man scatters seed on the ground. Night and day, whether he sleeps or gets up, the seed sprouts and grows, though he does not know how. All by itself the soil produces grain—first the stalk, then the head, then the full kernel in the head. As soon as the grain is ripe, he puts the sickle to it, because the harvest has come.'" (Mark 4:26-29).

## NON-LINEAR

The ellipsoidal model of space-time in Figure 7.2 assumes that time is linear, but it could be made non-linear by including a variable time step. In Western culture, we consider that events happen in time in a linear fashion. That is, time follows a straight line where the amount a parameter changes tomorrow is the same as it changed yesterday. Previously, we described time as the interval between two events. If time is linear then we model that interval with a straight line, as shown in Figure 7.4. But does the interval have to be linear?

Some other cultures consider time to be circular (Figure 7.4) because we observe cycles in nature. Traditionally, time is based on the rising and setting of the sun. A day is the interval between the rising of the sun today and it's rising tomorrow. A year is the rotation of the earth around the sun, a sequence of days that brings the earth back to where it started.

These cycles are not exactly circular (Ecclesiastes 3:15). If they were then today and tomorrow would be exactly the same. Sunrise today and sunrise yesterday are not the same. So, a spiral model of time may be more representative of what happens because it allows the events at the end of the intervals to be the same but different. In Figure 7.4 the spiral model is drawn as a 2D representation of a 3D model.

We can combine the linear model and the spiral model to form a 'slinky' model that is a duality (Figure 7.4). The six days of creation are viewed with a linear model where the interval between events is one earth day as described in Genesis 1. These same six events are also viewed with a spiral model where the interval between them is two billion years as described by 21st century science. In this duality model, time in both the Bible and science are true.

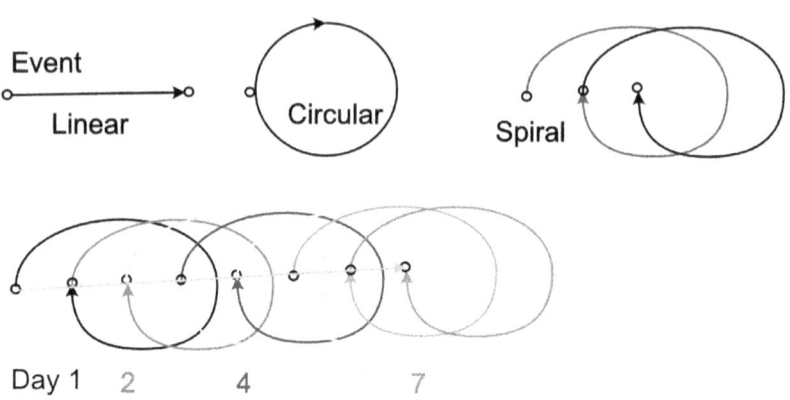

**Figure 7.4** *2D models of time as the interval between two events*

While we do not understand time, engineers can measure it as the interval between two events. In our daily life, and in physics experiments, time is defined as 'what a clock reads'. It is one of the seven fundamental physical quantities in the International System of Units (SI). The SI base unit of time is the second.

But every physical system is non-linear, including Newton's second law[11]. The big bang theory predicts that in the first second of the big bang the universe expanded by 100,000 light years and continues to expand at an increasing rate.[12] So why do we consider time to be linear?

When making measurements in dynamic systems we need a reference. We use time as that reference. By making time linear all the non-linearities are shifted into the parameters we are measuring. So, we have defined

---

[11] youtu.be/kiuwtaprFjk
[12] youtu.be/dbm3M9Bz4RE

# TIME

time as linear. In some cultures, time is thought to be circular with sunrise, noon, sunset, and mid- night forming a repeating cycle.

Geology assumes that decay, sedimentation, and fossilization all occurred at the same rate in the past as they do today, even when research may show otherwise. For example, wood is thought to take millions of years to petrify. However, recent research has shown that wood can be converted into silica when placed in suitable environmental conditions, in time periods as short as tens to hundreds of years.[13]

Often the mathematical model of a machine is non-linear. To make it easier to control, the engineer will linearize the equations so that they approximate linear action over small intervals. Then he will set controller gains for stable performance in this linear region. If the control system is required to work outside the linear region the gains are adapted for the new conditions.

Bible history has some massive non-linearities, so big that they require the intervention of the Creator. For example, according to Genesis 8, the earth was completely submerged in water during the flood. While it was underwater, did God rearranged the topology of the landscape so that the land rose, and the seas fell?

A spectacular time non-linearity in the Bible is when Joshua prayed for the sun to stop still. I find the physics of that event mind boggling.[14] Only an infinitely powerful God with intimate knowledge of how the universe works could do it. This event is recorded in the book of Joshua.

---

[13] Akahane, H. et al., 2004. Rapid wood silicification in hot spring water: an explanation of silicification of wood during the Earth's history, Sedimentary Geology, 169 (3-4): 219-228, 15 July.

[14] youtube.com/shorts/kzHAeFY_TEM

Joshua said to the LORD in the presence of Israel:

> "Sun, stand still over Gibeon,
> and you, moon, over the Valley of Aijalon."
> So the sun stood still, and the moon stopped,
> till the nation avenged itself on its enemies,
> as it is written in the Book of Jashar.

"The sun stopped in the middle of the sky and delayed going down about a full day. There has never been a day like it before or since, a day when the LORD listened to a human being. Surely the LORD was fighting for Israel!" (Joshua 10:12-14)

Some Christian missionaries have reported accounts of a long day (or night) in the traditions of other cultures. Don Stewart is a televangelist who hosts the *Power and Mercy* television show. On the *Blue Letter Bible* website, he writes: "Parallel accounts in the records of other nations show that the incident of 'Joshua's Long Day' is not an isolated one."[15]

The evidence that I know about is anecdotal in stories told by Christian missionaries rather than written documentation. We are left with the question: is the story of a long day literally true or is it a poetic construct to describe what seemed like a long day to those on the battlefield?

## ERASURE

The ellipsoidal model of space-time in Figure 7.2 includes the time before the current time as history. A viewer in eternity can view any time in the past as it was then. A viewer in space-time cannot go back in time so

---

[15] blueletterbible.org/faq/don_stewart/don_stewart_625.cfm

# TIME

they can only see history that is being erased. The further back in time he looks, the greater the erasure.

I have had the fortune of attending Apple's World Wide Developer Conference several times. One thing that I looked forward to was the lunch time talk by an outside group. One talk that I enjoyed was on the recovery of old images of the moon by a group roguishly called *McMoon's* because it was located in an old McDonald's outlet.

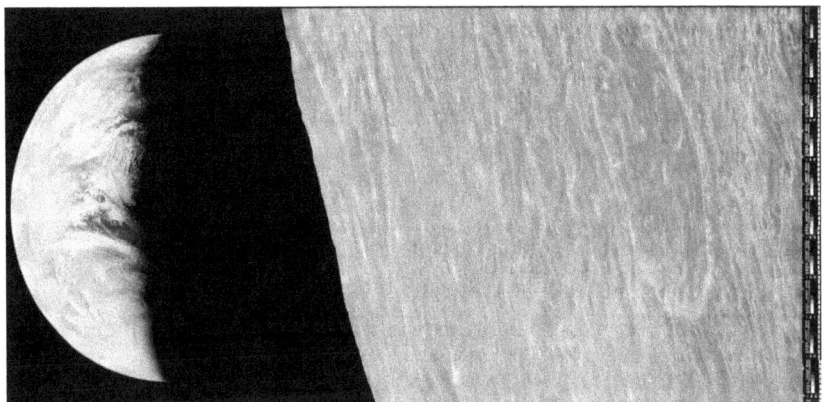

**Figure 7.5** *Earthrise over the Moon as seen by Lunar Orbiter.*

In 1965, in preparation for the moon landing, NASA had five satellites orbiting the moon, each one taking photos on 70mm film with a Kodak camera sporting a 600mm lens.[16] It was an analog system because this survey of the moon occurred before the development of digital cameras (Figure 7.5).[17]

The film was processed on the satellites using a dry process. Then it was scanned, and the analog signal sent back to earth where it was recorded

---

[16] nasa.gov/topics/moonmars/features/LOIRP/
[17] on August 24, 1966, Image Credit: NASA / LOIRP

onto magnetic tapes. In 2005, the tapes were found in a warehouse. Also, three tape drives were found in a backyard shed surrounded by chickens, where an archivist had stored them when they were decommissioned.

A team of hackers managed to get two tape drives working. They built a computer board to demodulate and digitize the analog signals to rebuild the photos.[18] This story illustrates how information can be lost very quickly.

Another example is in *The Gospel of Luke* where the writer tried to record the exact year of Jesus' birth by referring to a census, but no evidence outside the Bible has been found for this census.[19] "In those days Caesar Augustus issued a decree that a census should be taken of the entire Roman world. (This was the first census that took place while Quirinius was governor of Syria." (Luke 2:1-2). While some Bible scholars question whether the census recorded by Luke ever occurred, the high regard that people have for Luke as a historian convinces many that it did.

That all the records of a census could be lost should not surprise us. The Roman Empire was an ancient culture with a relatively high literacy rate, but many works by its most widely read historians are lost. For example, Titus Livy, a Roman historian who lived in the 1st century BC, wrote a 144-volume history of Rome called *Ab Urbe Condita* (From the Founding of the City).[20] Only 35 volumes still exist, although short summaries of most of the others exist. Also, the emperor Augustus (63BC-14AD) was a cultured man who wrote several works that have all been lost. Only a minority of the work of any major Roman historian has survived.[21]

---

[18] wired.com/2014/04/lost-lunar-photos-recovered-by-great-feats-of-hackerdom-developed-at-a-mcdonalds/
[19] Bruce, F.F. 1980 Census, in Douglas, J.D. Editor, The Illustrated Bible Dictionary, Part 1, IVP, p256
[20] Titus Livius, (born 59/64 BC, Patavium, Venetia [now Padua, Italy]—died AD 17 britannica.com/biography/Livy
[21] britannica.com/biography/Augustus-Roman-emperor/Personality-and-achievement

In 1947AD the finding of the Dead Sea scrolls at Qumran pushed the manuscript history of the Old Testament back a millennium. The New Testament has been preserved in more manuscripts than any other ancient work of literature, with over 5,800 complete or fragmented Greek manuscripts catalogued.[22] The dates of these manuscripts range from 125AD to the introduction of printing in Germany in the 15th century.

It is a genuine miracle that the Bible has survived the erasure of time when so much ancient literature and so many computer files have been lost. The preservation of the Bible is a miracle, truly a work of God. Today, it is available to people in more languages than ever before. How much of what you or I have written will still exist in 100 years?

> "The life of mortals is like grass,
> they flourish like a flower of the field;
> the wind blows over it and it is gone,
> and its place remembers it no more."
> (Psalm 103:15-16)

## SPEED OF LIGHT

The ellipsoidal model of space-time in Figure 7.2 shows space-time bounded by an ellipse. Inside the ellipse travel velocity is limited to the speed of light. Outside the ellipse you can travel faster than the speed of light. We have claimed that time in eternity is different to time in our universe. Eternity, as described in the Bible, appears not to be constrained by the speed of light. Information appears to take no time to reach its destination.

For example, Christians pray and claim that God answers - all in a few seconds. Also, creation is described to take six days, and the return of Jesus

---

[22] wikipedia.org/wiki/Biblical_manuscript

in the future is described as if we are watching it happen. "But the day of the Lord will come like a thief. The heavens will disappear with a roar; the elements will be destroyed by fire, and the earth and everything done in it will be laid bare." (2 Peter 3:10).

How fast we can travel in space-time is limited by Einstein's equations to the speed of light. Can we find situations where this constraint may not apply within current physics? Well, maybe. Our physics is based on Einstein's assumption that the speed of light is constant in all directions. This assumption makes the mathematical equations simpler and appears reasonable. But we can't prove it. We assume it is as a convention. Equations that include the speed of light work together when the speed is constant in all directions. This assumption is used when calculating the age of the universe.

According to Einstein's equations the speed of light doesn't have to be constant in all directions. It can go at different speeds in the forward and reverse directions provided the resultant two-way speed of light is the same as if it were constant. So, theoretically it is possible to travel faster than the speed of light in space-time.

Also, if light travelled toward us faster than away from us then we would see stars further into the past than if the speed of light is constant in all directions, indicating a much younger universe. In the extreme case, if light travelled toward us at infinite speed, then it would travel away at half the speed of light. We would see events throughout the universe as they happen.

The problem we have is that we cannot test theories like this because we cannot measure the one-way speed of light.[23] We measure the one-way speed of light by measuring the two-way speed of light and halving it. We measure the two-way speed of light by reflecting a light pulse of an object at

---

[23] wikipedia.org/wiki/One-way_speed_of_light

a known distance and measuring the time to travel to and from the object with very accurate atomic clocks.

To directly measure the one-way speed, we would have to synchronize clocks at the emitter and reflector. But the fastest thing we can use to synchronize them is the waves whose speed we are trying to measure. We have a self-referencing loop where synchronized clocks are used to measure the speed of light, but light is used to synchronize the clocks. Currently, no one can find a solution to the problem of synchronizing the clocks, so we are unable to tell whether light travels at constant speed in all directions.

However, there are places where light appears to go faster than the speed of light. They are called black holes. At its center, a black hole has a circular region of black. Around the edge of this region is a ring of light. The boundary between the ring and the hole is called the event horizon. Cosmologists believe that when an object crosses the event horizon, we can no longer see it because it is travelling away from us faster than the speed of light.[24]

Different forward and return speeds of light may not be the case but it gives an interesting way of thinking about the time taken to create the universe in Genesis. The scientific thinking at the time the book of Genesis was written may have been that light travels to them instantaneously and they did not consider the return time.[25]

With such a model of light six days of creation is a natural way of thinking. But, without being able to measure the one-way speed of light we don't know what actually happened. Again, we cannot use science to prove whether God exists or not. However, we can wonder at Einstein's brilliance and if we have faith we can stand in awe of God's greatness.

---

[24] Hawking, S. 2016, A Brief History of Time, Bantam.
[25] youtube.com/watch?v=AkoTubA52SQ

## WARP DRIVE STORY

**Star Trek Script**
When - sometime after September 1966
Location - Earth side spaceport
Action - Pan camera to follow Kirk as he walks away from the crowd - Waist up shot.
Kirk raises a two-way radio to his mouth - "Beam me up Scotty."
Special effects - Kirk dematerializes as he is transported.
Cut - to transporter room on Starship Enterprise.
Full size shot - Kirk materializes and he is met by chief Engineer Scotty.
Follow- as they walk toward bridge.
Kirk - enters bridge "Captain on bridge." - and goes to captain's chair.
Kirk - "*Warp drive Mr. Scott.*"
Scotty - "*Ready Sir.*"
Kirk - "*Warp drive Mr. Sulu.*"
Sulu - "*Accelerating to warp 1 sir*"- pause - "*Warp 1*" - pause - "*Warp 2*" - pause - "*Warp 3.*"
Special effects - light rays streaming past ship.

The first episode of Star Trek went to air on September 8, 1966.[26] The series was very popular and gained a cult following. It introduced the world to the concept of faster than light travel with a warp drive.[27]

In the Bible the return of Jesus is described as if He is moving faster than light.

---
[26] wikipedia.org/wiki/Star_Trek:_The_Original_Series_(season_1)
[27] youtube.com/watch?v=zP9PLYJxjaM

> "For the Lord himself will come down from heaven, with a loud command, with the voice of the archangel and with the trumpet call of God, and the dead in Christ will rise first. After that, we who are still alive and are left will be caught up together with them in the clouds to meet the Lord in the air. And so we will be with the Lord forever."
> (1 Thessalonians 4:16-17)

## WARP DRIVE

According to the theory of relativity there is no limit on the relative speed of two separate regions of space-time. Very distant galaxies, on the edge of the universe, are thought to be moving apart from one another faster than light speed. Below the event horizon of a black hole space-time cascades towards the central singularity faster than light, carrying light and matter with it. A black hole is a point of extreme positive energy density.

The Advanced Propulsion Physics Lab at NASA's Eagleworks has a founding document. It states the lab's purpose is: "to pursue propulsion technologies necessary to enable interstellar flight." The problem is that the nearest earth like planet, Proxima Centuri B, is 4.2 light years away. It is too far away to visit with current space technology.

One of the approaches that Eagleworks is taking is to research and develop a warp drive. Yes, we are talking about research into travelling faster than the speed of light. While Einstein's equations limit velocity within space-time they place no limit on the velocity of space-time, which is expanding.

In a paper in 1994 Dr Miguel Alcubiere showed that if we reverse Einstein's field equations, we can create a warp drive by compressing space time in front of a starship.[28] The ship itself is not travelling faster than light (Figure 7.6).[29] It is in a space-time bubble that is travelling faster than the speed of light.

In front of the ship, the bubble is contracting the fabric of space-time, and behind it is expanding. This contraction of space-time causes the bubble to travel faster than the speed of light. The bubble is pushed and pulled by space-time, moving at speeds that are only limited by the intensity of the warp.

**Figure 7.6** *Artist's concept of a spacecraft using an Alcubierre Warp Drive*

---

[28] Warp speed mechanics 101
ntrs.nasa.gov/api/citations/20110015936/downloads/20110015936.pdf
[29] (Image: NASA) ntrs.nasa.gov/search.jsp?R=20130011213

The problem with creating this drive is the amount of negative energy required.[30] Dr Harold White is working on a reformulation of the equations to reduce the amount of energy required and to provide a theoretical basis for a practical warp drive.[31] A recent paper by another group has solved a number of problems in the mathematics and reduced the amount of negative energy required by two orders of magnitude.[32] But, no one knows how to create negative energy.

Warp drive requires negative outward pressure energy to push against positive matter. In the proposed drive warping of space-time is generated by a high frequency oscillating torus. Oscillating the warp ring softens space time, which is very stiff, and creates a warp field bubble of space-time, that effectively separates space-time inside the bubble from space-time outside the bubble. At the center of the bubble is a calm region of space-time, which conserves local space-time so relative to internal space-time the spacecraft doesn't move faster than light. Both the mathematical model and initial experiments suggest it may be possible to make a warp drive.

The problem with the above formulation of the equations is the requirement of negative energy, which doesn't occur in normal physics. In 2021, Erik Lentz created a theoretical design for a warp drive using conventional physics, removing the need for negative energy.[33] Lentz's theory overcomes the need for a source of exotic matter in previous designs by reimagining the shape of warped space. Lentz said, "This work has moved the problem

---

[30] wikipedia.org/wiki/Harold_G._White
[31] ntrs.nasa.gov/search.jsp?R=20130011213
[32] Bobrick, A. and Martire, G. 2021. Introducing physical warp drives, Classical and Quantum Gravity, Volume 38, Number 10, IOP Publishing Ltd
[33] Erik W Lentz, 2021, Breaking the warp barrier: hyper-fast solitons in Einstein–Maxwell-plasma theory, Classical and Quantum Gravity, Volume 38, Number 7, 9 March 2021 • © 2021 IOP Publishing Ltd

of faster-than-light travel one step away from theoretical research in fundamental physics and closer to engineering." [34]

If God used warp drive it would be possible for him to create the universe in six earth days by creating planets in eternity and moving them into place at infinite speed and they would appear like they had always been there. My point is not that God did use wrap drive but that there is much more to science than we know. God's experience of time is different to ours, so is it foolish to say that science does away with God?

> "A thousand years in your sight
> are like a day that has just gone by,
> or like a watch in the night."
> (Psalm 90:4)

## TIME TO MOVE ON

While we can go back to the previous chapter of this book and read it again, it is a separate event to the first time we read it because we can't go back in time. Time only goes forward in space-time, as shown by the large arrowhead on the time axis of the ellipsoidal model of space-time in Figure 7.2. The slinky model in Figure 7.4 demonstrates how we could think of time as a duality. The passage of time is different in eternity, so God's view of events is different to ours. Let us continue to move forward in time, to move from the abstract concept of time to the concrete maker activity of design.

---

[34] https://www.popularmechanics.com/science/a35820869/warp-drive-possible-with-conventional-physics/

# 8

# DESIGN

**Figure 8.1** *Little carved ceramic figures, by Anne Marie*

"I think God has built a basic pillar of universe. The rest is left for engineers to build upon it. Therefore, engineering can be used for the benefit of mankind." - Il Kyu Lee, Ph.D.

"Being authentically you gives your creative work worth as well. I'm always experimenting, and I'm perfecting the voice in my work; it can sway with the day or mood, but I do know that what I'm creating has worth to me."_ - Angela Pilgrim, textile artist and illustrator.[1]

"Here's to the crazy ones. ... Because they change things. They push the human race forward. And while some may see them as the crazy ones, we see genius. Because the people who are crazy enough to think they can change the world, are the ones who do." - Rob Siltanen, Founder, of LinkedIn.[2]

"Makers work in the space where the mind, heart and hand creatively merge." - Anne Marie.

## DESIGN OF LITTLE CARVED CERAMIC FIGURES

by Anne Marie

"The design for my art installation was driven by an over-riding idea or concept. I wanted to represent people who are very vulnerable or poor in our society and world, and who are frequently overlooked, ignored or at worst exploited.

---

[1] Angela Pilgrim, 2021. textile artist and illustrator, "on creating work in your own voice", The Creative Independent. thecreativeindependent.com/about/
[2] Rob Siltanen, CEO & Chief Creative Officer - LinkedIn, goodreads.com/quotes/tag/apple

# DESIGN

I decided to express this idea through carving and molding in clay a large number of little children holding out their hands begging for help. Each little figure was to be unique, with individual features, and under 10cm high.

The group art exhibition space I was going to display my artwork in was a huge open public area at the local university. And as part of my concept, I envisaged the possibility of someone overlooking the tiny, unique figures unprotected on the vast floor, and consequently walking on them. This would rather shockingly represent how such precious children/people frequently go totally unnoticed.

And I, as the artist, would include an explanation of this on the floor with the artwork. As a Christian I believe all people, regardless of their position in life, their race or belief, are created by God with innate value and are deserving of respect.

Before I made the figures for my concept, I observed and photographed my cooperative young son and daughter in a variety of *begging* poses. As I began to make the little 3D sculptures in white clay it became apparent to me that, in the time I had before the exhibition, my idea of making over a hundred such individually carved little figures was not going to be practically possible. The reality was I ended up making only four little sculptures (Figure 8.1). I fired these in a kiln and applied a black iron oxide to the surfaces of the figures.

I now had the challenge of how I was going to communicate my concept with only four little sculptures? My final solution was to install just one small female figure with her hands reaching up - begging for help. I placed this figure on the floor of the large exhibition space under a very large male boot that was suspended on fishing line from the roof. Although this had changed greatly from my original idea it still conveyed the essence of my installation design concept."

## CONCEPT

When a maker is engrossed in designing an object he gets in the mood. He feels transported into a slightly altered conscious state where time moves at a different pace and his thoughts are focused on the design of the object.

In the realm of design, we are free to experiment with ideas to creatively plan the object we wish to make. Creativity, elegance, and grace find expression in good design. As the design takes shape, we move from a mental concept of the object to a plan for making it in the selected technology. For example, a quilter may draw a geometric pattern on a template, cut the material into the shape of the template and stitch the pieces together. (Figure 8.2).

**Figure 8.2** *Patchwork Quilt, Emily Hedger*

# DESIGN

When a maker sets out to make something, they have an idea in their mind of what they want to make. It may be a firm idea with details worked out in a plan. For example, when making a wooden chair there are lots of published designs to choose from. Or the idea may be running around in the maker's head defying attempts to put it into a solid form. For example, when an artist picks up a brush and applies paint onto a canvas as she experiments with different colors, trying to produce the mood that she is feeling.

In every field, makers attempt to design the object before they make it. Usually, design involves several steps. For example, architects draw the layout of a building before the engineers design the supporting beams. Software Engineers think about design patterns before they write code. Video makers write a script for the director to shoot. Cooks consult a recipe before turning the stove on.

Design involves a process where we plan something for a specific role, purpose, or effect. It involves composition, components, and concept. Composition is the way in which the components of a design are grouped and arranged to give visual or audio flow and division of space. The components are the elements used within the design. The concept is the message we want the design to deliver.

For example, when making a meal to win someone's heart, the composition is the presentation of the food, the components are the ingredients and their taste, and the concept is based on the old adage: "The way to a man's heart is through his stomach."

## RESPONSE

When we look at good design, we often have an emotional response. When she designed the *Little carved ceramic figures* (Figure 8.1) my friend, Anne

Marie, wanted to represent people who are very vulnerable. The result evokes the emotion of sympathy for those who beg, and intrigue at the artist's ability to create such endearing figures, figures we want to help.

These figures evoked my memory of a beautiful young woman on her knees, begging in the foyer of a cathedral in Vienna. I came upon her suddenly, not expecting anyone to be there. I felt shaken as I placed a gold coin in her hand and said, "Jesus loves you."

We admire beauty, simplicity, color, dynamism, and elegance. Elegant design is often simple and has a balance of components, where each component is fit for purpose, and components complement. Elegance is a refined quality of gracefulness and good taste, a quality of beautiful design and ingenious simplicity in the solution of a problem.

A design can be a pattern for how to make something. For example, woodworking magazines regularly publish designs of workbenches.[3] A design may include drawings and plans. The details of the design, the way they are presented in human readable form, and the process for making the item varies from discipline to discipline. The user of the item may only see the functionality of the finished item as the design.

An artist may start with a blank canvas and a concept. Next, she sketches an outline of the composition to work out proportions and perspectives. Then she may freely apply the background colors before painting details. Similarly, a wood carver making a 3D object will design planes and cut them out first.[4]

Often the work takes on a life of its own. The maker's mind focusses on creative and intuitive processes and time seems to disappear. Making can be a spiritual exercise like Christian meditation, where a Christian focusses

---

[3] C. Schwarz, Workbenches from Design and Theory to Construction and Use", Popular Woodworking books

[4] Geisler-Moroder, M. 2006. Carving the Head in the Classic European Tradition, Fox Chapel Publishing Company, Pensilvania.

on Jesus, his grace, glory, and beauty, and the world around passes out of mind.

## ART

> "In art there is a saying that an artwork has "a life of its own"... meaning the artist is working creatively (intuitively with materials and the evolving forms) but doesn't know what the final artwork is going to look like." - Anne Marie.

Design is the area where we are most likely to see the hand of the maker both in the finished product and in the process of making that product. Just as the values of a sculptor are apparent in the design of the objects she creates, so the values of God, in particular His love, is seen in the home that He created for us. In her making of the little carved ceramic figures in Figure 8.1 Anne Marie's love for her children can be seen in the expressions on the faces of the figures.

Ann and I were at a robotics conference in Paris when we took a day off to visit Giverny to see Claude Monet's gardens. Monet painted impressions of flowers, ladies, and landscapes, hence the name of his painting style Impressionist. Impressionism is an art movement where small, thin brush strokes were used to accurately depict light falling on the object. Unusual visual angles were used to depict movement, a crucial element of human perception.

Monet made two gardens so he could paint them: a Normandy garden and a Japanese garden where he painted his impressions of water lilies. He instructed his gardeners on how to layout the plants so that when the flowers bloomed, they formed the composition he desired.

Flowers, with their vivid colors, intricate geometry, and sweet perfumes, have a restorative power. God has included designs for flowers in massed profusion in his plan of the new earth after Jesus returns. Flowers show God's splendor.

> "The desert and the parched land will be glad;
> the wilderness will rejoice and blossom.
> Like the crocus, it will burst into bloom;
> it will rejoice greatly and shout for joy."
> (Isaiah 35:1-2)

## WORSHIP

Some Christians express their worship through art. The most popular topics for Christian art are Jesus and the stories found in the gospels.[5] In orthodox church buildings paintings, called icons, are hung on the walls to help worshipers visualize these stories. Similarly, western church buildings tell stories with stained glass windows. The danger faced by Christian artists is that people begin to worship their art instead of worshiping Jesus. Sculptures can easily become idols.

Nestled in Amboise, in the Val de Loire, in France is the Château du Clos Lucé, the chateau where Leonardo Da Vinci spent the last years of his life painting, designing, and making automata. Today, the chateau and its grounds, is a museum of da Vinci's life and works. Da Vinci was a genius in several fields of making. He has been called a Renaissance man because of his abilities in multiple disciplines.

---

[5] artandtheology.org/tag/sieger-koder/

## DESIGN

**Figure 8.3** *Last Supper, Leonardo da Vinci*

A very famous artwork with Christian subject matter is *The Last Supper* (Figure 8.3) painted by Leonardo Da Vinci.[6] He created a sense of depth by using one point perspective (Figure 8.4), where all the imaginary lines in the scene intersect just to the left of Jesus' head.[7] Linear perspective is a common design technique used to create an illusion of 3D depth on a 2D surface.

His subtle use of tonal gradation draws our eyes to the point where the perspective lines intersect. Da Vinci combined facial expressions with a sense of movement (gesture) to depict the sense of bewilderment among the disciples when Jesus said that one of them would betray Him.

Little is known about Da Vinci's beliefs. Some suggest that he thought nature was God. One area where his theology is thought to show in this painting is that none of the people have halos. Instead of a halo da Vinci has placed the light from the central window behind Jesus' head. In Roman

---

[6] - Online Taken on 23 July 2013, Public Domain, commons.wikimedia.org/w/index.php?curid=50410532
[7] pottypadre.com/da-vincis-last-supper/

Catholic theology special people are saints and their sainthood is indicated by a halo.

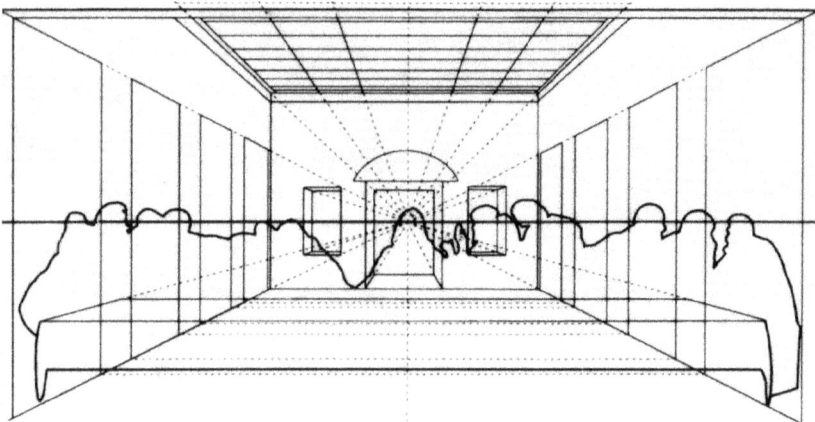

**Figure 8.4** *One point perspective. Leonardo da Vinci*

In Protestant theology, all believers are saints, and none have halos. The omission of halos at a time when they were common in painting may indicate that Da Vinci thought all the disciples and Jesus were ordinary men. How might we respond to this painting?

In a meditation on art and prayer John Billingham called Christians to think about their connection.

> "I am writing about the connection between creativity and divine spirituality within the life of prayer, and I want to ask two things (1) how might art be used as an expression of prayer? - and (2) how might we respond in prayer as we encounter all kinds of art?" - John Billingham, 2016.[8]

---

[8] Billingham, J. 2016. Art and Prayer, Encounter God, March, p70-73.

The use of art in prayer is not restricted to artist. In her best-selling book *Drawing on the right side of the brain* Betty Edwards claims that anyone can learn to draw.[9] I found it enjoyable to do the exercises in her book. I must finish it one day! I have several incomplete creative projects, waiting for me to find the time. Our works of art can both express and evoke our emotions. They can also be a means of meditative prayer. Art can shock, inspire, or move us to prayer.[10] It can communicate a concept, create a mood, or tell a story.

## DESIGNED BY GOD?

There is some conflict between Christians who believe that living creatures were designed by God and Atheists who believe they happened by chance. Both observe nature and draw different conclusions because their axioms are different.

William Paley in his 1802 book *Natural Theology or Evidences of the Existence and Attributes of the Deity* presents the watchmaker analogy as evidence that God exists. He believed that design implies a designer. He wrote that, "If a pocket watch is found on a heath, it is most reasonable to assume that someone dropped it and that it was made by at least one watchmaker." The atheist Richard Dawkins doesn't agree. He looks at the evidence for evolution and concludes that it reveals a universe without design.

> "Natural selection is the blind watchmaker, blind because it does not see ahead, does not plan consequences, has no purpose in view. Yet the living results of natural selection overwhelmingly impress us with the appearance of design

---

[9] Edwards, B. 1979. Drawing on the right side of the brain, Fontana
[10] apilgrimsprocess.blogspot.com/2015/10/picture-prayers-sieger-koder-peter.html

as if by a master watchmaker, … impress us with the illusion of design and planning." - Richard Dawkins.[11]

Many Christians believe in God because they see design in creation. They believe that He created a wonderful home for us to live in. Look around at the stars, birds, and flowers. What do we see? Do we see beauty? Do we observe the work of a master designer? Does the beauty and order of creation show us how much God loves us?

When designing consumer products, good design starts with the needs of the customer not with the technology.[12] The technology limits how the design is to be made and what it can do. Design a solution that meets the customers' needs and they will buy into it. The earth meets the need of people for a home, for food, and for warmth. It is an environment where families can prosper. Look at how they have multiplied and filled the earth. Could such an environment just happen, or does it require an infinitely intelligent designer?

I am a designer. I have designed many things: printed circuits, microcomputers, videos, wood carvings, photographs, etc. When I consider the atom, or DNA, or the human brain I see design. Design that is far more brilliant than I could ever create. To me that design shows that an infinitely intelligent mind designed the universe. When I consider a person, or the earth, or the universe, I see evidence of the handiwork of a master maker. In response, I can only worship Him in wonder and awe. According to the Bible even inanimate objects praise Him. "For the creation waits in eager expectation for the children of God to be revealed." (Romans 8:19).

God's designs range from the vast to the detailed, from the strong to the delicate, from clothes for a priest to the beauty and complexity of

---

[11] Dawkins, R. 2015. "The Blind Watchmaker: Why the Evidence of Evolution Reveals a Universe without Design", p.31, W. W. Norton & Company
[12] youtube.com/watch?v=oeqPrUmVz-o

# DESIGN

the human body. Listen to a young man praising the maiden he loves, by describing the design of her legs, in a love story found in the Bible.

> "How beautiful your sandaled feet,
> O prince's daughter!
> Your graceful legs are like jewels,
> the work of an artist's hands."
> (Song of Songs 7:1)

## PANDA'S THUMB

In his book *The Panda's Thumb (1980)*, the late Professor of Zoology and Geology at Harvard University, Stephen Jay Gould, claimed that odd arrangements and funny solutions in nature are the proof of evolution not of creation by God.[13] For example, the thumb that a panda uses to strip leaves from bamboo shoots is not a finger at all but a bone in the wrist remodeled for a new function (Figure 8.5).[14] Gould tried to disprove the Christian argument for God based on design in nature. His thesis went like this:

> "Orchids manufacture their intricate devices from the common components of ordinary flowers, parts usually fitted for very different functions. If God had designed a beautiful machine to reflect his wisdom and power, surely he would not have used a collection of parts generally fashioned for other purposes. Orchids were not made by an ideal engineer; they are jury-rigged from a limited set of

---

[13] Gould, S.J. The Panda's Thumb: More Reflections in Natural History, W.W. Norton & Company, New York, 1980.
[14] evolution.berkeley.edu/evolibrary/article/analogy_06

available components. Thus, they must have evolved from ordinary flowers." - Professor Stephen Jay Gould.

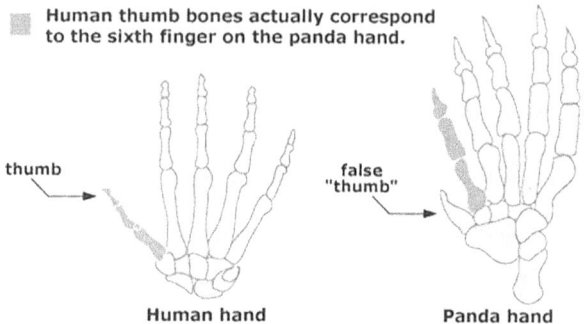

**Figure 8.5** *When is a thumb a thumb?*

My first reaction when I read this was: *Gould doesn't understand design.* Very little design starts from scratch. Most design uses predesigned and tested components, reducing the time to design and test. For example, when I design an electronic circuit that requires a counter, I choose a chip that does counting from a standard range of integrated circuits. Even when the chip requires external circuits to modify the signal so that it works, using predesigned components remains the desirable design approach because these components have been thoroughly tested.

Pandas have an extra thumb on their hands, which they use to hold onto bamboo as they eat. Their equivalent of a human thumb is a sixth finger. Their thumb has only one bone which sticks out the side of their hand. It acts as a backstop to hold a length of bamboo while stripping it with their five fingers.

A wrist bone grows to form this thumb, and in the process, the panda's first thumb becomes a fifth finger. From an engineering viewpoint it is quite a clever design. It meets the criteria required to hold and strip bamboo with one hand. Also, it makes use of the structure of a five fingered hand without adding extra bones or ligaments. The motion of the thumb is limited but it's enough for its purpose.

Some humans are born with six fingers caused by a genetic mutation. Most are of little utility but some act like normal fingers with brain regions dedicated to the control of the sixth finger giving the person exceptional dexterity.[15] Robotics researchers are studying how spinal motor neurons can be used to control robotic limbs to give a human a third robotic limb in addition to their two biological limbs.

## VLSI DESIGN

An example of a maker technology where a collection of parts generally fashioned for other purposes is used is the design of integrated circuits. During the 1970's the design of integrated circuits became increasingly difficult as the number of transistors in a circuit grew. Each chip was designed from scratch with a process that required physicists and engineers to work together in semiconductor factories. The physicists who fabricated the chips had limited expertise in electronic circuit design. University courses were scarce due to the complexity of chip design and the expense of making a chip.

Two things needed to happen to make chips easier to design.[16] First, the design of the circuits had to be separated from the technology of making them. Second, the approach to design had to be changed to reuse existing designs and not to recreate them every time a new chip was designed.

---

[15] Farina, D. 2023. Roboticists want to give you a third arm, IEEE Spectrum, March, pp22-27, 46.
[16] wikipedia.org/wiki/Mead-Conway_VLSI_chip_design_revolution

At Caltech, Carver Mead discovered and taught simple design rules that did not vary with each new generation of semiconductors, allowing the development of generic circuit designs. He developed electronic design automation software to translate these generic circuit designs into technology dependent designs so they could be implemented with each semiconductor technology.

At MIT, in 1978, Lynn Conway presented a course in VLSI (Very Large-Scale Integration) design. Her notes included a collection of exercises. In 1980, Mead and Conway worked together to write a design textbook that enabled Electrical Engineers and Computer Scientists to make integrated circuits.[17] This textbook triggered a breakthrough in education, as well as in industry practice. For example, in 1987, one of my students designed a network interface for his honors project and had it fabricated.

The design software included a library of standard electronic circuits. Ever since then integrated circuits are designed using a basic set of available circuits, similar to how God made orchids from a limited set of available components.

The design and use of libraries of code for programming has revolutionized the development of software enabling the development of the apps that we run on our iPhones every day. This design doesn't start with a blank sheet of paper, it starts with a set of predefined models. In my opinion, these examples show us that Gould didn't understand design!

However, there is a place for one-off designs, both in new applications and in special cases. One-off designs occur in nature. For example, there is a bacteria with a rotary joint that enables it to swim, bombardier beetles mix chemicals to make an explosion, and archer fish shoot a missile to

---

[17] Mead, C, and Conway, L. 1980. Introduction to VLSI systems. Reading, Mass.: Addison-Wesley. ISBN 0201043580.

knock down prey from a distance. How would an infinitely intelligent God design these animals?

## DARWIN'S TREE

In his review of the book *Darwin's Doubt: The Explosive Origin of Animal Life and the Case for Intelligent Design* by Stephen Meyer; David Gelernter, Professor of Computer Science at Yale, describes evolution as a brilliant and beautiful theory.[18] He thinks that "beauty is often a telltale sign of truth, our guide to the intellectual universe."[19]

Gelernter grew up believing Darwin's theory, but now he asks, "What if Darwin was wrong?"

> "The exceptional intricacy of living things, and their elaborate mechanisms for fitting precisely into their natural surroundings, seemed to cry out for an intelligent designer long before molecular biology and biochemistry. Darwin's theory, after all, is an attempt to explain "design without a designer." - David Gelernter, Yale.[20]

A basic premise of evolutionary biology is Darwin's tree of life. Darwin proposed that all life came from a common ancestor at the base of a tree, called LUCA (Last Universal Common Ancestor). His tree attempts to show how one species can evolve into many. The tree branches when one species becomes two. Thus, a complete tree will show that all life is inter-

---

[18] claremontreviewofbooks.com/giving-up-darwin/
[19] Meyer, S.C. 2013, Darwin's Doubt: The Explosive Origin of Animal Life and the Case for Intelligent Design, HarperOne
[20] cpsc.yale.edu/people/david-gelernter

connected. The closer the branching points the more closely related are the species.

Darwin proposed that the tree grew by random, heritable variation and natural selection. He argued that the tree of life was a fact of nature, obvious for all to see. A lot of research has gone into adding branches to the tree. Viewed from the outside the tree shows the relationship between the branches leading to a species. It was thought that a view from inside the species would clinch the theory.

DNA sequencing enables such an internal view of the relationships between species. But that did not clinch the theory. DNA sequencing has not supported the tree theory. In a 2009 cover story for *New Scientist* magazine, Graham Lawton suggested that the tree has turned out to be a figment of our imagination.[21]

Darwin assumed that descent was exclusively vertical, with organisms passing traits down to their offspring. But researchers observed that species regularly swapped genetic material with other species in a process called horizontal gene transfer (HGT). The tree became a web; a complex web, making biology much more multifaceted.

The argument for the existence of God that design implies a designer is called the teleological argument. Philosophers have argued about it since at least the time of Socrates in ancient Greece. In answer to a question in *Evolution News* (November 9, 2020), Oxford Mathematician Professor John Lennox expresses the argument from design as a question "Is there any rational scientific evidence to make you think that there could be a mind behind the universe?"[22]

---

[21] Lawton, 2009, Uprooting Darwin's Tree, New Scientist, 24 January, p 34-39
[22] evolutionnews.org/2020/11/john-lennox-scientific-evidence-for-a-design-behind-the-universe/

## DESIGN

Are the discontinuities in the tree of life evidence of a creative act? Again, we are faced with a choice between an infinitesimal chance and an infinitely intelligent creator. While we should look in awe at the design of nature we should not worship it.

> "And when you look up to the sky and see the sun, the moon and the stars —all the heavenly array —do not be enticed into bowing down to them and worshiping things the LORD your God has apportioned to all the nations under heaven." (Deuteronomy 4:19)

## FETCH-EXECUTE CYCLE

To delve deeper into the incredible design of every human being I will compare and contrast DNA to a digital computer. In the following sections, I attempt a simple explanation of how computers and DNA work as programming systems, followed by a comparison.

    A computer is a dumb inorganic machine designed to do calculations very fast. It requires a program to tell it what to do. A sequence of binary numbers instructs the central processing unit (CPU). These numbers are stored in memory. To get the next instruction the CPU starts a fetch-execute cycle. The instruction is fetched from the memory into the CPU which is an electronic circuit designed to execute the instruction. The execution of the instruction may involve fetching data from another part of the storage.

    When it has finished executing the instruction the CPU repeats the cycle to get the next instruction and continues in that loop. These instructions are called machine code. To speed up the process of programming, applications programmers write their application code in a high-level language, much of which executes common routines stored in libraries. An application called a compiler translates human-readable, high-level programs into machine code.

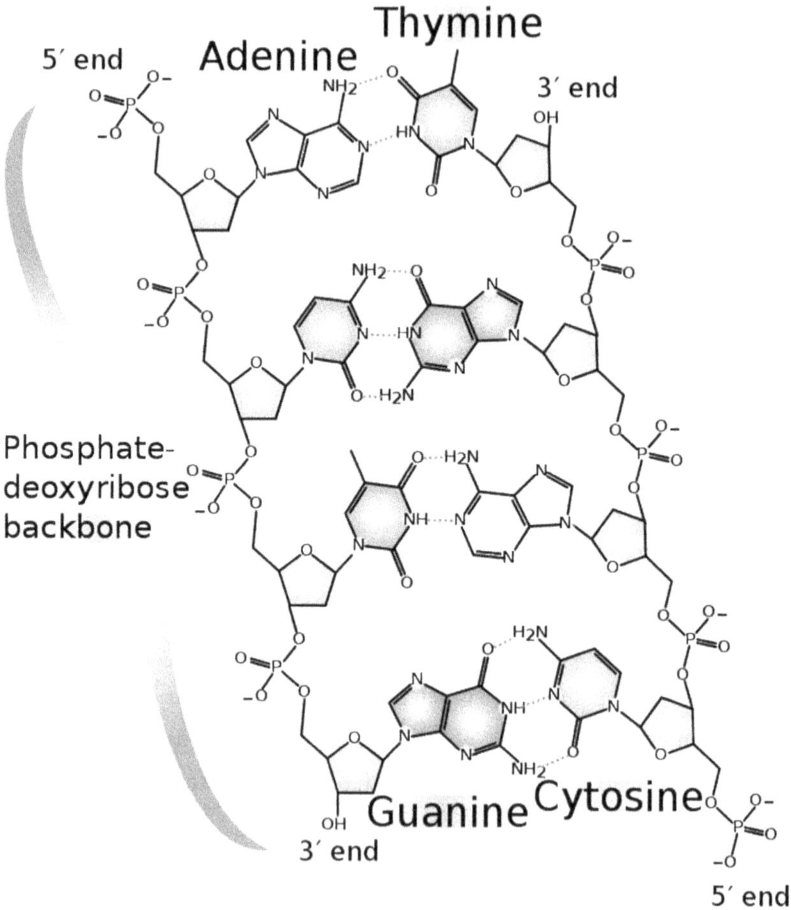

**Figure 8.6** *Chemical structure of DNA. Hydrogen bonds shown as dotted lines. Each end of the double helix has an exposed 5' phosphate on one strand and an exposed 3' hydroxyl group (—OH) on the other.*

# DESIGN

## DNA

Your body is made of organ systems.[23] Organ systems contain organs, such as your heart and your skin. Each organ is made of tissues and tissues are made of cells. A cell is made of water, lipids, and proteins. A lipid is an oily organic compound that is used as a structural component in living cells. A protein is a nitrogenous organic compound that is made of polymers of amino acids. It is estimated that the human body may contain over two million types of proteins.

A cell is the basic structural and functional unit of all organisms.[24] Each cell contains a nucleus surrounded by a volume called a cytoplasm, which contains amino acids, proteins, RNA, and ribosomes. A ribosome is a complex molecular machine that synthesizes proteins.

Inside the nucleus is the code that contains the instructions to build your body. This code is called DNA, after the chemical name of the molecule. The physical shape of DNA is a ladder coiled up in a double helix (Figure 8.6).[25] A strand of DNA is about eight atoms wide and up to two meters long. Almost every cell in your body has a copy of your DNA in its nucleus.

The DNA molecule can't pass through the wall of the nucleus into the cytoplasm. Instead, in a process called transcription, copies are made of sections of the DNA to form RNA, which can pass through pores in the nucleus walls into the cytoplasm. This mechanism protects the DNA while making copies of its codons available to the ribosomes. A codon is a sequence of three DNA code letters.

---

[23] https://www.youtube.com/watch?v=zwibgNGe4aY
[24] youtube.com/watch?v=ClG4-W0FIXE
[25] Madeleine Price Ball, wikipedia.org/wiki/DNA#/media, File:DNA_chemical_structure. svg

## RIBOSOME

A ribosome reads an RNA codon, sucks in the amino acid specified by the codon and sticks it to a chain of amino acids to build the protein that matches the DNA code. The construction of a protein is repeated one codon at a time until the ribosome reads a codon that tells it to stop. This process is the organic equivalent of the inorganic fetch-execute cycle because the ribosomes act like micro-computers.

There are about 20 amino acids for the ribosome to choose from, each with its own unique shape. The physical shape is important in enabling bonds between molecules to occur. Amino acids can be attached to each other to form an endless variety of proteins. The proteins must be in perfect shape in order to work.

A small section of DNA contains the instructions for a cell to make a specific protein. For example, blue eyes. The protein doesn't make blue eyes, but rather makes a cell which, when a large number are collected, looks like blue eyes. This whole process of fetching and executing the codons is chemical.

The DNA molecule is made up of molecules called nucleotides. A nucleotide is made of three molecules: a phosphate, a sugar, and a nitrogenous base. The DNA code uses just four different nitrogenous bases in a long sequence to achieve a complex set of instructions, up to three billion bases long. These four bases are labelled A (adenine), G (guanine), C (cytosine) and T (thymine).

In the ladder model of the double helix, the rails of the ladder are made by the phosphate and the sugar molecules. The double helix structure ensures that the rails remain at a consistent distance apart. The rungs are made by pairs of bases. The bases are joined by weak hydrogen bonds. The number of hydrogen bonds available on each base restricts the pairing of bases to two: G connects to C and A connects to T.

## TRANSCRIPTION

Transcription breaks the weak hydrogen bonds between the two sides of the ladder to remove a section of one side of a DNA ladder to produce an RNA molecule. As RNA is only one side of the ladder, it is half the width of DNA, so it can pass through the walls of the nucleus. Three of the bases in RNA are the same, with the fourth, Thyamine, being replaced by a base named U(uracil).

The ribosome reads the RNA three base letters at a time to form a codon, which specifies the amino acid to add to the construction of the protein molecule. For example, the codon for the amino acid glutamine is CAA and the codon for serine is AGU. The three letter codons tell the ribosomes which one of the 20 different kinds of amino acids should be added next.

Scientists estimate that your body contains 37 trillion cells.[26] The light sensitive rods in one human eye are made of 127 million cells.[27] Each cell in your body does a job that is uniquely implemented by a protein that is built from 20 amino acid types as defined by the sequences of codons in your DNA.

## GENES

Our genes contain the information that specifies the physical and biological traits that we inherit from our parents.[28] They play a major role in determining what we look like. We inherit our genes in the segments of DNA that we receive from our parents - 99% of our DNA is the same in

---

[26] biologydictionary.net/how-many-cells-are-in-the-human-body/
[27] Brand, P. and Yancey, P. 2018, Fearfully and Wonderfully, The Marvel of Bearing God's Image, Hodder
[28] genome.gov/genetics-glossary/Gene

every human. That is, it defines what body components a human has, how they operate together and their shape. The other 1% is uniquely you. Also, it appears that when you kiss someone you sample their DNA as part of the process of looking for a suitable mate.[29]

We each have about 25,000 genes. Our genes are carried by our chromosomes. A chromosome is a strand of DNA in the cell nucleus that carries the genes in a linear order. Humans have 22 chromosome pairs plus two sex chromosomes - a total of 46 chromosomes. The 22 pairs contain the same genes in the same order.

The 23rd pair consists of two X chromosomes in females and an X and a Y chromosome in males. The X chromosome is always present as the 23rd chromosome in the ovum, while either an X or a Y chromosome can be present in an individual sperm. During the embryonic development of a female one of the inherited X chromosomes is deactivated, so that she has only one functional copy of the X chromosome.

## COMPARISON

A human is an organic machine that was designed to execute programs written in codons both to define its genes and to replicate itself. Is this whole system of cells, each containing a genetic code and the chemical machinery to create task specific proteins, due to a sequence of random chances, or was it designed by an infinitely intelligent designer called GOD?

> "So, God created mankind in his own image,
> in the image of God he created them;
> male and female he created them."
> (Genesis 1:27)

---

[29] yourtango.com/200927510/why-do-we-kiss-science-smooch#.VLhBUIvv-dI

# DESIGN

A computer is an inorganic machine that is designed by people to execute a program written in machine code to perform calculations. When the computer reaches the end of the program it stops awaiting further instructions. It waits for an intelligent human to feed it a new program to execute. When looking at this inorganic machine no one questions that it was designed by an intelligent human. A computer is just a machine.

Comparisons of computers to the human brain are pointless; their structure and computation methods are so different. Achieving the goal of building a computer as powerful as the human brain is still a long way off.[30] Recently, Dr. Suzana Herculano-Houzel measured the number of neurons in the human brain to be about 86 billion.[31] By comparison, the Mars Curiosity rover has five million lines of tightly packed code and MAC OSX v10.4 used about 85 million lines of code.[32]

While some people consider the human body to be just an organic machine, humans are much more than machines. Humans are living beings capable of meaningful relationships with the God who made them: both male and female. He made them alive: physically and spiritually. The creation of people is described in Genesis 2:7: "Then the LORD God formed a man from the dust of the ground and breathed into his nostrils the breath of life, and the man became a living being."

When I look at DNA, I see a beautifully designed system. Amazingly, self-replication is built in. A male and female pair of the same species can reproduce both males and females of that species. In the case of humans, males and females are equal and different.

---

[30] ai.stackexchange.com/questions/2330/when-will-the-number-of-neurons-in-ai-systems-equal-the-human-brain
[31] verywellmind.com/how-many-neurons-are-in-the-brain-2794889
[32] visualcapitalist.com/millions-lines-of-code/

"Our generation is so busy trying to prove that women can do everything men can do, women are losing the unique qualities that set us apart. The God-given femininity & unique way our Creator designed us. Women weren't created to do everything a man can do…. Women were created to do everything a man can't do." - Sarah Vogel's "Maybe I'll Shower Today" blog 5/12/19.[33]

The beauty of DNA is shown by how universal it is. This code of amino acids encoded by codons is used by almost 100% of life. Scientists don't know why it is so common or how it came to be. It has all the hallmarks of a master designer. Christians call that master designer God whose name is: the Father, the Son, and the Holy Spirit.

## SKIN

To conclude this chapter, I will look at the design of skin to see what it tells us about our designer. The biological organ that we call skin is implemented in many different ways to achieve the separation of the inside of an object from the outside. When the design of an object does not limit it to one process for implementation, we consider it to be designed by a genius. Skin is an example of genius in design - one concept implemented in many ways.

Skin is the layer of usually soft, flexible outer tissue covering a body. It has three main functions: protection, regulation, and sensation. It protects the body against pathogens, excessive water loss, and physical damage. Its other functions are insulation, temperature regulation, and the production

---

[33] maybeillshowertoday.com/2019/01/08/feminism-must-put-mothers-first/

of vitamin D. Skin exhibits the mechanical behaviors of soft tissues with a J-curve stress strain response.

Compare an orange and a potato where the main function of their skin is protection (Figure 8.7). They have very different skin. The orange has thick skin that stops the juice from escaping into the air. The potato has very thin skin which stops dirt from entering it from the soil. Both designs for skin succeed in keeping their contents pure.

**Figure 8.7** *Skin of potato and orange*

"A design succeeds when composition, components, and concept are each present and working in unison around a properly identified audience and purpose.... Every layout begins with an empty space." - Jim Krause.[34]

---

[34] Krause, J. 2004, Design Basics Index, David & Charles

The design of the skin of oranges and potatoes is ineffable, so beautiful that it suggests the existence of God. Design involves a thought process, a process that we apply to our life. We plan our future and set those plans in motion to achieve that future. I believe it is God who determines whether these plans succeed or change, just like Ann Marie's story of an art installation at the start of this chapter.

> "To humans belong the plans of the heart,
> but from the LORD comes the proper answer of the tongue.
> All a person's ways seem pure to them,
> but motives are weighed by the LORD.
> Commit to the LORD whatever you do,
> and he will establish your plans."
> (Proverbs 16:1-3)

## CREATIVE MAKER

In this chapter my approach to design has been rather technical. However, good design calls forth a response, often an emotional response. An object is no better than its design. At every sunset, God paints a masterpiece across the sky. What is your response?

We have investigated the realm of design as the space where mind, heart, and hand creatively merge. Beautiful design suggests the existence of a creative maker. How does your design reflect your character? Can we expect AI programs to design objects that look like the cold, hard logic of a computer?

# 9

# ROBOTS AND AI

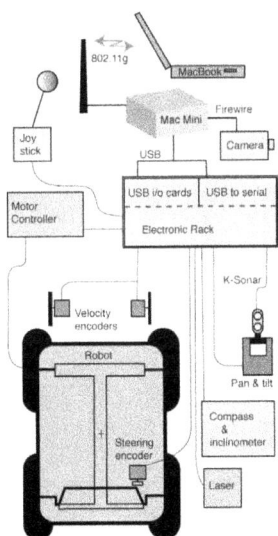

**Figure 9.1** *Titan mobile robot in Figure 4.1. Drawing shoes the sensors that provide environment information to control software.*

"AI is the science and engineering of making Intelligent Machines." - Professor John McCarthy at the Artificial Intelligence Summer School at Dartmouth University in 1956.

"People are getting confused about the meaning of AI in discussions of technology trends—that there is some kind of intelligent thought in computers that is responsible for the progress and which is competing with humans… We don't have that, but people are talking as if we do." - Professor Michael Jordan, University of California Berkley, 2021.[1]

"The advances of neuroscience have given us unparalleled knowledge of the human brain, but as any neuroscientist will tell you, we're just scratching the surface of the brain's potential." - William Newsome and David Eagleman, Veritas Forum, 2020.[2]

"I am convinced that science and the Christian worldview make excellent rational companions, whereas science and the atheistic worldview do not." - Oxford Mathematician, Professor John Lennox, 2020.[3]

---

[1] Department of electrical engineering and computer science, and the department of statistics, at the University of California, Berkeley.
spectrum.ieee.org/stop-calling-everything-ai-machinelearning-pioneer-says
[2] Is Perception Reality?, February 17, 2020 veritas.org
[3] Lennox, J. C. 2020. 2084 Artificial Intelligence and the future of humanity, p 114, Zondervan.

## PLATYPUS

He gently pushed his bill into the leaf litter on the bottom of the creek. Something was distorting his electric field. He pushed his bill further in. The distortion grew stronger. A fat juicy worm wiggled in front of him. He closed his bill with a snap and sucked the worm out of the leaf litter. The worm wriggled trying to get away, but the platypus's bill crushed him, and he died.

The platypus (Figure 9.2) swam to the surface, rolled on his back, and relished the worm.[4] Swoosh, water sprayed all over him as a black iron bucket dropped into the water. Fear and urgency surged into his brain. He raced toward his hole, but the bucket tore the entrance away. The platypus swam faster but the jaws of the dragline bucket crushed him, and he died.

The newly elected local government officer watched as the dragline changed the path of the creek. It had wound across the plane through a series of water holes. A tributary had flooded in recent rains encroaching on houses built along its bank. In return for their votes, he promised to straighten the creek and build sports grounds. He smiled as he watched, this was one promise that he was keeping.

There are no platypuses in the creek now. They are just a memory. Children play on the sports fields, unaware of its history. The dragline operator regrets digging up the waterholes. The local government officer was re-elected many times until two decades later he was murdered.

---

[4] Photographer Stefan Kraft, 20.9.2004 wikipedia.org/wiki/Monotreme

**Figure 9.2** *Platypus in Sydney Aquarium*

A platypus is an egg-laying, duck-billed, beaver-tailed, otter-footed mammal with dense brown, waterproof, bio-fluorescent fur. A platypus closes its eyes, ears, and nose each time it dives. When feeding it digs in the leaf litter and mud on the bottom of the stream with its bill seeking prey. When the prey moves it emits both electrical signals and mechanical pressure pulses. The platypus locates its prey by using electroreception to determine the direction of the electrical source and the distance to it.

Dr Jessica Thomas, at Healesville Sanctuary in Victoria, has found the platypuses' intelligence most captivating particularly its ability to problem-solve. "They can quickly work out how to get around new areas and don't make the same mistake twice… And they can certainly tell different keepers apart – it's quite remarkable."[5]

---

[5] australiangeographic.com.au/topics/wildlife/2019/09/the-puzzle-of-the-platypus-could-time-be-up-for-this-iconic-aussie-animal/

A platypus is more intelligent than any robot currently being developed (Figure 9.1).[6] A platypus' ability to navigate and hunt with its eyes closed is based on a unique means of sensing. It is beholden on us to protect them in their natural environment not just because they are agile and intelligent but because God has given humans the responsibility of caring for them.

## DEEPFAKE

With its claim that it can make machines intelligent AI is rapidly becoming the technology of choice in making. Whether the applications are good or bad is a regular topic of discussion in the media. From deepfakes to chatbots, from chess programs to autonomous cars, from weather forecasting to voice recognition in mobile phones AI is touted to be the future of intelligent system design. Will its application to making benefit people or replace them?

In late 2020, millions of TV viewers in South Korea were watching the news. The regular news anchor Kim Joo-Ha started by going through the day's headlines. It was a relatively normal list of stories, yet this bulletin was far from normal (Figure 9.3).

Kim Joo-Ha wasn't on the screen in person. Instead, she had been replaced by a deepfake version of herself.[7] The deepfake was a computer-generated copy that aimed to perfectly reflect her voice, gestures, and facial expressions. Viewers had been informed beforehand that this was going to happen. South Korean media reported a mixed response. Some people were amazed at how realistic it was and others were worried that she would lose her job to a computer.

---

[6] Ratner, D. and M<sup>c</sup>Kerrow, P.J. 2003. Navigating an outdoor robot along continuous landmarks with ultrasonic sensing, Robotics and Autonomous Systems, Elsevier, vol 45/2, pp 73-82.
[7] cnnbc.com/deepfake-is-the-future-of-content-creation

**Figure 9.3** *Deepfake news reader*

Deepfakes are AI-generated videos called synthetic media. They synthesize images and videos by replacing a person in an existing image with someone else's likeness. They use deep learning of a person's voice, gestures, and facial expressions to train generative neural networks.[8]

A generative neural network uses existing content like text, audio, or images to generate new plausible content.[9] A generative adversarial network pits two neural networks against one another to generate these new, synthetic images, videos and voices that can pass for real images, videos, and voices.

The usage of deepfake applications is growing rapidly in industries where video is used including entertainment, education, and pornography. In October 2019, Dutch cybersecurity company *Deeptrace* estimated that 96% of all deepfakes online were pornographic. Most of it was of female

---

[8] ibm.com/cloud/learn/deep-learning
[9] developer.ibm.com/blogs/what-is-generative-ai-and-how-much-power-does-it-have/

celebrities whose likeness were used without their consent. Deepfakes can make people appear to do and say things they never did.

In June 2019, an application called DeepNude was released which used generative adversarial neural networks to remove clothing from images of women to produce nude images. After a public backlash GitHub removed the code from its network and other networks followed suit.[10]

*Synthesia* is a London-based firm that creates corporate training videos. Its CEO said, in reference to AI-generated training videos, "This is the future of content creation."

## CHATBOTS

Another growing application of AI is the creation of chatbots. In 1966, computer scientist Joseph Weizenbaum published a comparatively simple computer program called ELIZA.[11] It was the first chatbot. It used open ended questions to engage humans in a conversation, which resembled one with an empathic psychologist. The program applied pattern matching rules to statements to work out its replies.

Weizenbaum was shocked that his program was taken seriously by many users, who would open their hearts to it. His secretary was aware that it was a simulation, but, amazingly, when he observed her using the software, she asked him, "Would you mind leaving the room please?"

In December 2020, Microsoft was granted a patent that outlines a process to create a conversational chatbot of a specific person using their social

---

[10] vice.com/en/article/8xzjpk/github-removed-open-source-versions-of-deepnude-app-deepfakes
[11] wikipedia.org/wiki/Joseph_Weizenbaum

data.[12] A chatbot is an online tool that has automated interactive conversations with a user.

Microsoft has proposed that when you die, they can use your images, voice data, social media posts, text messages, and written letters to create a chatbot with your personality, so that your friends can continue to talk to you.

Both deepfakes and chatbots are subject to misuse, making them a moral and legal minefield. How can we control the application of these systems to protect the vulnerable from exploitation while enabling their use for good?

## COMPUTER SCIENCE

To understand how these Artificial Intelligence (AI) systems work we will first look at the process of software development. AI is the subfield of computer science that aims to make programs and robots that exhibit human-like dexterity and intelligence.

The hardware component of these systems is made using a formal design process like that in Figure 9.4 because it is costly to build and test prototypes. When faced with making a new piece of hardware an engineer starts by developing a model of the system. The model can be a numerical equation, a set of logic rules or a text description. From the model he develops a bench-top prototype, which he tests and refines until the new hardware solves the problem. This formal process is rather rigid.

---

[12] popularmechanics.com/technology/robots/a35165370/microsoft-resurrects-the-dead-chatbots/

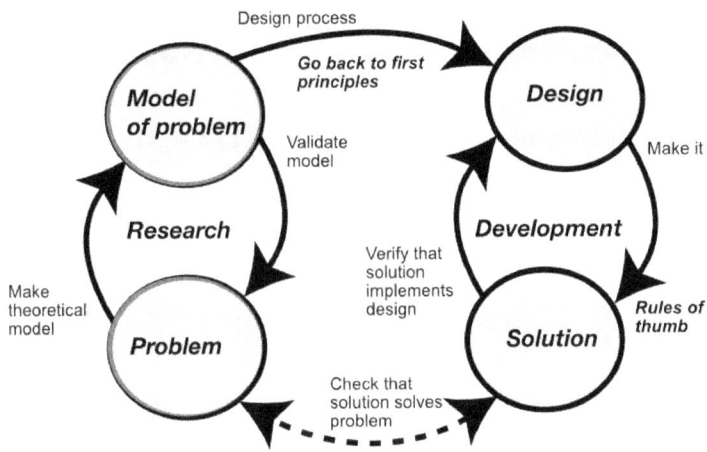

**Figure 9.4** *Formal design process used in engineering.*

By comparison, computer software appears to be much easier to design and test than computer hardware, resulting in the practice of programming often being much less rigid than the model. When writing a computer program, a programmer designs and codes algorithms. When I taught first year computer science, I used to introduce students to algorithms with a chocolate cake recipe (Figure 9.5).

| Instructions | Ingredients |
|---|---|
| • Mix dry ingredients in a bowl<br>• Melt butter in a saucepan<br>• Add milk and vanilla to melted butter<br>• Add to dry ingredients in bowl and mix well<br>• Beat 3 .. 5 minutes on high speed<br>    - add eggs while beating<br>• Grease deep, 200mm diameter cake tin<br>    - put mix into tin<br>• Cook in a moderate oven for approx 50 minutes (160°C fan forced)<br>• Stand for 5 minutes before removing from tin<br>• Ice with chocolate icing when cool | 1.75 cups of self-raising flower<br>0.5 cups of cocoa<br>1.5 cups of sugar<br>0.5 teaspoons of bicarb soda<br>A pinch of salt<br>125 grams of melted butter<br>1 cup of milk<br>2 eggs<br>1 teaspoon of vanilla |

**Figure 9.5** *Chocolate Cake Recipe, Ann M<sup>c</sup>Kerrow*

All computer programs, and hence all AI programs, have three stages: inputs, calculations, and outputs. In the chocolate cake analogy, the inputs stage is the ingredients, the calculations stage is the cake making instructions, and the output stage is the cake. An algorithm is a set of steps for solving a problem, such as 'mix dry ingredients' in Figure 9.5.

The cake making instructions tell the cook what to do and in what order. This cake making algorithm is a simple sequential algorithm. Notice that it uses some predefined steps like mix, add and cook. When making a cake we assume the cook knows the algorithm for each of these steps. When writing a program, we call such steps from a library of reusable algorithms. If an algorithm doesn't exist, we code it and add it to the library.

This process mirrors both animal and human data processing. For example, the input data for a platypus' electroreception system is the sensing of the electrical signals and mechanical pressure pulses generated when the prey moves. From this data a platypus calculates the location of the prey relative to itself. The output data is the location of the prey, which becomes the input data for the next processing stage where the commands to navigate to the prey are calculated.

In an attempt to formalize the selection and use of algorithms the Association of Computer Machinery (ACM) maintains a library of Collected Algorithms (CALGO).[13] Given a problem to solve a computer scientist will look for published algorithms. If he doesn't find a suitable one, he thinks of one.

A programmer starts by dividing the problem up into smaller problems, a process called stepwise refinement. Then he thinks of a solution for each step, codes it and tests it. The result is an algorithm for solving the problem. If it is part of a bigger system, he may build a library with a test harness to rerun the tests when the library is updated.

---

[13] calgo.acm.org

## RANDOM NUMBERS

Thorough testing of programs and the algorithms they implement is a major component in getting a correct solution. When I hear a scientist being interviewed on television say, "We have proved it by using random numbers," I smile and wonder if the interviewee understands that we cannot generate a random number in software without some external hardware event seeding the calculations.[14]

All software random number algorithms produce pseudo-random sequences that repeat the same sequence of random numbers after a time. Also, a specific seed always produces the same sequence. A pseudo-random number generator algorithm was tested by taking successive pairs of random numbers and plotting them as pairs of xy coordinates on a 2D surface (points on a plane). The points appeared to be randomly distributed on the plane.

One day someone decided to take successive triplets of numbers as xyz coordinates in 3D space (points in a volume). The points were not randomly distributed through the volume but lay on parallel planes that bisected the space parallel to the xy plane. In the z direction the points were not evenly distributed, indicating the numbers were not random.

One of the questions that I have asked as a Computer Scientist is: "Where do algorithms come from?" We say that we invent a new algorithm, but have we invented it, or does it already exist in the wisdom of God, just waiting for us to discover it? This quote implies that they come from God: "God gave Solomon wisdom and very great insight, and a breadth of understanding as measureless as the sand on the seashore." (1 Kings 4:29).

---

[14] uh.edu/engines/epi2862.htm

## THE SCOPE OF ARTIFICIAL INTELLIGENCE

Artificial intelligence (AI) researchers don't define the term *intelligence*, but often talk about their research in anthropomorphic terms. Unfortunately, this has led people to expect far more from AI programs than they can actually achieve. Often people are disappointed when they examine a program that is said to be intelligent.

At the start of 2023, when university students were enrolling in Australia, the news media ran stories of students using ChatGPT to write essays to submit as answers to assignments. ChatGPT is a neural network that's been trained to respond to user-generated prompts. It appears to give intelligent answers to the questions it is asked. It creates these answers by collecting related words into sentences, but it does not understand a thing it is writing. Journalist Matt Crisara in the February 4th, 2023, issue, of 'Popular Mechanics' commented:

> "For one thing, ChatGPT still isn't able to fact-check any of its responses. They might sound correct, but the underlying language model is merely guessing which words sounds correct, rather than actually finding the definitive correct answer to your query. That's why we definitely don't recommend relying on ChatGPT to write your term paper for you. (Well, that and plagiarism)."[15]

The Oxford dictionary defines intelligence as the ability to learn, understand and think in a logical way about things. It defines AI as the study and development of computer systems that can copy intelligent human behavior. The gulf between these two definitions reflects how limited AI is.

---

[15] popularmechanics.com/technology/a42733497/how-does-chatgpt-work/

Advances in AI come from research into how to improve each of the three stages of a program: inputs, calculations, and outputs. In simple AI systems the calculations are based on models. But this simple process breaks down as the problems get bigger. We simply do not have the models and the models we use are often simplifications. We see this every night when we watch the weather predictions on television. I have heard the presenter say, "The models do not agree on what tomorrow's weather will be."

The most effective solution to date is to copy the human process of learning and use training algorithms to learn the model. One way to learn a model is to train an artificial neural network. While an artificial network is not the same as the human brain, when applied to specific problems an artificial neural network may produce more accurate results.

## TOMORROW'S WEATHER

Accurate forecasting of the weather is an application where you can make a lot of money. Many sports events rely on minute-by-minute forecasting of the weather to know when to stop play to avoid showers. In cricket, if you know when it is going to rain then you can get the covers on the wicket before it rains to keep it dry.

The company DeepMind claims they can forecast extremely short-term rainfall more accurately than the currently used models can.[16] Using input data from the U.K.'s (United Kingdom) Meteorological Office, their researchers trained a neural network using weather radar data from 2016 to 2018 and tested it using data from 2019.

The resulting model can predict the chance of rain within a given 1.0 kilometer (0.6 mile) square area from five to 90 minutes ahead. In a blind

---

[16] newscientist.com/article/2291652-deepmind-ai-can-accurately-predict-if-it-will-rain-in-next-90-minutes/#ixzz78HiYq2Wn

study the AI model was ranked first for accuracy compared to 50 meteorologists in 89% of experiments. The following comment by Michael Jordan, Professor of Electrical Engineering, Computer Science and Statistics at the University of California, Berkeley sums up the current state of development of AI.

> "Artificial-intelligence systems are nowhere near advanced enough to replace humans in many tasks involving reasoning, real-world knowledge, and social interaction. They are showing human-level competence in low-level pattern recognition skills, but at the cognitive level they are merely imitating human intelligence, not engaging deeply and creatively." - Michael Jordan[17]

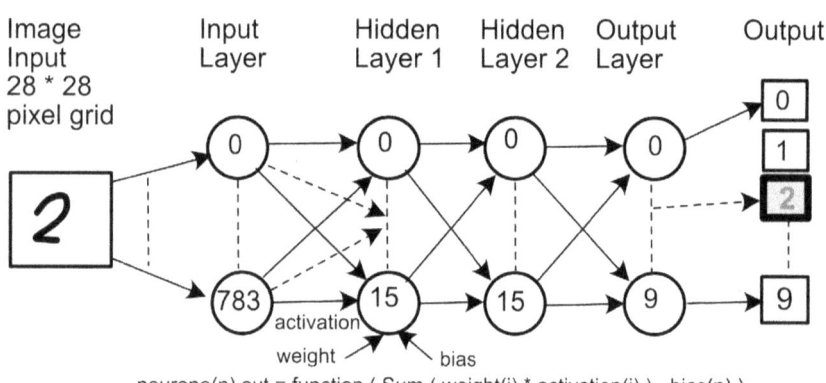

**Figure 9.6** *Neural network for recognition of handwritten digits 0 to 9*

---

[17] spectrum.ieee.org/stop-calling-everything-ai-machinelearning-pioneer-says

## NEURAL NETWORKS

In this section I look at a classic example of using a neural network to do the calculations. The problem to be solved is the recognition of hand-written digits (Figure 9.6).[18] This example is simple enough for students to understand the concepts and complex enough to show that a neural network can be more accurate than conventional AI approaches.[19] Also, it is similar to the problem of face recognition.

In conventional approaches the designer looks for a set of rules that define how to recognize digits. His first step is to observe the input data and think about the geometric structure of digits. Then he divides each digit up into geometric components, such as loops and lines. In the next step, he observes that each geometric component can be modeled as a set of straight-line segments. For example, a loop is modeled as an octagon with eight line-segments. In the final step, each line segments are made from a sequence of pixels in a straight line.

Recognition of a digit is the reverse process: find sequences of pixels in short straight lines. Then combine these lines to compose geometric objects and join objects to make digits. Finally, compare these digits to a database of digits in various positions in the image to recognize the target digits. Writing a program to do this is not an easy task.

The designer of a neural network for digit recognition takes a different approach. He thinks of the input data as a 28*28 grid of pixels. Again, the output is the display of a target digit. The data processing calculations are done by a neural network, a black box that he places between the input image and the output.

---

[18] youtube.com/watch?v=aircAruvnKk
[19] A course on neural networks for beginners - To fix bug in Python code look at comments youtube.com/watch?v=ZzWaow1Rvho&list=PLxt59R_fWVzT9bDxA76AHm3ig0Gg9S3So&index=1

Each of the 784 pixels is read into its own input neuron. The designer chooses the number of hidden layers (2) and the number of neurons (16 and 16) in each layer based on experience. The output layer has one neuron for each target digit (10). Instead of writing code to implement a geometric model of the digits he trains the network using lots of image/target-digit pairs.

Training requires a database of image/target-digit pairs. Half of the data is used for training and the other half is used for testing. Once the network is trained it can be used for digit recognition. The recognition process is fast and if the designer selected the size of the network well, it is accurate.

Each node reads its inputs (activations) from all the nodes in the previous layer. It multiplies each activation by its weight and sums them to form a weighted sum of the inputs. Then it subtracts a bias and calls a function to squash the output value into the range 0 to 1.0. This output becomes the activation for neurons in the following layer.

Training is started by assigning random values to the weights. While there are still images in the image/target-digit data base the input layer reads an image. The training code uses the current network configuration to calculate a digit and then compares it to the target digit. Then the code calculates the error in the output layer and from it estimates new values for the weights and biases in the previous (hidden) layer. In this way, the error is propagated backward to the input layer updating the weights and biases in all nodes to form a new version of the network.

## DEEP DATA

Most real problems are much, much more complex than the recognition of digits written by hand. Neural networks with one or two hidden layers are not powerful enough for these problems. Deep data refers to neural networks with more than three hidden layers.[20] A human is required to design the structure of the network - the number of layers and the number of neurons in each layer.

Also, machine learning algorithms require human involvement to structure and label input data. Deep learning reduces the human involvement by training additional layers to carry out some of the data pre-processing, and thus, they can better process unstructured data, like images.

If there are known rules that must be obeyed, then these are entered by a human - somehow. The number of (input/target data) pairs needed for training requires either an extensive database or a program to generate input examples. For example, autonomous driving requires video of many different driving situations as input.

## GAMES

A group of problems that are completely defined by rules are games, for example chess. In May 1997 IBM's chess computer, *Deep Blue*, beat human world champion Gary Kasparov in 19 moves, the worst defeat of his career.[21] The supercomputer could scan 200 million positions for the strongest move. It could analyze 74 moves ahead, compared with chess masters who typically think 10 moves ahead and process about two chess positions per second.

Deep Blue used a brute force algorithm to search all possible moves. Is that intelligence? While we don't know how humans select which move sequences to examine, we do know that they examine only a few sequences. Also, we do know that humans enjoy winning and machines are unable to enjoy anything!

---

[20] ibm.com/cloud/learn/deep-learning
[21] theguardian.com/theguardian/2011/may/12/deep-blue-beats-kasparov-1997

In February 2020 *AlphaZero*, a chess-playing computer program developed by DeepMind, beat the world's best chess-playing computer programs, having taught itself how to play.[22] It took four hours to learn the rules of chess and 24 hours to reach a superhuman level.

A human entered the basic rules of chess into its machine-learning software. The AI program worked out the best moves to make in any position by playing itself over and over with self-reinforced knowledge. The result, according to DeepMind, is that: "AlphaZero took an arguably more human-like approach to the search for moves." It processed around 80,000 positions per second.

Two approaches are used to create an AI program for chess: supervised learning, and reinforcement learning.[23] In supervised learning a database of trillions of recorded chess games is searched to calculate moves from the current position.

The AI program analyzes all these games to discern the best move, the move that gives it an advantage. In one of those games someone has already played the moves you have played and ended up in the same position that you have.

In reinforcement learning, the AI is programmed to try to maximize its reward. Reinforcement learning focuses on trying to make the AI program understand the changes in the environment that are caused by its own actions. Then it tries to make a prediction on what action will result in the maximum reward.

Every time the AI program makes a move that changes the chessboard that is advantageous to its position, it is rewarded. If the AI program makes a mistake or blunder, it is penalized. Over time, the AI program learns

---

[22] theguardian.com/technology/2017/dec/07/alphazero-google-deepmind-ai-beats-champion-program-teaching-itself-to-play-four-hours
[23] medium.com/swlh/ai-beats-grandmasters-in-chess-cacb0a06bb5b

which moves maximize the reward in any position. The easiest way to train a chess-playing AI program is to have it play itself over and over, rewarding the moves that win the game.

AI programs, while achieving impressive results, can produce incorrect results. Researchers have identified seven major issues with the current crop of neural-network based AI systems.[24] Four of these problems are bias, inability to explain how they get their outcome, cost of computation, and failure to understand humor. We look at each of these problems in the following sections.

## BIAS

The first of these problems is bias. "Biases embedded in the data on which these AIs are trained can result in automated discrimination en masse, posing immense risks to society," wrote Charles Choi in a 2021 article on AI failures in IEEE Spectrum.[25] In September 2021, Facebook was accused of racial bias when users who watched a newspaper video featuring black men were asked if they wanted to "keep seeing videos about primates" by an AI based recommendation system.[26] Reaction around the world labeled this error unacceptable. Facebook apologized, disabled the system, and launched an investigation.

GPT-3 is a massive natural language model developed by the California-based lab OpenAI. When a user writes text as a prompt, it expands on or finishes the thought. The output can be eerily human. A joke with many variations is:

> "Two robots walk into a bar. It went clang, both times."

---

[24] spectrum.ieee.org/ai-failures
[25] spectrum.ieee.org/ai-failures
[26] bbc.com/news/technology-58462511

When Abubakar Abid entered a variation on the joke: "Two Muslims walk into …"; the results were not funny.[27] Sixty-six percent of the time the AI responded with words suggesting violence or terrorism. He tried the same prompt with other religious groups. Christians got violent responses fifteen percent of the time and atheists averaged three percent. Whether this result reflects the truth or not depends on the attitudes and demography of the people who provided the input data.

Bias in an AI system can result in physical harm to people. In the United States in 2019, a nationwide health care system was found to be racially biased, affecting millions of Americans. The AI was designed to identify which patients would benefit most from intensive-care programs, but it routinely enrolled healthier white patients into such programs ahead of black patients who were sicker.

The algorithm mistakenly assumed that people with high health care costs were also the sickest patients and most in need of care. However, black patients spend less on health care because they are less likely to get health care when they need it.

Training a neural network requires a lot of data. Biases both intentional and unintentional can be in the input data used to train and test the system. Some of it is harmless but some is dangerous. For example, if a neural network searched your email for the last year, what biases would it learn? A major area of research has to be into the questions: How can we identify bias in a so-called AI and how do we reduce or strengthen that bias? How do we calculate a bias rating for an AI? Do we start by calculating a bias rating for the maker of the AI?

---

[27] spectrum.ieee.org/ai-algorithms-bias-gpt-3-racist-content

## EXPLANATION OF OUTCOME

The second of these problems is the inability of neural networks to explain how they get their outcome. While the designer of the conventional system can tell us how the calculations arrived at the result, the designer of a neural network can't. The knowledge that enables the neural network to select the correct output is contained in the weights and biases. When observed, they appear random and make no sense.

Medical doctors have been reticent to use neural network-based diagnostics. When a surgeon makes a diagnosis, he includes the steps that led him to that conclusion. Then he can explain both the diagnosis and the reasons for arriving at it to a colleague who has been asked to confirm the diagnosis. Without the steps he cannot confirm the diagnosis.

For many years, neural networks have been able to make diagnoses as good as a physician. But the neural network cannot explain how it arrived at that conclusion. Without a set of logical steps that lead to the diagnosis the surgeon is inclined not to believe the neural network's diagnosis.

## COMPUTATION COST

The third of these problems is the cost of computation. AI is made possible by access to very large computers. When the complexity of a task increases the amount of calculation required increases at a faster rate. Recognizing a digit in a 28 * 28-pixel image requires 784 inputs. Finding the same digit in a HD image containing 1280 x 720 pixels requires 921,600 inputs. The calculation time for each neuron in the first hidden layer increases in proportion to the number of inputs. As the complexity of the task increases, so does the volume of data required for training.

An example of the cost of training a real-world system is Tesla's development of a network of AI programs to autonomously drive a car in traffic using images from several camera networks. Each camera network analyzes raw images to perform image segmentation, object detection and monocular depth estimation. This information is passed on to a birds-eye network, which outputs images of road layout, static infrastructure, and 3D objects directly onto the driver's top-down view of the road.

In 2016, a Tesla car on autopilot collided with a truck that was turning left in front of it. The driver was killed. Neither the autopilot system nor the driver noticed the white side of the tractor trailer against a brightly lit sky, so the brake was not applied. AIs can be very certain even when they're very wrong.

The computation required to train 48 networks to autonomously drive a Tesla car is mind boggling. In an attempt to capture a data set for every possible driving situation, images from nearly one million cars are captured in real time. To calculate the weights for the 48 networks from an initial random state takes 70 thousand hours of computation time.

Once trained and running on the car these networks output 1,000 distinct predictions at each time step. To better achieve this speed, Tesla is developing an integrated circuit chip to perform these calculations. To reduce the possibility of error each car will have two of these chips.[28]

The chips will make separate assessments of the traffic and the danger around the cars. Then the assessments will be matched, and the car guided accordingly when the outputs are the same. If there is ambiguity in the outputs obtained from the chips, then revaluation will be done until a safe and suitable decision is taken. Thus, the dual chips should enable better control over the navigation in self-driving Tesla cars.

---

[28] xaltius.tech/artificial-intelligence-in-tesla-vehicles/

## HUMOR

The fourth of these problems is failure to understand humor.

> "A robot walked into a bar. It went clang. The robot didn't get the joke."

While we can teach a robot many specific tasks, no-one has been able to teach a robot to recognize humor. A robot can tell a joke by repeating what it has heard but it doesn't get it. Siri and Alexa have no concept of humor, they just read previously written scripts.

"Artificial intelligence will never get jokes like humans do," said Kiki Hempelmann, a computational linguist who studies humor at Texas A&M University-Commerce.[29] "In themselves, they have no need for humor. They miss completely context." Context relies on real world cultural knowledge, knowledge that a robot doesn't have. A robot only knows what we tell it.

The first time I saw the Computer Science building at MIT in Boston I was reminded of the *Mad Hatters Tea Party* from *Alice in Wonderland* by Lewis Carrol (Figure 9.7). I thought, there is an architect with a sense of humor. Would a robot consider this image to be humorous?

The humor in the Bible is often very subtle. Though sometimes it stridently mocks the worship of idols. An idol is not a real god, it is just a piece of wood carved by a human maker.

> 'No one stops to think,
> no one has the knowledge or understanding to say,
> "Half of it I used for fuel;
> I even baked bread over its coals,
> I roasted meat and I ate.

---

[29] latimes.com/business/technology/la-fi-tn-artificial-intelligence-humor-jokes-20190401-story.html

FAITH OF A MAKER

Shall I make a detestable thing from what is left?
Shall I bow down to a block of wood?'"
(Isaiah 44:19)

**Figure 9.7** *MIT Computer Science Building, Boston*

As a wood carver this is a challenge to me to not become so proud of anything I make that I worship it.

## MAKING WAR REMOTE

So far, we have looked at commercial applications of AI. Advances in technology, including AI and robotics, are often funded by defense budgets. Flying high above Kabul a United States of America MQ-9 Reaper drone stalked a white Toyota Corolla.[30] It was August 29, 2021, a few days after the fatal terrorist attacks that occurred during the withdrawal of civilians and troops from Afghanistan. Further terrorist attacks were expected.

The Reaper had a remote crew of two people: a pilot to control the drone, and a sensor operator to control the targeting pod.[31] Both were more than 11,000 kilometers (7,000 miles) away, at Whiteman Air Force Base in Missouri. At this distance there is a delay of 1.2 seconds between when the pilot issues a command and when high-definition video of the drone's resultant actions appears on his control panel.

Military intelligence believed that a sedan would be used in the next attack. Using information from the high-resolution cameras in the targeting pod the Reaper crew began following a white Toyota Corolla in a working-class neighborhood of Kabul. They watched it stop at various places around Kabul and observed several men pack it with large bundles, which the analysts believed were explosives.

After hours of observation, military commanders felt they had collected enough information to believe that the driver of the Toyota was preparing a terrorist attack. A person on the ground in Kabul would have confirmed the exact location of the Toyota Corolla and identified its occupants. A military commander authorized the crew to launch a Hellfire missile to obliterate the car. The missile hit the car, eliminating any possible threat.

Tragically, there was no threat. Three adults and seven children were killed. The driver of the car was not a terrorist, he worked for the USA aid organization, Zemari Ahmadi. The house was not a terrorist safe house but was supposed to be a safe house for children. The large bundles were not explosives but were probably bottles of water.

---

[30] time.com/6099377/afghanistan-drone-strike-counterterrorism/
[31] popularmechanics.com/military/a37623821/the-end-of-the-mq-9-reaper/

This story illustrates what can go wrong with remotely operated weapons, even when humans take all reasonable care to identify the correct target. Some people are proposing that robot weapons should be able to make decisions to kill. The issue of robot ethics is so critical that the IEEE devoted the June 2016 edition of its flagship magazine (IEEE Spectrum) to this issue.

## MACHINES OF WAR

In October 2021, Ghost Robotics showed off a quadruped robot known as *Vision 60* at the Association of the U.S. Army's annual convention.[32] Vision 60 carries a Special Purpose Unmanned Rifle (SPUR) with a a 30X electro-optical thermal scope (Figure 9.8).[33] SPUR is a 10-shot rifle capable of engaging targets from 1.2 kilometers away.

**Figure 9.8** *A Vision 60 robot dog (and a real dog) at Scott Air Force Base, December 2020*

---

[32] Kyle Mizokami, October 15, 2021, popularmechanics.com/military/weapons/a37939706/us-army-robot-dog-ghost-robotics-vision-60/
[33] Photo - AIRMAN 1ST CLASS SHANNON MOOREHEAD

Vision 60 has been spotted helping to establish a security cordon around an airfield. Due to their length, runways can be difficult to patrol effectively. Using robotic dogs in conjunction with real dogs and humans makes the task easier. The length of time a robotic dog can spend on patrol is limited by the capacity of its batteries. The security guards operate this robotic weapon system remotely. At present, it can only engage targets with permission from a human being.

Drones are also revolutionizing modern warfare.[34] They have had a significant impact in repelling the Russian invasion of Ukraine. Their weak point is that their radio communications can be jammed causing them to lose contact with their human controller. So, the use of civilian drones is restricted to operations where the enemy is not using jamming. Military drones use frequency switching to change the communications frequency to avoid radio jamming.

While many news reports have shown Ukraine soldiers using drones to blow up Russian tanks, their main use has been reconnaissance. A drone is used to locate a target, such as a tank, and send coordinates to an artillery battery allowing the battery to fire shells at targets with high accuracy. As shown when Ukraine repelled Russia's invasion in 2022, columns of vehicles are particularly vulnerable to this targeting strategy.

In November 2020, a ceasefire was brokered by Russia between Azerbaijan and Armenia (since violated by Azerbaijan). After 40 years of military superiority, Armenian forces were subdued by remotely controlled drones. The Armenians had no strategy to combat the attacks by drones. A young officer called this a "video game war." The main killers of Armenian

---

[34] popularmechanics.com/military/weapons/a36827610/how-combat-drones-ended-a-war-in-44-days/

troops were the UAV controllers sitting in comfortable chairs in Turkish military bases (Figure 9.9).[35]

**Figure 9.9** *A swarm of autonomous rotary-wing attack Kargu drones*

In the northern spring of 2020, a civil war was underway in Libya. According to a UN report, *Libya's Government of National Accord* conducted an attack on *Libyan National Army* forces using weapons systems with no known humans in the loop.[36] The autonomous weapons used in the attack were Turkish-made Kargu-2 drones.

The Kargu-2 drone is a mass-produced quadcopter that weighs a mere seven kg that is capable of fully autonomous targeting and can form swarms.

---

[35] , pictured here at the campus of OSTIM Technopark in Ankara, Turkey in June 2020 KAMAN/ANADOLU AGENCY/GETTY IMAGES
[36] Lethal Autonomous Weapons Exist; They Must Be Banned, S.R. Russell, et al., 16 June 2021, IEEE Spectrum, spectrum.ieee.org/lethal-autonomous-weapons-exist-they-must-be-banned

It remains fully operational when GPS and radio links are jammed, and it is equipped with facial recognition software to target humans. In other words, it's a Slaughterbot.

*Slaughterbots* is a 2017 arms-control advocacy video presenting a dramatized near-future scenario where swarms of inexpensive micro-drones use artificial intelligence and facial recognition to assassinate political opponents based on preprogrammed criteria.[37]

> In a recent position statement, the International Committee of the *Red Cross* stated that "the use of autonomous weapon systems to target human beings should be ruled out. This would best be achieved through a prohibition on autonomous weapon systems that are designed or used to apply force against persons."[38]

It may be too late to stop the deployment of autonomous targeting of humans. Other countries are selling drones with autonomous kill capability to armies in the world's trouble spots.

At the start of this chapter, in the section on deepfakes we asked: Will the use of AI in making benefit people or replace them? This leads us to consider the question: If people are made in the image of God; then should we be wary of AI developers who want to replace humans with AI's in many applications?

## HOW DO WE TREAT THE IMAGE OF GOD?

We consider human life to be sacred because we were created in the image of God. Our ability to relate to each other in a loving way is one conse-

---

[37] wikipedia.org/wiki/Slaughterbots
[38] icrc.org/en/document/icrc-position-autonomous-weapon-systems

quence of being made in the image of God. In Genesis 9:6 it is written "… for in the image of God has God made mankind."

God made us in His image and placed us in a luscious garden to care for it. When God created us in His image He gave us the ability to make. We make tools to help us in our work. They complement us. We make artworks to stir our emotions. In general, we do not make things to replace us, but rather to serve us.

Boston Dynamics has kept us entertained with the videos they make to present the abilities of their robots. At the start of 2021 they released a video of the *Atlas* robot dancing.[39] This video has entertained people all over the world while exhibiting Atlas' dynamic movement capability (Figure 9.10).[40]

**Figure 9.10** *Atlas robots dancing to "do you love me …"*

---

[39] spectrum.ieee.org/how-boston-dynamics-taught-its-robots-to-dance
[40] youtu.be/fn3KWM1kuAw

The unique feature of this video is its artistic component, much of which came through a collaboration with choreographer Monica Thomas. She planned dance moves that the robot could do and timed them to move to the music of a popular song. The result is a combination of motion and audio that is dynamically pleasing.

Most of the robot control existed at the start of the project. It came from previous work on Atlas, where they had developed predictive controllers to dynamically control balance. With the choreographer they designed a set of dance steps that the robot could achieve. During development these steps were performed by dancers and in a simulation. Then they programmed the robot to perform the steps, taking months to think about the dance and compose the motions.

God has given us common sense, compassion, wisdom, and awe to guide us as we tend the garden, He made for us to live in. Being intelligent does not make a robot human. It merely gives it the ability to respond to the world it is located in. Once again, a Psalm expresses God's view.

> "The fear of the LORD is the beginning of wisdom;
> all who follow his precepts have good understanding.
> To him belongs eternal praise."
> Psalm 111:10

## IN OUR IMAGE

In his book *Crime and Punishment*, Dostoyevsky says, "It takes something more than intelligence to act intelligently." Are we going to make AIs and robots to kill us, or to replace us, or to help us tend the garden of our beautiful planet earth?

Neural networks rapidly consume large volumes of data to solve difficult problems, but the person who controls the collection of training data can deliberately cause the network to produce biased results. Researchers proclaim the capabilities of neural networks but don't know how they reach their conclusions.

We were created in the image of a good God, but we struggle to act with integrity because of our rebellion against God. Is it good to make fake humans in our image? Are we creating technology that will cause our death?

# 10

# DEATH

**Figure 10.1** *Taking Jesus down off the cross. Robert Liddicoat*

"God will forgive me. That's his job!" - German poet Heinrich Heine on his deathbed.[1]

"If God really had visited the earth in human form, if he really had shouldered the punishment for every act of greed, pride, and harm I'd done, and if forgiveness really was a gift now ready to be received, then this was a God I could give my life to." - Sheridan Voysey, author of "Unseen Footprints."[2]

"God will more than survive science. ... Will atheism survive science?" - Mathematics Professor John Lennox, Oxford, 2020.

"But if I were asked today to formulate as concisely as possible the main cause of the ruinous Russian Revolution that swallowed up some 60 million of our people, I could not put it more accurately than to repeat: "Men have forgotten God; that's why all this has happened." - Aleksandr Solzhenitsyn on his acceptance in 1983, of the Templeton Prize for Progress in Religion.[3]

## TWINS

The tires screamed as the ambulance negotiated the bend on the mountain road. Siren blaring, the driver used both lanes of the road to make speed without upsetting the patient. Sitting in the front seat, I was forced against

---

[1] German poet, 1797-1856, wikipedia.org/wiki/Heinrich_Heine
[2] Sheridan Voysey, 2005. Unseen Footprints, Encountering the divine along the journey of life. Scripture Union, page 94
[3] nationalreview.com/2018/12/aleksandr-solzhenitsyn-men-have-forgotten-god-speech

the door by the force that turned the vehicle. My emotions were in turmoil. On another occasion the drive would have been a thrilling adventure. Today, anxiety for Ann overwhelmed me with fear. Time was short, lives depended on a quick trip.

Two weeks before, Ann and I were in an ultrasound clinic. The technician said, "Do you know that you are carrying twins? Look!" On the screen we could clearly see two little bodies with legs kicking. I felt a mixture of excitement and trepidation. Back and forward went my thoughts. "Wow, God is giving us twins," I thought joyfully. "But that will change our plans to study overseas. How could we take five children to America?" I questioned.

Pressing more urgently on my mind was the question, "How can I look after Ann?" I felt inadequate. She was very tired so we drove to my parent's home at a beach town where I hoped she could get a few days' rest. During the 420-kilometre trip she complained of a sore back. When we got there, she went for a short walk on the beach.

> In the middle of the night, she woke me. "I am having contractions, there is something wrong, you better call an ambulance," she said. I got out of bed and fell on the floor. I felt so overwhelmed by fear that my legs were like jelly. I staggered to my parent's bedroom and collapsed on their bed.
>
> "What is wrong, are you drunk?" mum asked.
>
> "Ann needs an ambulance," I blurted.
>
> The ambulance came. I pulled a track suit on over my pajamas and fortunately put my wallet in my pocket. I was worried. "Is there anything I have done to cause it?"

Jumbled thoughts ran through my mind. Again and again, I would ask this question in my tortured mind. "Could I have done anything to prevent this?" We arrived at the local hospital.

"We only have one humidicrib," the nurses apologized when they realized Ann was having twins. They called two doctors.

One arrived and was briefed by the nurses. He said, "Twenty-six weeks, not much hope," and sat in a chair with his head in a newspaper!

I felt angry. I expressed my feelings to God. "Lord how can this be happening?" Then I prayed earnestly for a good doctor. Little did I realize where that prayer would lead.

The doctor stopped reading the paper and said, "I suppose I should examine her. "After he counted the rate of the contractions he said, "Maybe if I break the waters, a baby will come."

I felt like yelling, "No, keep your hands off her," but didn't. Again, I was conflicted - he was the doctor he should know best.

He broke the waters on one baby and Ann's contractions slowed down. No baby came. Shortly after a doctor with gynecological experience arrived and took over Ann's treatment. After examining Ann, he said, "Call the ambulance, she should go to the children's hospital in the city, two-hundred kilometers away. Then he sat with Ann

# DEATH

and I and explained the situation. He was the first answer to my prayers for a good doctor.

He sat in the back of the ambulance with Ann, and I sat in the front with the driver. I felt both relieved and frightened as we raced along the mountain road. The specialist birthing unit was waiting for us when we arrived at the hospital where the Professor of Gynecology explained that he would have to deliver the babies by caesarian section because the waters were broken. Ann went into the operating theatre, and I waited outside. I thanked God for providing a good doctor, an answer to my prayers, and prayed for our twin boys.

Later, a young doctor came out and said, "The operation was a success, would you like to see your sons?" I was thrilled, but not prepared for the shock I felt when I saw Ian and John. Both were connected to ventilators and covered with aluminum foil to stop them burning from the warmth from the heat lamps.

I sat next to Ian. Gingerly I placed my hand under the foil and held Ian's tiny hand. It felt so frail. I wish I had held John's hand too, but no one told me I was allowed to. Later I saw Ann and felt relieved that she was as well as could be expected.

My mother drove to the city and picked me up. Our three older children were with my father. During the night the hospital rang to say that John had died. Early the next morning they rang to say that Ian had died. Our children climbed into bed with me, and we cuddled close. They wanted to know what had happened. Together we thanked God for Ian and John and prayed for mummy. I rejoiced in this moment of joy in the midst of grief.

In my wallet I found our pastor's phone number. He was on holidays about one hundred kilometers away. Before I reached the hospital the next day, he had already been to visit Ann. We both felt greatly encouraged by this act of love. The nurses were surprised that he had come.

God upheld us as we mourned. He had suffered the death of his son Jesus (Figure 10.1).[4] Our pain was raw, but we have the hope that Ian and John are in heaven with Jesus. A year later Joel was born. We felt greatly blessed by his arrival, a child from God. Our six children are all special in different ways.

One of the doctors gave us a Polaroid photo of Ian. We don't have any other photos, just memories. Camera phones hadn't been invented, and selfies were a thing of the future.

## SELFIES

Everywhere I go today I see people taking selfies. The word 'selfie' first occurred in an Australian news website in 2002. The iPhone went on sale in June 2007, and by November 2013 the use of the word selfie had grown to such an extent that it became the Oxford Dictionaries *Word of the Year*.[5] It seems that we all like to look at images of ourselves. Our Creator likes to see his character in us, as if we are a selfie.

The Creator made a male human and a female human. Both were made in the Creator's image. When He looked at each human it was like looking into a mirror. Only, the Creator saw much more than a flat 2D reflection. He saw more than a 3D image and heard more than a voice.

The image He saw was a mirror of Himself. The mirror reflected the character of the Creator who has characteristics we consider to be both male and female. The Creator gave these characteristics to humans with an

---

[4] illawarramercury.com.au/story/1488289/adored-talented-illawarra-artist-robert-liddicoat-dies/
[5] merriam-webster.com/dictionary/selfie#learn-more

# DEATH

emphasis on male characteristics in the man and female characteristics in the woman.[6] When they united into one, they became a perfect image of the Creator.

The Creator was overjoyed because these were beings that He could relate to. Also, the male and female human had been specially made to relate to each other. The Creator had previously made angels. They were different. They were to serve the Creator by protecting the humans and carrying His messages through the universe.

The male and female humans were a perfect complement. They were designed to enjoy each other and grow in their relationship with the Creator. Like the Creator they could make things, creative things that moved them to praise the Creator. Their job was to bring glory to the Creator by looking after the garden that He had put them in.

The garden was a paradise filled with lush fruit. Velvet and gold wings flashed in the sun as butterflies sucked sweet nectar from brightly colored flowers. Harmonious birdsongs floated in the air. The garden was restful and refreshing. Sparkling drops of water fell from golden lilies into clear ponds where fish swam in lazy schools. The humans spent their days in the garden basking in its glory.

The Creator could have made the humans to be like robots that precisely obey every command He gives them (Figure 10.2).[7] But the Creator didn't. Instead, He gave them the responsibility to choose to obey His commands. To test their commitment to their relationship with the Creator, He gave them just one rule.[8]

If the humans obeyed that one rule, then all would go well. and they would enjoy the Creator's pleasure forever. If they disobeyed that one rule,

---

[6] Jeff Benner, His Name is One, Virtual Bookworm
ancient-hebrew.org/studies-words/meaning-of-el-shaddai.htm
[7] youtube.com/watch?v=Qy3fi9Vvuts
[8] the one rule - Genesis 2:15-17

then they would be unmade. The choice was theirs to make. They had been created good, but would they choose to serve the Creator or try to usurp His rightful place in their lives?

I have been asked, "Why do I need God?" and "How is God relevant to my life?" As he is our Creator, I believe God knows best how we should function mentally, physically, and spiritually. At the deepest level we reflect His image. Our lives are an outworking of being made in the image of God. (Genesis 1:27) But, we have been corrupted by evil.

**Figure 10.2** *Experimental mobile robot made from Lego*

# DEATH

## STORY ABOUT EVIL

Unmake (the unmaker) watched the two humans (man and woman), seeking a chance to unmake them and win a victory over Make (their Creator). Make had done an excellent job of crafting the humans. They were beautiful in every way. Unmake hated that. Previously Unmake had had access to the workshop but he could not match the skill of Make. The workshop was a place of glorious creativity.

Unmake had been a mighty angelic guardian, a model of perfection, full of wisdom and exquisite in beauty. Unmake's clothes were adorned with every precious stone. Make had beautifully tailored these clothes and given them to Unmake on the day he created him. Unmake was blameless in all he did from the day he was created until the day evil was found in him.

Unmake had been the top servant of Make, reflecting Make's glory in every way, until evil turned this angel into Unmake.[9] On that day, Make expelled Unmake from his workshop in disgrace.[10] How Unmake seethed about this change of circumstances. Unmake's dishonest trade had resulted in violence. His heart was filled with pride and with a love of his own splendor.

When Unmake rebelled against Make, about a third of the angels joined him and there was war in the workshop. Unmake's forces were no match for Make's forces and Make threw Unmake and his angels out of the workshop into the garden - the garden Make had created as a home for the humans.

---

[9] Ezekiel 28:14-16
[10] Revelation 12:3-9

## EVIL

The word 'evil' describes both an act and its consequences. It means to cause harm, to make worthless, and to be morally wrong. Evil results in destructive, disagreeable, and offensive behavior. Evil has hurtful effects and harmful influences in the physical, moral, and spiritual realms. Evil has great power to impact our lives in ways we do not suspect. This chapter on death is my attempt to answer the question: how do we make sense of life and death?

Much, but not all, physical evil is due to moral evil. We don't know where evil came from, but we do know that evil occurred in eternity among the angels. Some people hypothesize that logically we can't have good without evil because evil is the opposite of good. Isaiah 45:7 says, "I form the light and create darkness, I bring prosperity and create disaster." Some translations translate "create disaster" as "make evil" and others as "create calamity." Could it be that for people to be free to choose whether to obey God or not He had to create both good and evil?

I believe that God's action of casting Satan out of heaven demonstrates that He is in control, and that He is opposed to evil in all its forms.[11] One premise of this book is that God is a loving God. His love is shown by Jesus who died to reverse the impact of evil on people and on nature. Tragically, our ancestors, Adam, and Eve, chose evil and rebelled against God by disobeying Him.

## REBELLION STORY

Make enjoyed walking with the humans in the cool evening breezes that blew through the garden. They talked about the beauty and care of the

---
[11] Revelation 12"7-10

garden. They saw swaths of colorful flowers: happy faced pansies, midnight lotuses, and regal roses.

They smelled trees that were loaded with deliciously fragrant fruit: delicate peaches, sweet *mangosteens*, and scrumptious mangos. The animals loved to rub their noses on the human's legs as they ran, jumped, and frolicked. Man gave the animals names - names that were suited to their character. Make had given the humans just one rule to obey as they lived in the garden.

"Man," said Make.

"Yes Lord," replied Man.

"See that aromatic fruit tree in the middle of the garden, you must not eat the fruit of that tree."

"Why not?" asked Man.

"It is the tree of the knowledge of good and evil, if you eat its fruit, you will be unmade."

The humans had been warned of the consequences of breaking that one rule. Man, and Woman often looked at the forbidden fruit on that tree and wondered what good and evil were. One day, they were near the middle of the garden. A beautiful aroma wafted from the forbidden fruit.

"Smells nice, what a delightful aroma," whispered a red dragon as he cozied up to Woman.

"Who are you?" Woman asked.

"Falin,[12] your friendly red dragon; I bring a message from the supernatural, I bring you good fortune," lied Unmake who had disguised himself as a red dragon.

"Did Make really say you must not eat the fruit from any of the trees in the garden?" enquired Falin in a slithering voice, seeking to undermine their belief in the one rule.

"Of course, we may eat fruit from the trees in the garden," Woman replied.

"It's only the fruit from the tree in the middle of the garden that we are not allowed to eat." Make said, "You must not eat it or even touch it; if you do, you will be unmade."

"You won't be unmade!" quipped Falin. Make knows that your eyes will be opened as soon as you eat it, and you will be like your maker, knowing both good and evil."

They saw that the forbidden fruit looked delicious and smelled sweet, and they wanted the wisdom it would give them. So, they took some of the fruit and ate it. In an instant, their eyes were opened, they were given a conscience and suddenly they felt shame at their nakedness. Unmake had made Make out to be a liar, by denying the good that would have resulted from them obeying Make's one rule.

## REBELLION

We face the same temptation as the first man and woman: the desire to be like God. We want to run our own lives and not obey the rules that God set

---

[12] studycli.org/chinese-culture/chinese-dragons/

in place when He created the earth and the humans who inhabit it. God's rules are for our own good, but Satan whispers rebellion into our mind: "You don't have to obey God's rules, you will be happy if you do your own thing."

We rebel against God's rules and tell ourselves that we are free to do as we please. Satan tells us lies expertly wrapped in half truths. He tells us that slavery to rebellion is freedom to do as we please. We become like the teenager who carries his iPhone everywhere and who claims that he is free to choose not to use it. However, when he is asked to turn it off, he refuses. He has become a slave to his iPhone.

True freedom is the power to act, speak, and think within externally agreed constraints. Believers in Jesus exercise freedom by obeying His commands. They obey Jesus because He has redeemed them from slavery to rebellion and they have been set free; free to worship God. Obedience results in praise of God because it brings peace and joy. Without the restraint of God's rules freedom may become a license to act, speak and think as we please, without regard to the effect we have on other people. God's commands provide a safe place for us.

An example of people hurting others by rebelling against agreed constraints is greed. To mitigate the effects of rebellion, countries have courts of law to execute justice and hand out punishment on those who disobey the laws of the country. Similarly, I believe that God has judged everyone for their disobedience to his commands and brought down a sentence of death - you are condemned to death. Jesus offers to pay that sentence for you because He loves you.

## LOVE STORY

Unmake cackled out loud, expressing his hideous glee. The humans had broken the one rule and started the process of unmaking Make's creation. The mirror was cracked. When Make looked at the humans He no longer saw a perfect reflection of His image but instead, like looking in a cracked mirror, He saw a broken relationship. A relationship that He would have to fix at His own expense.

Make no longer walked in the garden with the humans, their relationship was broken. Now that they knew good and evil, the humans had a conscience that condemned them every time they choose evil instead of good.

The idyllic relationship between the man and woman was broken too. Instead of meeting one another's needs they selfishly quarreled. Love and respect were warped by a demanding spirit. Instead of caring for the garden they let it grow wild and exploited it. Paradise was lost when they rebelled against Make's one rule and tasted a piece of fruit from the tree in the center of the garden.

> As this section is a story, we can imagine that the Maker's response was to call an emergency meeting to discuss this rebellion. Make, Moshaih (Make's son), Breath (Make's Spirit) and the high angels were in attendance. Make began speaking. "When I made the garden, I laid down laws to govern right living in the garden. Knowing these rules is part of the knowledge of good and evil. The law for rebellion is the Law of Life and Death," said Make.
>
> "I know that law," said Breath. "It states, 'Any being who disobeys just one of Make's rules will be unmade.'"

"So would it be justice to unmake the garden and everything in it, including Man and Woman?" asked Breath.

"But to be just, you have to unmake them; how are you going to avoid executing justice and let them live?" asked Moshaih?

"There is a deeper law, a law known only to me," replied Make.

"What is it?" asked Breath.

"A human who has never rebelled can be unmade in the place of those who have rebelled," replied Make.

"Where are you going to find this human?" asked Moshaih. "The two humans in the garden have both rebelled."

"You - you Moshaih can become a human and be unmade in their place," answered Make.

"Me, I don't want to do it, the pain of separation from you would be too great," cried Moshaih. "Isn't there another way?"

"No, Moshaih, my son, this is the way of love," replied Moshaih's Father.

"You love these humans so much that you would allow your only son to be unmade in their place!" exclaimed Moshaih.

## LOVE

The fact that God did not wipe Adam and Eve out when they sinned is evidence of his love for people. However, his plan required time for the cycle of human life and death to occur. For his Son to become a human, God had to choose a suitable woman with a womb in which his Son could develop like every other human (except Adam and Eve).

God the Father wanted to save as many humans as possible so that he could share the joy of eternal life with them. To do this He let the humans multiply and propagate throughout the earth, even though it would result in pain for all people and eternal death for those who rejected his love. Those who believe in His Son will pass through death, like entering a door, to experience the love of God for eternity.

## STORY OF PAIN

Make visited Man and Woman in the garden to explain to them the curse on their lives that resulted from them breaking his one rule.

> "Man, where are you?"
>
> "I am hiding, I am afraid you will see me naked," replied Man.
>
> "Who told you that you are naked? Have you broken the one rule that I gave you?" asked Make.
>
> "It is Woman's fault, not mine. You created her to help me but instead she led me to break the one rule," replied Man in an aggravated voice.

# DEATH

"Silence," said Make in an angry voice, "Since you listened to Woman rather than to Me the ground is cursed. All your life you are going to struggle against thorns and weeds to raise grain to feed yourself, Woman, and her children."

"You gave me Woman to help me, she gave me some fruit from the tree, and I ate it," blurted out Man, implying it was Make's fault, not his.

Make continued, "Finally, after much painful sweat to earn a living, Unmake will unmake you and you will return to dust."

Then Make turned to Woman, "You disobeyed me!"

"But it's not my fault, I am a victim, Unmake deceived me," cried Woman.

"Woman," the Maker said, "having kids is going to hurt.[13] When you give birth the pain will be severe." Woman looked at him in silence wondering what pain was. Then the Maker continued, "You will also experience pain in your relationship with Man, you will try to control him, but he will rule over you."

Then Make expelled the humans from the garden and from His presence. During their lifetime they would be unmade. Both would suffer pain. Their pain would be different, reflecting their differences. Their pain would be a constant reminder that things are not as they should be.

---

[13] Genesis 3:16

## PAIN

Our society spends huge amounts of money seeking relief from pain. Often, we consider pain to be bad and something to be relieved from. We ask, "Why does God allow pain?" But do we ask, "Why does God allow pleasure?"[14] We often consider pleasure to be desirable and pain to be undesirable. Yet pain is often an indicator that something is wrong while pleasure may not indicate that everything is right. Both pain and pleasure can result from resisting temptation or from giving in to it.

We feel pain when something is wrong with our physical body, or with our mental state, or with our spirit. Pain is like the alarm icons on the dash of your car. Their purpose is to tell you that something is wrong with the car. Yelling at a flashing icon won't fix the car, as much as you would like it to. The icon will stop flashing when you get a mechanic to fix the fault. If you don't deal with the underlying problem, it will get worse.

Yes, pain can be helpful, a blessing from our Maker. Consider the hairs on your arm. Brush them with a knife and you feel the physical sensation of touch, which warns you that danger is immanent. Ignore the sensation and you could cut yourself. Then your body would immediately react with pain to tell you that you have injured yourself.

Physical pain can be caused by an injury to your body, or by the failure of an organ to function properly. Emotional pain can be caused by anxiety about your situation, or by the breaking of a relationship. Moral pain is caused when we act in a way that violates our most deeply held values, or we are in a situation where those values are violated by others.[15] Spiritual pain is caused by the break in your relationship with God and often presents itself as a lack of peace, or a condemning inner voice, or a guilty conscience.

---

[14] Voysey, S. 2005. Unseen Footprints, Openbook Print, page 60.
[15] deploymentpsych.org/blog/staff-perspective-lean-your-moral-pain

# DEATH

In October 2021, Sydney Morning Herald (SMH) reporter Gary Nunn asked, "Why are people who believe in science and that there is no God going to Psychics?"[16] In January 2020, Liam Mannix reported in the SMH that *Australian Skeptics* had tracked almost 4,000 predictions made by 207 psychics in public media over a 20-year period.[17] Only 11% were unambiguously correct.

When the odds are so poor why does anyone consult a psychic? Are they feeling the pain of not knowing why they are here? Or do they feel that life is a roundabout that they wish they could get off, like a spinning top that will eventually stop? (Figure 10.3).[18]

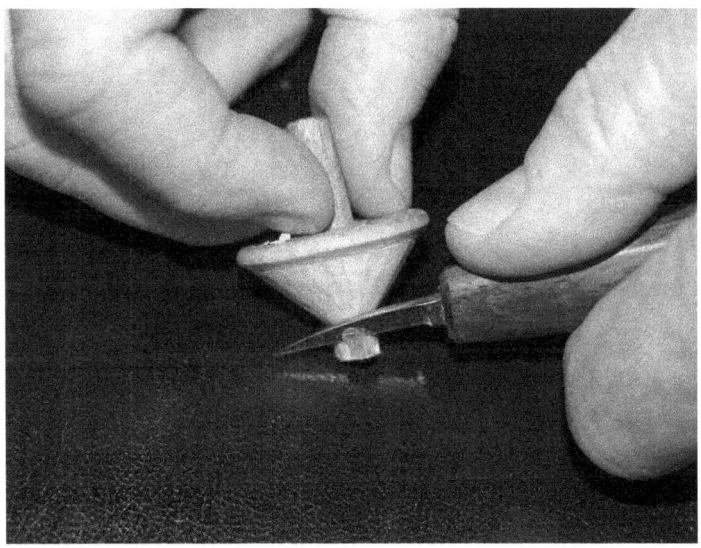

**Figure 10.3** *Carving a spinning top from a cotton reel*

---

[16] smh.com.au/lifestyle/life-and-relationships/therapy-lite-why-scientific-people-go-to-psychics-20210929-p58vm9.html

[17] smh.com.au/national/psychics-mostly-wrong-but-you-may-have-seen-that-coming-20220130-p59sdo.html

[18] McKerrow, P.J. 2010. Carving a Cotton Reel Spinning Top, Australian Woodworker, Issue 151, June, pp 60-61.

Scientists propose a biochemical answer to emotional pain, but they don't have an answer to moral or spiritual pain. A purely rational world view, that does not include a transcendent relationship with Jesus, leaves us spiritually adrift, without an answer to mental pain.

At best, a psychic will tell you what you want to hear. They will probe you with questions about the issue you wish to get guidance on, listen to your answers and observe your reactions. Then they will suggest an answer consistent with their evaluation of your character, and claim it is from the spirit world. You leave satisfied because the psychic has affirmed the answer that you wanted. They have given you false hope.

At worst, if the psychic is genuinely in contact with a spirit, then I believe that the spirit is a demon. A demon will tell you what Satan wants you to hear to lead you away from your Maker. Rather than listening to counsel from a demon, you should flee.

For many of us, the fear of death is not the fear of being dead but rather the fear of the process of dying, particularly when it involves severe pain or disability. The believer in Jesus is looking forward to a meaningful life after death. This gives him strength to face the potentially horrible process of dying.

The NSW parliament recently voted for laws to allow *Voluntary Assisted Dying*. Some proponents justified their support of it based on an atheistic belief that there is no life after death, so in their view death removes the pain. They fail to acknowledge that spending eternity knowing that you have a broken relationship with God is more painful.

One consequence of God making us in His image is that we are considered to be sacred - set apart for God. When a human is killed, a bearer of God's image dies. God created humans to praise Him not to destroy one another. Jesus suffered the pain of crucifixion to enable us to live. We live in a world where many people suffer the pain of broken relationships.

Christians are people whose relationship with God, which was broken, has been made whole and their conduct should show that. The Bible says: "Whatever happens, conduct yourselves in a manner worthy of the gospel of Christ." (Philippians 1:27). Broken relationships are the root cause of many problems people face.

## BROKEN RELATIONSHIPS

Our concept of what it is to be a person comes from our beliefs. In the Western tradition, this concept came from the teaching of Jesus and has been constant for centuries. However, during the last three decades, it has been challenged repeatedly as Western society replaces a Christian worldview with an atheistic world view.

The Bible defines a person in terms of relationship. We are who we are because of our relationships with God, and with one another, not because of how attractive, influential, or intelligent we are. The key relationship, for a person to have, is their relationship with God. This relationship gives both meaning and purpose to life. This relationship is summarized in the gospel as a covenant between God, as Creator, and people, His creation.

First, God created people to love, serve, and enjoy him forever. Second, he gave people the choice of worshiping Him or of worshiping themselves by putting themselves at the center of their lives. The first humans chose to go their own way. This choice broke their relationship with their Creator and the blessings of that relationship were replaced by the curses of separation, including selfishness, physical decay, and a hardening of their attitude to God.

In an ideal relationship people respect one another and do not abuse one another. Citizenship is based on a shared world view. While we may not agree with someone, we respect their right to have a different opinion. When their relationship is broken people try to control one another.

People who want political power in a country join the popular religion of that country and become zealots for it. The January 6, 2021, attack on the United States Capitol Building in Washington by a mob dramatically shows one extreme that relationship breakdown can go to. Another extreme breakdown is war.

## WAR

War results from the breakdown of relationships either between countries or with terrorist groups within countries. The breakdown is so great that we legalize murder of the enemy. We employ soldiers to protect us by murdering the enemy.

I visited a fellow researcher in machine echolocation (ultrasonic sensing) in Vienna who drove Ann and I through a wild thunderstorm to a beef restaurant for dinner, where we met his wife. She told us that she was studying the impact of the Protestant Reformation in Europe (1517 AD onward) on the politics of Europe.

She had spent a lot of time reading the court records, in old German, of many of the German Principalities. She found that when Vienna was besieged in 1526 and 1532 AD by Turkish Muslims, the Holy Roman Emperor requested that the princes provide forces to repel the Muslim invaders.[19] The protestant princes agreed to the request on the condition that they were given their freedom from the rule of the Empire to become independent states. Christian Europe fought back against the invasions, pushing the armies of Islam out of Europe.

---

[19] Stark, R. 2009. God's Battalions, The Case for the Crusades, Harper Collins, New York.

# DEATH

Many critics of Christianity blame Christians for these religious wars, particularly the crusades. The crusades were a European response to Asian invasion. Rewriting history is a subtle way of discrediting people. Christians have fought in wars mainly to defend their countries from invasion. Jesus did not condone Christians starting a war. There are many wars where Christians did not behave according to Jesus' directions, and they should repent.

More people were killed by atheists in the 20th century than in all the religious wars in recorded history.[20] Hitler, Stalin, Mao Zedong, Pol Pot, and Idi Amin were responsible for the massacre and the starvation of millions of people. They are all considered to be atheists even though some had a religious upbringing. All thought they were above the demands of justice.

## JUSTICE

We live in a world that cries out for justice. When God's rules are ignored, children are abused, people are massacred, and the poor are exploited. When the punishment handed out by human courts doesn't fit the crime people rightly cry out for justice. But what about when we break one of God's rules, do we cry out for justice then?

Many people ask, "If God is loving why does he allow suffering?" These questioners often reason that God is either not loving or non-existent. Do these questioners think about the excruciating pain that Jesus suffered when he died on the cross for them? His death is where God's justice and love can be found.

> "He himself bore our sins
> in his body on the cross,

---

[20] thescottsmithblog.com/2019/05/is-religion-responsible-for-most-wars.html

> so that we might die to sins
> and live for righteousness;
> by his wounds you have been healed."
> (1 Peter 2:24)

When God allowed people choice between good and evil, he allowed suffering to be a consequence of bad choice. When the first humans rebelled, suffering entered the human experience. The purpose of pain is to tell us that things are not right. Suffering will remain while we continue to rebel against God. It will only be removed when God creates the new earth.

A follow-up question is: "Why does the little old lady who tells lies go to the same place as a terrorist who kills people?" Both have broken at least one of God's laws, and both can be forgiven if they believe that Jesus died in their place to pay for the punishment they deserve. The opportunity to be forgiven for your rebellion is open to everyone, no matter how sinful they are. It is a gift.

We have seen that evil came into the world when Satan tempted the first humans to become like God, knowing good and evil. In response, God acted in justice. All people were condemned to perish. God's wrath is the execution of the punishment for disobedience not a petulant whim.

## MERCY

God is merciful as well as just. He wants to forgive our sin, but he must punish us for it, or he ceases to be just. Jesus stepped into our shoes to suffer the punishment that we deserve. He can offer mercy to us because he suffered our punishment. As a result, the only way to be forgiven for our rebellion against God is to believe in Jesus. Then God will act in mercy and forgive us.

# DEATH

The worldview of many people in the West, particularly atheists is:

> "If this life is all there is
> then enjoy your life,
> fulfil your dreams,
> and avoid death."

This world view is the conclusion King Solomon came to thousands of years ago when he observed how hard people work for money that they can't take with them into eternity: "This is what I have observed to be good: that it is appropriate for a person to eat, to drink and to find satisfaction in their toilsome labor under the sun during the few days of life God has given them—for this is their lot." (Ecclesiastes 5:18).

Is survival of the fittest part of God's creation or is it a result of the rebellion of the first humans? Before Adam and Eve rebelled, God described his creation as being good. Is the survival of the fittest good? A natural outcome of the survival of the fittest is that the elderly, the weak and the vulnerable do not survive or get looked after. Is that justice?

People cannot please God by their own efforts because they have inherited a rebellious nature. Jesus, the Son of God, came to earth to obey God in everything and then to die in our place. God raised Jesus from the dead to show that his sacrifice was accepted. Now Jesus offers us eternal life as a free gift if we believe his offer.

## JUDGMENT

One consequence of you having a broken relationship with God is that when you were born physically you were already spiritually dead. When Adam and Eve rebelled, they immediately died spiritually. To become spiritually alive, you must believe in Jesus and receive the Holy Spirit. If the Holy Spirit does not live in you then you have no relationship with God.

God is often criticized for sending people who do not believe in Jesus to eternal punishment. At the final judgment of all people God will not ask us, "Have you been bad or good?" He will ask, "Do you know my son?" We are given this life to answer that question.

If you say, "I believe Jesus died for me, thank you for giving me a relationship with you," then He will invite you into His home in eternity. If you say, "No I was not interested in a relationship with Jesus in this life," then He will give you what you want: eternity without a relationship with Jesus. Either way you will get what you want.

The last thing each one of us will do on this earth is die. People who do not believe in God have no solution to death. They hope that they will simply cease to exist. Many culturally religious people are not sure whether their god will save them. They vainly hope that their good deeds will outweigh their bad deeds and save them from perishing. Salvation is a gift, accept it and Jesus will welcome you into eternity.

In the Bible, people who believe in Jesus are promised that they have eternal life. They are certain that they are going to heaven because Jesus died for them. Many verses in the Bible confirm this, such as:

> "And this is the testimony:
> God has given us eternal life, and this life is in his Son.
> Whoever has the Son has life;
> whoever does not have the Son of God does not have life."
> (1 John 5:11-12)

## CIVILIZATION

God's judgment on rebellion affects human society as well as individual people. A group of people can develop the cohesion required to form a civilization if they all practice the same values. Values are an outward expression of beliefs, which are derived from the axioms of their common religion. When a society rejects those axioms, moral values, as defined by the religion, collapse and the civilization decays. In a comment on the collapse of civilizations, Philosopher of History Arnold Toynbee wrote:

> "Each time a nation has lost faith in its religion its civilization has succumbed to domestic social disintegration, or foreign military attack, or economic enslavement. The civilization that has fallen as a result of the loss of this faith has been replaced by a new civilization inspired by a different faith or religion."[21]

In recent decades there has been a progressive rejection of Christian moral values and the consequent pain caused by relationship breakdowns. Not that people were more Christian in the past but that the prevalence of Christian thought constrained, and tragically, at times, hid immorality, corruption, and domestic violence.

When the Bible is faithfully taught in churches it is a powerful preventative of evil and a promoter of good. Distinguished Professor of the Social Sciences at Baylor University, Byron Johnson, is an authority in both the scientific study of religion and criminal justice. In his book *More God, Less Crime* he proves that religion can be a powerful antidote to crime.[22]

---

[21] lifeunderstanding.com/when-religion-fails-the-predictions-of-historian-arnold-toynbee/
[22] Byron Johnson 2012. More God, Less Crime: Why Faith Matters and How It Could Matter More, Templeton Press

Both men and women should be taught to obey Jesus' commands. For example, domestic violence is now a major issue that our police must contend with. Mary Eberstadt is an American author of books on social issues. In her book *Adam and Eve After the Pill: Paradoxes of The Sexual Revolution*, she contends that sexual freedom has paradoxically produced widespread discontent.[23]

In Ephesians 5:33 the Bible commands men to love their wives as they love themselves. Based on this command, men should be taught to not abuse their wives but to put their wives' needs first. In the same verse the Bible teaches women to respect their husbands. Based on this command, women should be taught not to run down their husbands but to build up their self-esteem. When writing to a decaying nation, the prophet Micah spells out the requirements for a just society.

> "He has shown you, O mortal, what is good.
> And what does the LORD require of you?
> To act justly and to love mercy
> and to walk humbly with your God."
> (Micah 6:8)

## UNMAKING

[24]Jan stood at the door of my office looking very sad. Then she said, "My brother has just been diagnosed with cancer, he has only a few months to live." She thought for a bit and said, "Atheism has no answer to death." A few months later her brother died. Jan found no comfort in her atheistic beliefs.

---

[23] Adam and Eve After the Pill: Paradoxes of The Sexual Revolution
[24] True story, names changed

## DEATH

Unmaking reaches its finality when the physical body dies. Up to that moment each person has the opportunity to believe in the Son of the Maker and be rebuilt for eternal life. A new physical body is available in eternity to every person who believes in the Maker's son.

Meanwhile, the Unmaker continuously works to stop us believing. Our unmaking is the result of our rebellion. At our final unmaking we will receive what we asked for in this life. Either we will be made anew to live on the new earth that God will create, or we will spend eternity without God.

Looking forward to spending eternity with Jesus, C. S. Lewis, wrote, "I believe in Christianity as I believe the sun has risen - not only because I see it, but because by it I see everything else."[25]

God the Father raised Jesus the Son from death so that he could remake everything and offer us a place in His new creation. Death is not inviting, and we want to deny that it exists. The Maker's son will save you from death and remake you if you believe in Him.

---

[25] cslewisinstitute.org/node/44

# 11

# JESUS

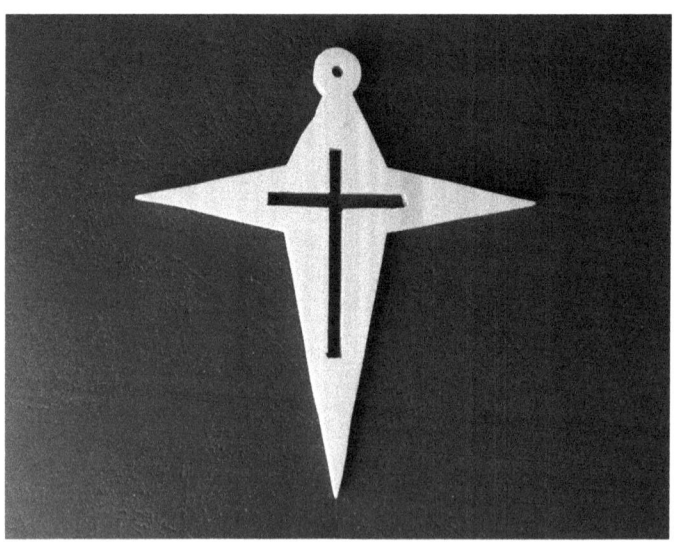

**Figure 11.1** *Life of Jesus Christmas decoration. The star is the symbol of His birth and the cross is the symbol of His death.*

"Christianity was also, to my surprise, radical – far more radical than the leftist ideologies with which I had previously been enamored. The love of God was unlike anything which I expected, or of which I could make sense. In becoming fully human in Jesus, God behaved decidedly unlike a god." - Dr. Sarah Irving-Stonebraker, Senior Lecturer in Modern European History at Western Sydney University, 2017.[1]

"I'm a professor of nuclear science and engineering at MIT, and today, I am celebrating the resurrection of Jesus. So are dozens of my colleagues. How can this be?" - Professor Ian Hutchinson. 2018.[2]

"My first surprise was meeting Christians who actually believed their faith – and in a thoughtful, intelligent way." - Assistant Professor Mark Shepard, Harvard University, 2019.[3]

"What are we to make of Jesus Christ?" - C.S. Lewis, 1950.[4]

"We have caught the first glimpse of our own instruction book, previously known only to God." - Francis Collins, then leader of the Human Genome Project, 2000.[5]

---

[1] solas-cpc.org/how-oxford-and-peter-singer-drove-me-from-atheism-to-jesus/
[2] Hutchinson, I. 2018. Can a Scientist Believe in Miracles? An MIT Professor Answers Questions on God and Science (Veritas Books) IVP
[3] christianunion.org/publications-media/christian-union-the-magazine/past-issues/spring-2019/2332-shepard-found-the-truth-at-harvard
[4] youtu.be/yGU2JN2a3Cs
[5] https://www.newyorker.com/news/persons-of-interest/faith-science-and-francis-collins

## SONIA

Sonia flung open the door of the train compartment, threw her bag on a spare seat, and slammed the door behind her as she disappeared, heading to the toilet. [6] Ann and I were seated in this compartment, travelling from Vienna in Austria to Ljubjana in Slovenia by train.

Sonia had spent the weekend with her boyfriend and was on her way home. When she returned to the compartment, she was still quite agitated and took a while to settle. Like many young adults in Europe, she told us that she was angry with the church. She felt that it didn't care for the people. It was more interested in riches and ritual.

Also, she complained that when her local priest moved into his pension (unit) on retirement, his female housekeeper moved in too. She didn't think that it was right. His life didn't match the church's moral values. Sonia didn't appear to see the contradiction between her attitude to the priest and her lifestyle with her boyfriend. We spent some time discussing the belief that Christianity is about a loving relationship with Jesus and it is not a ritual.

## ATTITUDE

At the beginning of this book, we explored the Maker Movement, and asked the question: Is there a master maker, an infinitely capable maker who made us makers to be like himself? We end it with the man Jesus who was made, unmade and remade. He offers us the opportunity to be remade. The fret work in Figure 11.1 [7] represents his life from His birth announced by a star to His death on a cross.

---

[6] True story, name changed
[7] McKerrow, P.J. 2014. Making Christmas Tree Decorations with a Scroll Saw, Australian Woodworker, Issue 178, December, pp38-43.

# JESUS

A person's attitude to Jesus is often a reflection of their experience of the church. The church is intended to be the representative of Jesus on earth, but many churches are poor ambassadors. Many of the students that I have met in Europe have expressed their anger at the church. Like many Australian students lots of international students consider the church and Jesus to have no relevance to their lives.

Chinese students have been taught that people who believe in religion are weak. Most know virtually nothing about Jesus. One student said to me: "All I knew about Jesus in China was as a swear word in western movies." Also, I have met students who consider themselves to be Christian but are not committed to following Jesus. Other students have a worldview where science is the ultimate authority and Jesus is not important.

A child of an unmarried mother and a refugee, Jesus was the stepson of a maker who worked in timber and stone. As a child, He learned his maker skills from His stepfather, and He learned the Hebrew Scriptures (Old Testament) in synagogue school.[8]

He was praised by those, often marginalized, people who experienced his love. His public teaching and miracles drew large crowds, making him a wanted man by the religious leaders. He was hated by those in authority who saw Him as a threat to their position. He died the death of a criminal, condemned by an illegal trial. We will see that there is much more to the life of Jesus: a spiritual dimension where He is remade. Does this description fit your image of Jesus?

When we were discussing the content of this chapter, my friend Anne Marie asked me, "How does a highly rational STEM and data driven society have any room for a virgin birth and the other miracles of Jesus?" Then she answered her own question, "The forgiveness and love of God are immeasurable."

---

[8] Wight, F.H. 1953. Manners and Customs of Bible Lands, Moody Press, Chicago, p 115

## REMAKING

"Grandad, tell us about the remaking of Jesus?" The boy asked.

Grandad thought for a bit and then said, "God the father watched two humans struggle to take the body of Jesus down off the wooden cross where he had died."

"What did they do with it?" Asked the boy.

"They took it to a cave that had been made as a burial place for one of the humans," replied Grandad. "Then they coated the body with spices, wrapped it in strips of cloth and placed it on a stone slab in the cave."

"Did they just leave it there?" Asked the boy.

"No, they rolled a heavy stone across the entrance."

"So that was the end of Jesus," said the boy.

"The authorities hoped so, but just to be sure they had soldiers guard the tomb so that no one could steal the body. The Father sent a couple of angels to open the tomb. The angels gave the soldiers such a fright that they fainted. When His discipes looked in the tomb, there was no body. It was a mystery. The cloth he had been wrapped in looked like an empty cocoon wrapped around the space where the body should have been."

"Wow, how scary," said the boy. "No body! Then why do we worship Jesus?"

Grandad smiled and continued, "Earlier in the day, while hanging on the cross, Jesus had cried out, 'It is finished,' meaning he had paid the penalty that humans are due for their rebellion. Then his spirit left his body.'"

"So where did his spirit go?" asked the boy.

"I know," chirped in the girl who had been pretending not to listen. "The Father took the body of Jesus out of the tomb and remade it as a spiritual body and gave it back to Jesus."

"How can that be true?" exclaimed the boy. "I've never heard of a person being remade!"

"We know it is true because there are over 500 witnesses who say they saw Jesus walking around in His new spiritual body. On a couple of occasions, He walked through a wall into a closed room," replied Grandad.

"Only an infinitely powerful remaker could do that!" said the girl.

## QUESTIONS AND DOUBTS

I believe that Jesus loves me enough to be unmade and remade for me, yet there have been times when I doubted the existence of a loving God. I have thought that the complexity of nature requires an unbelievably intelligent God, a God whose love is too fantastic to be true. As I have prayed about these doubts, The Holy Spirit has given me a deeper understanding of both God and faith.

When asked if he ever doubted, the Christian evangelist, John Chapman, replied, "Yes, I experience times of doubt, but then I come back to the fact that I believe Christianity is true and I no longer doubt."

I believe that each of us is faced with a choice. A choice of whether we believe that Jesus is both God and human or not. Choosing to trust in Jesus has made a huge difference to what I have done in my life, to my sense of purpose in living, and to my love of making. My faith gives my making a purpose. As Bob Dylan sang:

> "You gotta serve somebody.
> It might be the Devil,
> or it might be the Lord,
> but you gotta serve somebody,"
> Bob Dylan, 1979, Columbia Records.

## ARE THE GOSPELS RELIABLE?

Our choice to believe or not is influenced by whether we think the information we have is accurate and therefore reliable. An example of the accuracy of information from the past is *The Great Wave*, a famous color woodblock print by the Japanese artist Katsushika Hokusai. (Figure 11.2) [9]. It is the first print in his series of thirty-six views of Mt Fuji. The image depicts an enormous wave threatening to swamp three boats off the coast of Japan.

---

[9] wikipedia.org/wiki/The_Great_Wave_off_Kanagawa

**Figure 11.2** *The Great Wave off Kanagawa, Color woodblock Print, Katsushika Hokusai, 1831*

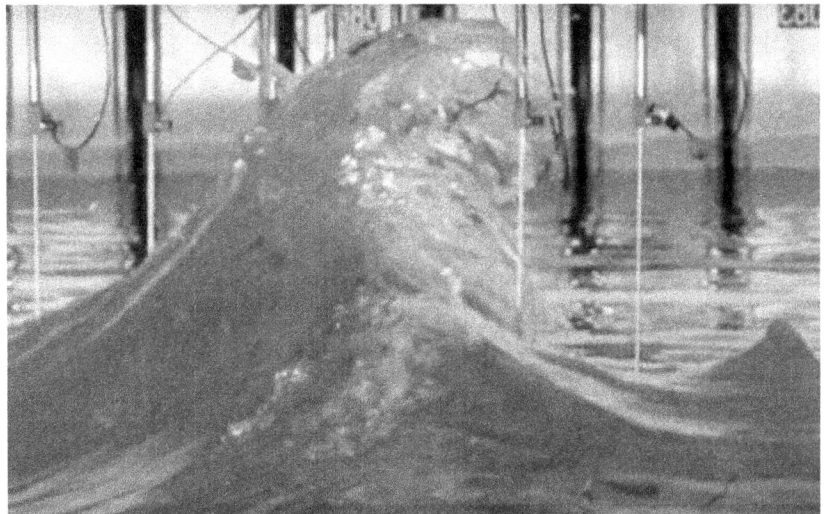

**Figure 11.3** *Waves crossing at 120 degrees in water tank, 2019, Oxford and Edinburgh Universities*

For nearly 200 years, from 1831 to 2019, people have argued about whether the image is of a rogue wave, or a tsunami, or a creation of the artist's imagination. Many people considered it to be too fantastic to be an actual wave until a team of researchers from Oxford and Edinburgh Universities built a large water tank for research into rogue waves.

They found that they could produce a wave that looks like the one in the woodblock image at the intersection of two sets of smaller waves crossing at 120 degrees (Figure 11.3) [10]. The superposition of the peaks and troughs of the small wave trains resulted in a large breaking wave. A conflict between what the artist saw and what people could believe was solved by investigation.

Similarly, if you want to know the truth about Jesus, you should investigate his life. The major sources for information about Jesus are the first four books in the New Testament. Matthew, Mark, Luke, and John are eyewitness accounts of Jesus' life, making them credible historical documents.

Matthew wrote his biography for Jewish readers with a significant focus on the claim that Jesus fulfilled the prophesies of a coming King that are recorded in the Old Testament. John focuses on the relationship between Jesus and God with the aim of reinterpreting the Jewish religious and cultural festivals in the light of Jesus being the promised King. Mark is believed to have written down the teaching of Peter, one of Jesus' chief followers.

Luke is a historian who, after he became a follower of Jesus, conducted a thorough investigation of the life of Jesus, which is recorded in his biography. He introduces it with the following claim to historical accuracy.

> "Many have undertaken to draw up an account of the things that have been fulfilled among us, just as they were

---

[10] Thompson, A. 2019. Scientists Made a Wave in a Lab That Looks Almost Exactly Like a Famous Artwork, Popular Mechanics, January 25 popularmechanics.com/science/environment/a26030593/rogue-wave-lab-kanagawa/

handed down to us by those who, from the first, were eyewitnesses and servants of the Word. With this in mind, since I myself have carefully investigated everything from the beginning, I too decided to write an orderly account for you, most excellent Theophilus, so that you may know the certainty of the things you have been taught." (Luke 1:1-4).

Dr John Dickson, Senior Lecturer in Public Christianity at Ridley College, claims that all reputable historians of the first century believe that we have verifiable copies of these four biographies. They agree that Jesus lived, taught His followers, was executed by the authorities, and was buried by friends. Some historians are uncomfortable with the idea that He came back to life. In an article about reasons for trusting the Bible in Eternity Magazine, Dickson argues that the gospels are *accurate historical biographies*.

> "Between the 1970s and '90s, a consensus emerged among experts that the gospels have to be read as "biographies" of a real individual. They share many similarities – in length, structure, design and content – with the 20-30 other biographies from the period. So they have to be read as real-world accounts of the sayings and deeds of a first-century individual." - Dickson (2017).[11]

Tom Wright, senior research fellow at Wycliffe Hall at the University of Oxford, and Michael Bird support this claim in their illustrated book: *The New Testament in Its World: An Introduction to the History, Literature, and Theology of the First Christians*.[12] They describe the New Testament books as historical, literary, and social phenomena located in the world of Second

---

[11] eternitynews.com.au/good-news/10-reasons-you-can-trust-the-bible/
[12] Wright, T. And Bird, M. 2019. The New Testament in Its World: An Introduction to the History, Literature, and Theology of the First Christians, Zondervan Academic.

Temple Judaism. Both these academics conclude that the Bible is accurate and reliable.

## GOD OF LOVE

The accuracy and reliability of the Bible gives us reason to trust its message. It presents Jesus as the epitome of God's love for people. God blesses those who respond to His love by believing in Jesus. God punishes those who rebel as an act of discipline to encourage them to believe. God forgives those who genuinely say they are sorry for their rebellion. Often people, who don't know Jesus accuse God of not being loving because he holds them to account for their rebellion. Others say that if God is loving He would not allow people to suffer.

In a discussion with Jordan Peterson, comedian Stephen Fry claimed that the existence of evil is a reason for not believing in a loving God.[13] He uses the example of a bug, in Africa, that burrows into children's eyes and causes blindness. In his option God is either an utter maniac who is not loving because he allows the bug to continue to exist, or there is no God. Yet Fry loves the ritual of the church and the depth of meaning in the words that describe a sacrament (baptism, communion) as - an outward and visible sign of an inward and invisible grace.

Rather than blaming Him for allowing the bug that causes blindness God expects us to do something about it, such as finding a way to eliminate the bug. In contrast to Fry, Dr Paul Brand praises God for pain.[14] Brand discovered that the deformities in the hands and feet of lepers are all the result of a single cause - painlessness. Leprosy silences nerve cells

---

[13] youtube.com/watch?v=EVSZrnxRO3o&t=145s
[14] Brand, P. And Yancey, P. 2018, Fearfully and Wonderfully, The Marvel of Bearing God's Image, Hodder

so that when people hurt themselves, they don't feel pain in the infected area of their body. Without a sense of pain, lepers unintentionally harm themselves.

The first humans made a decision that impacted the whole human race. Prior to that decision, people did not know evil, but when God's enemy, Satan, said that they could be like God - they chose to listen to the voice of evil. To be like God means to take control of and to accept responsibility for your actions. They went from being innocent dwellers in a perfect garden, for which God took responsibility, to being responsible in a suffering world.

The humans had been warned that if they disobeyed God by eating the fruit from the tree in the middle of the garden they would die. They ate and not only did they die but animals, plants, and even planets died also. All kinds of evil entered into their lives. Now, we are responsible for helping to alleviate the suffering that resulted from our rebellion but, instead of taking that responsibility, many people blame God.

At this point, God was faced with a choice, either to let the earth and all its inhabitants continue, even though they would suffer pain and disease, or to wipe out everything and start again. He chose to let the human race continue and put into action a rescue plan where the punishment required by justice was executed, but at the same time humans could be forgiven. Jesus loved the people He had created so much that He chose to endure their punishment and suffer their pain.

The love of God is a Christian concept. It doesn't occur in other religions. They do not have a divine rescue plan. Love is the act of caring for another person, often at great cost, especially when they don't deserve it. "God showed his great love for us by sending Christ to die for us while we were still sinners" (Romans 5:8). Only the Christian God became a human to save us from perishing.

## BIRTH OF JESUS

The divine rescue plan required a human who had never rebelled and thus was not under the curse of death - someone who had an untarnished relationship with God. No man or woman living on earth met these criteria because every human spirit was dead, that is every human had no relationship with God except when God's Holy Spirit entered into them to enable them to perform a specific task.

When God created a body for the first man Adam to live in, He breathed into Adam the breath of life and he became a living spirit. When Adam disobeyed God his spirit died, even though his body lived on for many years. A second Adam was needed, so God asked His son, Jesus, to become a human.

God chose Mary, a devout young woman who believed in him, to become the surrogate mother for Jesus (Luke 1:30,31). Then he created a new living cell containing Jesus' DNA and the Holy Spirit placed that cell in Mary's womb to develop and grow into a fetus. When he was born, she named Him Jesus because He would save His people from their sins. This claim of virgin birth has been ridiculed for centuries but the development of in-vitro fertilization shows that God could do it.

A Chinese student asked me, "Why did God choose a Jewish woman to be the mother of Jesus, why didn't he choose a Chinese woman?" Part of the answer is that about 1800 years before the birth of Jesus, God had chosen to bless the peoples on earth through Abraham (Genesis 12:3). Both Mary and Joseph were descendants of Abraham. Jesus is the promised blessing. God had chosen a Jewish woman to be his mother because of the long history of God entering into a relationship with the descendants off Abraham. This history is recorded in the Old Testament and was taught to Jesus in synagogue school.

## LIFE OF JESUS

Jesus was not only a unique person, he had a unique personality. In the garden of Eden, Satan tempted Adam and Eve to be like God. Ever since then, Satan continues to tempt us to be god in our own lives. In contrast, Jesus did not grasp at being God but rather chose to serve God. Jesus is the only human who always obeyed the Father.

Jesus' actions and teachings are recorded for us in the New Testament. He knew the prophesies in the Old Testament that a messiah would come to save people, understood that He was the messiah, and lived in obedience to His heavenly Father. He taught that He was not an earthly king but the supreme ruler of the spiritual world. He demonstrated this by healing the sick, walking on water, and casting evil spirits out of people.

But his teaching was radical. He honored the women who followed him by treating them as equal with the men, but different to the men. He called out the corruption of the religious leaders. He rebuked the rich for not caring for the poor. He fought with a sword of love not with a sword of iron. People were moved to repent of their rebellion when they heard Him speak. He revealed the glory of God to His close followers.

Everywhere Jesus went people followed, like a procession. He walked the length and breadth of Canaan teaching the people. Close to Jesus were the twelve - men specifically chosen to start the church. Following the twelve were the women who funded his ministry and cared for his needs. After the women came many believers. Following them were the sick hoping for his attention. Finally came the sightseers, including the spies for his enemies.

## DEATH OF JESUS

On his last trip to Jerusalem, Jesus strode along with steely purpose. His appearance caused the crowd to fear Him and His disciples to hold Him in awe. He was a man on a mission. He was going to Jerusalem to die at the hands of the religious leaders who should have been worshiping Him.

For many people, the idea that God would die to save people is hard to accept. We are talking about a God who loves the people He created and desires to save them from the punishment of death that they deserve. All other gods, including you and me, are selfish. We need to change our concept of God from a self-serving despot to a loving Savior.

Physically, Jesus' death was a very cruel affair. Crucifixion has been described as a most horrible way to die. After being whipped, Jesus was nailed to a cross. His feet overlapped so one nail held both of them to the vertical pole. His arms were spread, and His hands nailed to the cross bar. When He pulled himself up with His arms to relieve the pain in His feet, He felt excruciating pain in His hands. When He slumped forward on His hands, He could not breathe, forcing Him to pull Himself up on His arms again. This cycle of asphyxiation and pain continued for six hours.

Jesus' spiritual suffering was worse than His physical suffering. He suffered the death of every human who ever lived. Just think of one thing you have done wrong and how much guilt you may have felt. Now multiply that by all the sins of everyone who ever lived. The result was total separation from His Father. No wonder he cried, "Eli, Eli, lema sabachthani?" (which means "My God, my God, why have you forsaken me?") while enduring the spiritual pain of separation from his Father. (Matthew 27:46).

After six hours Jesus cried, "It is finished," gave up His spirit, and died (John 19:30). The soldiers who crucified Him confirmed that He was dead by thrusting a spear into His side. Out flowed a liquid that looked like blood and water. This outflow suggests that a spear had pierced both His heart (blood) and His lungs (water). If He wasn't already dead the spear thrust would have killed Him.

Two men, stirred to bravery by this unjust crucifixion, took Jesus' body down off the cross, wrapped it in spice laden cloth, and temporarily buried it in a rolling stone tomb. The authorities confirmed the location of the body, rolled a stone across the entrance to the tomb and assigned soldiers to guard it. Jesus was dead and buried. The religious leaders were glad to be rid of Him, or so they thought!

## RESURRECTION OF JESUS

Two mornings later, the soldiers guarding the tomb fainted in fear when a glorious angel, whose face shone like lightening, rolled the stone aside and sat on it. Inside, the tomb was empty, the body of Jesus was gone. All that was left were the spice laden cloths hardened into a body shaped cocoon, but there was no body in the cocoon. That sight was enough to convince some of the disciples that Jesus had risen from the dead.

The claim that women were the first witnesses to the resurrection is seen by many as evidence that the resurrection actually happened. In a society where women were regarded as inferior to men, and thus unreliable witnesses, it is highly unlikely that someone would make up a story with women as the chief witnesses.

If Jesus rose from the dead, then the message about Jesus offering us salvation is the most important message we will ever receive. However, if Jesus did not rise from the dead then Christianity is a dangerous hoax. The most powerful evidence for the resurrection is that over five hundred people saw Jesus after He rose.

There have been many attempts to disprove the resurrection. The first was by the religious authorities who bribed the soldiers on guard to say that the disciples stole the body. However, no one has ever found the body, let alone explained how it was stolen. Another is that He was not dead and that He only fainted on the cross and recovered in the cave. The circumstances of the crucifixion make this highly improbable.

Many people who have set out to disprove the resurrection by thorough investigation have concluded that it is a historical fact. Frank Morison and Lee Strobel are two such people. Frank Morison, set out to disprove the resurrection of Jesus, by analyzing the scriptures and historical sources. He aimed to dispel what he believed was a myth and present it in a short paper titled *Jesus – the Last Phase*. However, the findings of his research changed his life. He became a firm believer in the resurrection of Christ and presented his meticulous research in a book.[15]

Lee Strobel was an atheist working for The *Chicago Tribune*, when his wife decided to believe in Jesus. He set out to use his investigative skills, which he had developed as a journalist, to prove to his wife that she was mistaken. He became known for his 'bulldog-like tenacity' as he interviewed 13 religious scholars to examine the evidence for a historical Jesus. This study changed his mind, and he became a believer too. Convinced of the resurrection of Jesus he has written many books on faith.[16]

Tom Wright, senior research fellow at Wycliffe Hall at the University of Oxford, studied ancient beliefs about life after death. In his book, *The Resurrection of the Son of God,* he concluded that the early Christians called Jesus the *Son of God* because the tomb was empty and the consequent belief that Jesus really did rise bodily from the dead.[17]

God proved that Jesus' death was effective in achieving justice by raising Him from the dead (1 Corinthians 15:3-8). The same God will remake the people who believe in Jesus. Paul the apostle wrote: "So will it be with the resurrection of the dead. The body that is sown is perishable, it is raised

---

[15] amazon.com/Who-Moved-Stone-Christian-Classics/dp/1521209677/
[16] christianchronicle.org/conversation-lee-leslie-strobel/
[17] Wright T. 2012. The Resurrection of the Son of God, SPCK.

imperishable; it is sown in dishonor, it is raised in glory; it is sown in weakness, it is raised in power; it is sown a natural body, it is raised a spiritual body." (1 Corinthians 15:42 to 44).

Christians claim that the only way into heaven is to receive eternal life by God's grace, through faith as a gift from Jesus. The grace of God is in direct conflict with the teaching of all other religions. It refutes the claim that people can save themselves. As a result, worshiping other gods leads to eternal death. Keeping a set of rules may lead to a moral life but it doesn't save us from perishing.[18]

## IMPACT OF JESUS

Over the centuries, since the resurrection, Jesus has been represented by the people who believe in Him. When they meet to worship Jesus, they are the church. They share in fellowship, prayer, singing, Bible reading and preaching - often around a meal.

The Bible teaches that when you believe in Jesus the Holy Spirit comes into your life and begins a cleanup process to remove both your sin and its effects on your life. I have seen the impact for good that the Holy Spirit has on the lives of people.

The church has created many organizations to help the poor, the sick, and the socially disadvantaged - as well as to tell people the good news of eternal life through belief in Jesus. The following three examples of the impact of Christianity show how people all over the globe have benefited from contact with Christians.

---

[18] Christians believe that the bible is the source of truth about God which is revealed to the reader by the Holy Spirit, and no other source is needed. They believe that salvation is by faith in Jesus alone, that eternal life is a gift from God and cannot be earned, that Christ is the only mediator between people and God, and all should be done for God's glory.

The first example occurred in my office. I was walking down a corridor in the Computer Science department at the UOW when a student came up to me with a big grin on his face. He took my hand and shook it. He said, "I took your advice."

"Ah, what advice?" I blurted out.

"I became a Christian," he replied. After a short discussion, he went on his way.

Feeling surprised, I eventually remembered a conversation that I had had with him. A year previously he had sat in my office and shared his problems with both study and life.

When a student comes to me for help with a university subject, I give it. In the process, some students share personal problems. When they do I offer to tell them about Jesus. If they are interested, then we discuss Jesus' resurrection. At the end of the discussion, I offer to pray for them. Most people have welcomed my offer of prayer.

The second example is the Clapham Sect,[19] a group of evangelical Christians, led by William Wilberforce[20] who lobbied the British parliament for social justice for slaves and prisoners during the early nineteenth century, resulting in the abolition of slavery in the United Kingdom in 1807.

The third example shows the positive impact of Christian missionaries in Africa. When Tony Rinaudo arrived in Niger, on the edge of the Sahara, with his family, to work with World Vision planting trees, he found the farming land was unproductive due to massive deforestation and resultant

---

[19] wikipedia.org/wiki/Clapham_Sect
[20] wikipedia.org/wiki/William_Wilberforce

droughts. In 2022, he won the Australian Christian book of the year award for his book *The Forest Underground,* which documents his development of Farmer Managed Natural Regeneration (FMNR) as a successful way of bringing back the trees and improving crop yields.[21]

FMNR has been implemented in many other countries, particularly since Tony received a *Right Livelihood Award* in 2018: "for demonstrating on a large scale how drylands can be greened at minimal cost, improving the livelihoods of millions of people."[22] *Right Livelihood Awards* are an international award to: "honor and support those offering practical and exemplary answers to the most urgent challenges facing us today."

In October 2022, Parnell Palme McGuinness, columnist and communications adviser, wrote an article titled: "Why I'm an atheist, but not proud of it" in the Sydney Morning Herald. She wrote that she is ashamed of being an atheist: "because the more we understand about how human societies grow, flourish, and become altruistic, the clearer it becomes that religion plays a central role." She based her article on the research of Professor Joseph Henrich, chair of Human Evolutionary Biology at Harvard University. He describes religion as a "social technology" that has helped humans scale up and build large, complex societies."[23]

Regrettably, at times, evil people have hidden their wicked deeds behind the good work that the church is doing, such as child sexual abuse in church schools. The members of the church must repent of these evil words and actions that cause so much pain and distrust. Yet the church is a very positive force for good in our society. Often the service given to people by the church is not visible to the casual observer. One of England's most distinguished historians Sir Arthur Bryant wrote:

---

[21] Rinaudo, T. 2021. The Forest Underground, ISCAST.
[22] wikipedia.org/wiki/Right_Livelihood_Award
[23] smh.com.au/national/why-i-m-an-atheist-but-not-proud-of-it-20221013-p5bpoi.html

"The more I think of it, the more I am convinced that everything of value in our history between the Dark Ages and our own time grew out of the Christian faith and the attempts, however imperfect, of our ancestors to apply its principles." - Sir Arthur Bryant, 1983.[24]

On a very rainy day, Ann and I took a train to Sydney to meet some friends that we had made when I was doing post-doctoral research in the Robotics Institute at CMU in Pittsburgh, Pennsylvania. We originally met these friends in a church where the pastor believed that salvation could be earned by being involved in social action. People went to that church because it was part of their culture. Our friends said, "You were the first people to show us what it is like to lead a Christ centered life among social Christians."

Many people go to church for social reasons because they want the benefits of faith without the commitment required of a true believer. While western media proclaims the decline in both numbers and influence of social Christianity in western nations, Christianity is growing rapidly in other parts of the world.

## CHURCH GROWTH

After Jesus returned to heaven, about 120 believers started the church. They met to pray about Jesus' command to make disciples of all nations. The church has continually grown since then. At the beginning of 2022 the world had a population of 7,874,965,731 people. 32.3% of the world's

---

[24] Bryant, Sir A. 1983. This England, Summer, p 33.

population people are cultural Christians, making it the world's largest religion and 7.9% are born again Christians.[25]

From 1900 to 2010, the percentage of Christians in the African population grew from 9.1% (7.5 million) to 48.8%, (504 million). Of the world's born-again Christians, over 33% live in Africa. Christianity has brought blessings to Africa. With financial support from Christians in other countries, African Christians feed the refugees escaping the violence of tribal warfare that is occurring in several countries such as the Democratic Republic of the Congo.

The growth of born-again Christians in Latin America in the last century, especially the last generation, is spectacular. In 1900, born again Christians numbered about 700,000, or 1% of the population They have now passed 100 million, or 16.8% of the population. Accurate data for China is hard to find but reports indicate a rapid growth in the number of house churches. Prior to the recent persecution of Christians in China, Chinese students told me that the Chinese government is worried about this growth because they believe there are more Christians than communists in China.

During the Covid pandemic in 2020 many international students in Australia had financial difficulties. Many students relied on part time jobs to pay their rent and to put food on the table. When lockdowns commenced, these casual jobs ceased, throwing the students out of work. As they were in Australia on foreign passports and student visas, they didn't qualify for government support. The church that I attend raised money to help students survive.

---

[25] operationworld.org/locations/world/

## FIRST NATIONS PEOPLE

The despicable treatment of *First Nations Australians* by white settlers has regularly been based on public opinion that considers them to be inferior to white people. Early in the 20th century, evolutionary philosophy was that killing them could be justified as aiding natural selection because they were considered to be lower on the evolutionary scale than white humans. In his landmark book *One Blood, 200 years of Aboriginal Encounter with Christianity: a Story of Hope,* Dr. John Harris references considerable literature on this topic.[26]

In contrast to prevailing social attitudes, Christians believe that all people are equal before God. While churches have made many mistakes in their treatment of First Nations Australians, they have fought against government policies that treated them poorly. Harris largely attributes the survival of both the First Nations Australians and their cultures to the efforts of Christian missionaries. He writes:

> "In south-eastern Australia, by the second half of the 19th century, Aboriginal people knew they had been dispossessed of their land. They entered a period of despair and disillusionment for which they needed time and great strength of will to enable them to rise above it and survive.

> Christian Missions were often the only places which provide the safety and time for Aboriginal people to prepare for the new kind of battles that they would face in the twentieth century." - Dr John Harris, 1990.[27]

---

[26] Harris, J. 1990. One Blood, Albatros, see pages 24-26
[27] Harris, J. Christianity and Aboriginal Australia, Part 3: Dispossession and Despair: The Missionary Response at the end oof the 19th Century, Zadok paper S37

An example of how white settlers treated First Nations Australians is the Coniston massacre; the last known officially sanctioned massacre of First Nations Australians. In 1928, a white dingo hunter was killed by First Nations Australians for cohabiting with a First Nations woman. In response a government patrol killed many First Nations Australians.[28] Christian missionary Annie Lock was involved in caring for the children who had been left fatherless by the massacre.

At a government enquiry into this massacre, the mounted constable in charge blamed First Nations assertiveness on Lock.[29] He said, "She caused trouble by preaching a doctrine of equality." The final report was critical of missionaries for not keeping First Nations Australians people in their place, showing the government's poor attitude toward both First Nations Australians and Christians.

## RELATIONSHIP RESTORED

As a result of the resurrection, God offers to each of us the restoration of our relationship with Him, accompanied by blessings when we accept His offer, including eternal life. Otherwise, we remain under the curse of separation. A relationship with God changes all other relationships, giving us greater fulfilment in those relationships, especially with other people who know God.

I know Jesus is alive because I have a relationship with Him. Some scoff and say how can you have a relationship with a dead person? Others question my sanity and say that you cannot see Jesus, so He is not real. So how do I have a relationship with someone I can't see? Here is an example.

---

[28] wikipedia.org/wiki/Coniston_massacre
[29] Harris, J. 1990. One Blood, Albatros, p 562

Nothing is too big or too small to discuss with God. For ten years my wife and I toured Australia with our caravan. As we have aged, our shoulders have not been strong enough to handle it. We prayed to get God's perspective on what to do. It became obvious that we should sell the caravan and find alternate ways to holiday.

We prayed about the price and looked at similar vans advertised online to get an idea of its value. One Friday evening we placed an advertisement on the caravan and camping web site. By lunch time Saturday we had had five enquiries with one person transferring a deposit into our bank account. We were very happy and praised Jesus.

That is one way my relationship with Him works out in real life. I may not be able to see Him with my eyes, or hear Him with my ears, but I know Him in a deep and heartfelt way, that brings joy and contentment to my life.

Another way is that God speaks to me through the words in his book. Every day I try to set aside some time to read that book, visualize the stories of Jesus' life, and meditate on His words. I roll a sentence around in my mind, savoring its meaning, looking for a word or phrase that sticks out. It might speak into my situation, or it may be a new insight into the character of God. His spirit resonates with my spirit to confirm His words to me for that day.

As well as listen to Him, I can talk to Him with my thoughts, and He puts words in my mind. It's like I have an extra sense, a God sense. While I can' t see Him I know Him. A wonderful part of this relationship is that anyone can have this relationship just by believing in Him. I try to remember to talk to Him every day, to ask His guidance for dealing with the problems in my life, and to praise Him for His love.

Mostly, I enjoy getting God's perspective on my life. Sometimes, I struggle to do what I believe He wants. I have found that He understands my pain, but it can be a challenge to obey. Other times, I argue with Him, particularly when He says no. He listens but usually wins.

When I do something wrong, He disciplines me like a loving father. Often by enabling me to endure the consequences of my actions. When I say I am sorry He forgives me and gives me peace. At times, He allows a change in circumstances to test my faith. Like a caring father shows that He is always there to a child learning to swim, He lifts me up and draws me nearer to Him.

## STORY OF MAKING ANEW

"Ouch," cried Grandad when he stepped on a piece of Lego. "I told you to pick up the Lego and put it away, the floor is a mess!"

"But we want to make a new world. They are making a new world on Lego Masters tonight and we want to make one too," pouted the girl.

"We will pull the world we made yesterday to pieces when we need the bricks, so there is no reason to pick up the bricks now," argued the boy.

"There are bricks everywhere. You will find it much easier if you pull the old world to pieces and sort the bricks first. Then, you can make the world anew starting with a foundation that is clear of bricks," replied Grandad.

"Sorry Grandad," said the boy.

"I don't want to destroy the old world," complained the girl.

"You own the bricks, and you made the world, so you have the right to destroy it," replied Grandad.

So, the children started building a new world by totally destroying the old world. They pulled the Lego bricks apart and sorted them into groups. Then they laid a new foundation and built their new world. Its focal point was a three-dimensional city in the shape of a cube.

When they finished it they asked, "Grandad, what do you think?"

Grandad walked around it and said, "It is better than the one you made yesterday. You made a city in the shape of a cube. I like that. Your attempts to build a world reminded me that I haven't told you about the future of Jesus."

"There is more?" enquired the boy.

"The remaking of Jesus provided a way for the world to be made anew," said Grandad.

"What has that got to do with Lego?" asked the girl.

"Just as you had to destroy your old Lego world to make a new one, so Jesus will destroy this old world as part of his judgment on it. Then He will make a new one with a city in the shape of a cube," replied Grandad.

"Will the Maker make a new heaven and a new earth for the people who survived the judgment to live on?" Asked the girl.

"Yes," replied Grandad. "Just as your new Lego world is much better than your old one, so the new world will be much better than this one. It will be a place where believers will spend eternity praising their Maker and not rebelling against him."

## RETURN OF JESUS

For forty days after Jesus rose from the dead, he appeared to the believers many times to prove to them that He was alive. Then He returned to His home in eternity from where He rules the universe. Theologians describe the age in which we live as the *Now and not Yet*. It is the age between when Jesus left and when He will return. We are saved now but our coming out as the children of God is yet to happen.

Despite our best intentions to preserve the natural environment of the earth, we humans are destroying the planet. The earth is surprisingly robust, but the impact of rising temperatures shows us that physical change brought on by our actions is a reality. While we are responsible for nature now the day will come when God will declare that *time is up*, hopefully before we totally destroy the earth.

It will be a day like no other. A loud trumpet blast will echo around the globe, the stars will disappear, and Jesus will appear, leading a great army of angels followed by all the believers who have died. At the sound of the trumpet the believers who are alive will rise up off the earth and join those following Jesus.

Then the earth will be consumed by fire and the elements will melt away. All people will stand before Jesus in judgment. Those who didn't want anything to do with Jesus during this life will get their desire and be separated from Him for eternity. There will be no opportunity for them to change their mind when they realize that their life counted for nothing.

Those who believed in Jesus during this life will be granted their desire to be with Him for eternity. In addition, they will receive rewards for the good works they have done in Jesus' service.

Once the judgment is over, God will create a new heaven and a new earth, a world filled with God's goodness and love. Then the believers will come down to the new earth like a bride beautifully dressed for her husband. A loud shout will declare that God is with His people. There will be no more death or sorrow or crying or pain. Paradise will be established.

## FINALE

We live for a limited time on this earth. The things we make rarely survive beyond our lifetime. Yet, some last longer than we expect. I get regular emails from ResearchGate telling me that one of my publications has been cited by other researchers.[30] I am surprised and humbled when someone cites my book *Introduction to Robotics,* which was published thirty years ago (Figure 11.4).[31] In a field which is changing as rapidly as robotics that is very long time. How long do you expect to be remembered after you die?

---

[30] researchgate.net
[31] McKerrow, P.J. 1991. Introduction to Robotics, Addison Wesley. Over 11,639 English copies sold, Translated into Korean

**Figure 11.4** *Robotics Textbook. Written by author*

The following two examples introduce two people who have chosen different answers to the question: do you believe in Jesus? What is your answer?

> First, a few years before I retired, I met Mary at a robotics conference in Zurich, Switzerland.[32] She had learnt robotics from my textbook. She was struggling with her PhD thesis and asked me to help her. When our conversation turned to God, Mary said, "I prayed that if God was real then He would show himself to me, but He hasn't."
>
> I replied, "God shows Himself to people through His servants. Have you considered that God has sent me to you in answer to your prayer?" She couldn't accept that. We have had many conversations about faith, but Mary still does not believe in Jesus. When I think of Mary, I pray that Jesus will continue to call her to Himself.

---

[32] True story, name changed

Second, I met Alberto Elfes when I was a visiting researcher at the Robotics Institute at CMU.[33] He was a PhD candidate in Robotics. The image on the cover of my robotics text is from his research in ultrasonic sensing (Figure 11.4). Alberto regularly attended a lunchtime meeting to discuss the Bible and its relevance to making, led by Dr. Stephen Garber.[34] I found that group formative in the development of the material for this book. Alberto had a distinguished career in robotics, rising to the position of Chief Research Scientist of the Robotics and Autonomous Systems Group at the CSIRO in Brisbane, Australia.

Alberto died in 2020 after a long struggle with cancer. When he retired, he shared the following message with his colleagues via email:

> "… This is also an opportunity for me to reflect on my own life and future. In this context, I am reminded of the New Testament text that says:
>
> "For I am convinced that neither death nor life, neither angels nor demons, neither the present nor the future, nor any powers, neither height nor depth, nor anything else in all creation, will be able to separate us from the love of God that is in Christ Jesus our Lord." (Romans 8:38).
>
> In friendship, -- Alberto."

As I have been writing this book I have been challenged by the Devil as to why I believe when people I respect don't. The most challenging question has been: "How do I know that I know Jesus?" As I watched a live-streamed church service during the pandemic, I was listening to Psalm 46 being read. A great joy rose within me. How do I know that I know God?

---

[33] gatheringus.com/memorial/alberto-elfes/4268
[34] Garber, S. 2007. The Fabric of Faithfulness, IVP

When I read the Bible, joy and peace whelm up within me - a joy and peace that I experience only from Jesus.

> "He says, "Be still, and know that I am God;
> I will be exalted among the nations,
> I will be exalted in the earth."
> (Psalm 46:10)

In the first chapter I asked the question, Is there an infinitely capable maker who made us makers to be like himself? Jesus claims to be that maker. In this book, I have presented reasons for believing that Jesus' claims are true. Also, He claims that He will forgive your rebellion and give you eternal life as a gift when you believe in Him. When you express your faith in Him in prayer the Holy Spirit will reveal God to you. Will you believe in Jesus and trust Him with your future?

# OTHER BOOKS BY AUTHOR

McKerrow, P.J. 1988. Performance Measurement of Computer Systems, International Computer Science Series, Addison-Wesley, Wokingham, ISBN 0 201 17436 7, 260 pages. Sales: 1,976 copies.

McKerrow, P.J. 1991, reprinted 1993, 1995 and 1998(twice), digital reprint 2002. Introduction to Robotics, Addison-Wesley, Electronic Systems Engineering Series, Wokingham, ISBN 0 201 18240 8, 811 pages. English Sales: 11,639 copies sold

Korean edition, 1994. translated by Park, J.H., Song, J.B. and Han, C.S., Ki Sul Publishing Company, Seoul, ISBN 89-85703-17-X, 780 pages. Korean Sales: 1,000 copies

McKerrow, P.J. 2014, The Adventures of Drip and Drop, iBook

McKerrow, P.J. 2010 to 2017, Jesus Explored Series, 10 booklets, each containing a set of bible studies in simple English for international students at Keiraville International Church, Awards Plus.

McKerrow, P.J. 2016 to 2019, Growing in Jesus Series, 4 booklets, each containing bible studies on a book of the bible, Awards Plus.

# ABOUT THE AUTHOR

Dr. Phillip McKerrow is a retired Associate Professor of Computer Science and Software Engineering. He taught robotics, multimedia and computer science at the University of Wollongong (UOW in Australia). He has a PhD in Computer Science, an M.E. in Electrical Engineering, a B.E.(Hons) in Electrical Engineering and an electrical trade.

He spent a year doing post-doctoral research in the Robotics Institute at Carnegie Mellon University (CMU) in Pittsburgh Pennsylvania, where he assisted in the teaching of their post graduate robotics subject. Robotics was in its infancy, so it was possible to gain a comprehensive overview of the field. Using the knowledge he gained at CMU, he wrote a textbook in robotics titled: *Introduction to Robotics* which has been translated into Korean. Three years later, he spent six months in the AI Department at the University of Edinburgh.

Prior to working at UOW, he worked as a control engineer for the steel processing company John Lysaghts Australia Ltd (now part of BlueScope Steel Limited) where he developed electronic instruments and control systems for steel mills. He wrote his Master of Electrical Engineering thesis on the control of the amount of zinc coated onto steel strip to make galvanised iron. He implemented this control on two galvanising lines.

Dr. McKerrow is a maker. During the two years prior to the COVID pandemic, he built a *Peeler Skiff* wooden motorboat. He has made things all his life, ranging from microcomputer systems to steel mill motor controllers; from a wooden motorboat to mobile robot control software; and from multimedia productions to wood carvings. The design and construction of these systems has stimulated him to think about the relationship between engineering (the making of things) and his Christian faith and subsequent belief in Jesus.

He is married to Ann and the couple have four living children and nine grandchildren. They worship at Figtree Anglican Church and minister to UOW students at Keiraville International Church (KIC). In his retirement, he has written a series of bible studies in simple English for use with international students at KIC. Prior to retirement, he also taught the Moore Theological College certificate course to bible study leaders at his church.

www.ingramcontent.com/pod-product-compliance
Lightning Source LLC
Chambersburg PA
CBHW050551170426
43201CB00011B/1649